Co-Planning

Co-Planning

Five Essential Practices to Integrate Curriculum and Instruction for English Learners

Andrea Honigsfeld

Maria G. Dove

Illustrated by Claribel González

FOR INFORMATION:

Corwin
A SAGE Company
2455 Teller Road
Thousand Oaks, California 91320
(800) 233-9936
www.corwin.com

SAGE Publications Ltd.
1 Oliver's Yard
55 City Road
London EC1Y 1SP
United Kingdom

SAGE Publications India Pvt. Ltd.
B 1/I 1 Mohan Cooperative Industrial Area
Mathura Road, New Delhi 110 044
India

SAGE Publications Asia-Pacific Pte. Ltd.
18 Cross Street #10-10/11/12
China Square Central
Singapore 048423

President: Mike Soules
Associate Vice President and Editorial Director: Monica Eckman
Program Director and Publisher: Dan Alpert
Senior Content Development Editor: Lucas Schleicher
Associate Content Development Editor: Mia Rodriguez
Project Editor: Amy Schroller
Copy Editor: Karin Rathert
Typesetter: C&M Digitals (P) Ltd.
Proofreader: Dennis Webb
Indexer: Sheila Hill
Cover Designer: Rose Storey
Marketing Manager: Sharon Pendergast

Printed in the United States of America

Library of Congress Cataloging-in-Publication Data

Names: Honigsfeld, Andrea, 1965- author. | Dove, Maria G., author.

Title: Co-planning : five essential practices to integrate curriculum and instruction for English learners / Andrea Honigsfeld, Maria G. Dove.

Description: Thousand Oaks, California : Corwin, [2022] | Includes bibliographical references and index.

Identifiers: LCCN 2021023330 | ISBN 9781544365992 (paperback) | ISBN 9781544366067 (epub) | ISBN 9781544366074 (epub) | ISBN 9781544366050 (pdf)

Subjects: LCSH: English language—Study and teaching—Foreign speakers. | Teaching teams. | Interdisciplinary approach in education. | Curriculum planning.

Classification: LCC PE1128.A2 H5857 2022 | DDC 428.0071—dc23
LC record available at https://lccn.loc.gov/2021023330

This book is printed on acid-free paper.

22 23 24 25 10 9 8 7 6 5 4

Contents

Visit the companion website for
Co-Planning resources and related materials at
resources.corwin.com/CoPlanningforELs

Acknowledgments

We are so very grateful for the countless educators who support and promote our work on teacher collaboration for the sake of multilingual learners in its many forms. For this volume, so many of you shared your personal stories and experiences in the field with us, that in turn, gave substance and credence to our life's work. We have been able to include many of those brief glimpses of meaningful practice or more detailed accounts of success with collaborative planning here.

We so very much appreciate our dear friend and editor, Dan Alpert, who believes in our work and in us as a collaborative writing team. We could not have completed this project without his patience and support. Our sincere appreciation goes to the entire Corwin team, especially to Lucas Schleicher, Mia Rodriguez, and Amy Schroller for their work on the manuscript preparation and production process.

We are continually inspired and energized by the educational warriors who advocate for multilingual learners everywhere we go—traveling around the country, going abroad, or moving across the pages of social media. It is often these brief yet powerful encounters that influence, drive, and affirm our work.

We are indebted to our critical friends and peer reviewers, Patrick Kane and Kristina Robertson, for their recommendations and validations of our work. We also wish to acknowledge friends and colleagues who have encouraged us to pursue this project, including those at Molloy College, Rockville Centre, New York.

And finally, we could not have completed this project without the loving support of our dear families and friends. Without them, this project would never have been completed.

About the Authors

Andrea Honigsfeld, EdD, is associate dean and professor in the School of Education and Human Services at Molloy College, Rockville Centre, New York. She directs a doctoral program in Educational Leadership for Diverse Learning Communities. Before entering the field of teacher education, she was an English-as-a-foreign-language teacher in Hungary (Grades 5–8 and adult) and an English-as-a-second-language teacher in New York City (Grades K–3 and adult). She also taught Hungarian at New York University.

She was the recipient of a doctoral fellowship at St. John's University, New York, where she conducted research on individualized instruction. She received a Fulbright Award to lecture in Iceland in the fall of 2002. In the past 18 years, she has been presenting at conferences across the United States, Canada, China, Denmark, Great Britain, the Philippines, Sweden, Thailand, and the United Arab Emirates. She frequently offers professional development, primarily focusing on effective differentiated strategies and collaborative practices for English-as-a-second-language and general-education teachers. She coauthored *Differentiated Instruction for At-Risk Students* (2009) and coedited the five-volume Breaking the Mold of Education series (2010–2013), published by Rowman and Littlefield. She is also the coauthor of *Core Instructional Routines: Go-To Structures for Effective Literacy Teaching, K–5 and 6–12* (2014) and author of *Growing Language and Literacy* (2019), published by Heinemann. With Maria Dove, she coedited *Coteaching and Other Collaborative Practices in the EFL/ESL Classroom: Rationale, Research, Reflections, and Recommendations* (2012) and *Co-Teaching for English Learners: Evidence-based Practices and Research-Informed Outcomes* (2020). Maria and Andrea also coauthored *Collaboration and Co-Teaching: Strategies for English Learners* (2010), *Common Core for the Not-So-Common Learner, Grades K–5: English Language Arts Strategies* (2013), *Common Core for the Not-So-Common Learner, Grades 6–12: English Language Arts Strategies* (2013), *Beyond Core Expectations: A Schoolwide Framework for Serving the Not-So-Common Learner* (2014),

Collaboration and Co-Teaching: A Leader's Guide (2015), *Co-Teaching for English Learners: A Guide to Collaborative Planning, Instruction, Assessment, and Reflection* (2018), and *Collaborating for English Learners: A Foundational Guide to Integrated Practices* (2019), seven of which are Corwin best sellers. She is a contributing author of *Breaking Down the Wall: Essential Shifts for English Learner Success* (2020).

Maria G. Dove, EdD, is professor in the School of Education and Human Services at Molloy College, Rockville Centre, New York. She teaches preservice and inservice teachers about the research and best practices for implementing effective instruction for English learners, and she supports doctoral students in the EdD program in Educational Leadership for Diverse Learning Communities. Before entering the field of higher education, she worked for over 30 years as an English-as-a-second-language teacher in public school settings (Grades K–12) and in adult English language programs in the greater New York City area. She frequently provides professional development for educators throughout the United States on the teaching of multilingual learners. She also serves as a mentor for new ESOL teachers as well as an instructional coach for general-education teachers and literacy specialists.

With Andrea Honigsfeld, she has coauthored multiple best-selling Corwin books, including *Collaboration and Co-Teaching: Strategies for English Learners* (2010), *Common Core for the Not-So-Common Learner, Grades K–5: English Language Arts Strategies* (2013), *Common Core for the Not-So-Common Learner, Grades 6–12: English Language Arts Strategies* (2013), *Collaboration and Co-Teaching: A Leader's Guide* (2015), and *Co-Teaching for English Learners: A Guide to Collaborative Planning, Instruction, Assessment, and Reflection* (2018). Along with other Corwin top-named authors, she coauthored *Breaking Down the Wall: Essential Shifts for English Learner Success* (2020). In addition, she coedited, *Coteaching and Other Collaborative Practices in the EFL/ESL Classroom: Rationale, Research, Reflections, and Recommendations* (2012) and *Co-Teaching for English Learners: Evidence-based Practices and Research-Informed Outcomes* (2020), published by Information Age. With Audrey Cohan and Andrea Honigsfeld, she coauthored *Beyond Core Expectations: A Schoolwide Framework for Serving the Not-So-Common Learner* (2014), published by Corwin, and *Team Up, Speak Up, Fire Up! Educators, Students, and the Community Working Together to Support English Learners* (2020), published by ASCD.

About the Illustrator

Claribel González is a staff developer in Western New York. She supports administrators, teachers, and other stakeholders in achieving academic excellence for multilingual learners. Her passion for language and equity started at a young age as a result of her participation in bilingual and ESL programs. As an avid doodler, she celebrates creativity and the power of sketch notes as a vehicle to synthesize information. Claribel has also served as a bilingual classroom teacher and instructional coach.

Much of this book was written during the COVID-19 outbreak of 2020. During these difficult times, we were profoundly moved by educators who, as first responders to the crisis, worked with children, families, and other teachers removed from the familiarity of their schools and placed in remote learning environments, where they had to reinvent themselves and their teaching methods every day. Overnight, teachers across the U.S. and beyond our borders found themselves thinking about their jobs and their students very differently. The why of their call to educate and create equitable, meaningful learning experiences had been amplified; their how had to change even more. One consistent pattern of teacher action we have observed and supported throughout these months of physical distancing was virtual teacher collaboration. This book is dedicated to those teachers whose perseverance, ingenuity, and commitment embody the spirit of collaboration!

We also dedicate this book to our respective families who are our daily inspirations, Howie, Benjamin, Jacob, and Noah; Tim, Dave, Jason, Sara, Christine, Meadow, Gavin, and Rohnan.

Introduction 1

"It does not take a lot to do a lot for ELLs."

—Madison Altorfer, elementary teacher
Boise Public Schools, Idaho

"Co-planning doesn't need to be a time-consuming chore. Great teachers work smarter, not harder, and co-planning time, when used effectively, can actually ease the workload for teachers through the collaborative sharing of strategies. It's such a helpful tool for ALL educators!"

—Jody T. Nolf, ESOL coordinator
School District of Palm Beach County, Florida

"If we are to serve the needs of ALL learners, we must work together to design learning experiences that are accessible and inclusive. This is possible when educators with varied expertise and experiences come together to design and deliver the curriculum. Collaboration among teachers also models this key life skill for our students."

—Mahima Bhalla, high school learning support teacher
American Embassy School, New Delhi, India

Collaboration is not just an action people take to work together; it requires practice—trial and error—much like developing a complex skill that takes time to master. With this in mind, we have been collaborating around the topic collaboration for the sake of English learners/multilingual learners (ELs/MLs) for a long time as we continue to refine our abilities to master the art of collaboration! Taking many unique angles in our work, we have focused on establishing an integrated collaborative service delivery model for English language development (ELD) (Honigsfeld & Dove, 2010, 2019), unpacking the collaborative instructional cycle with a special emphasis on seven co-teaching models (Dove & Honigsfeld, 2018), advocating for teamwork on all levels of instruction (Cohan et al., 2020), and offering research support for collaboration and co-teaching (Dove & Honigsfeld, 2020a; Honigsfeld & Dove, 2012). And we are not done yet! The old adage attributed to Aristotle, "The more you know, the more you know you don't know," seems to find its way into our research and practice as well with a bit of a twist: the more we know, the more we want to know and understand what there is still to learn and uncover!

In this book, we are returning to our topic of teacher collaboration only to take a deep dive into one practice we often identify as a nonnegotiable in the collaborative instructional cycle: co-planning. Yet it is impossible for us to begin to discuss co-planning without putting first things first: *you do not need to be co-teaching to engage in co-planning*. However, the reverse is also true—*you cannot co-teach without co-planning!* With these basic premises in mind, we hope to reach our largest possible audience, that is, every teacher who works with English learners, dual language learners, multilingual learners, or other culturally and linguistically diverse student populations in any program model or context, be it stand-alone, collaborative, integrated, bilingual or dual language, or general education classes. The fact of the matter is that no one should be planning instruction alone! In writing this book, our most fervent goal is to support the daily work of teachers preparing high-quality, impactful lessons through collaborative planning—working with colleagues together to support the learning of ELs/MLs from all possible angles.

Before we get into our topic, we would like to offer a quick note about terminology. In our previous publications, we referred to the subgroup of learners whose home languages are not English as ELs or English language learners (ELLs), which suggest these youngsters are lacking something and they need to learn English to be complete. In this book, we are intentionally switching to ELs/MLs to recognize the strengths and assets these students bring to school, to affirm that they already are fluent speakers of one or more languages, while we also note that all students are academic language learners (Ottow, 2019; Soto-Hinman & Hetzel, 2009). WIDA (2020a) defines multilingual learners as "all children and youth who are, or have been, consistently exposed to multiple languages. It includes students known as ELLs or dual language learners (DLLs); heritage language learners; and students who speak varieties of English or indigenous languages" (para. 2). We too believe what García and Kleifgen (2018) so emphatically claim:

> Always [...] the starting point would be the students' rich unitary language system and a view of the students' linguistic system as capable of adapting to new sociolinguistic situations and able to expand, whether the instruction is monolingual or bilingual, and whether the goal of instruction is monolingualism or bilingualism or biliteracy. (p. 64)

ELs/MLs may feel marginalized in their schools—lacking a sense of belonging, feeling anxious, seemingly without the motivation to connect with others, and remaining silent about feeling undervalued (Dove & Honigsfeld, 2018; Yoon, 2008). With this in mind, we want to lift up these students to be recognized as capable and valued members of the school community with unique and rich language and academic abilities and potentials.

Why Is There a Need for a Book on Collaborative Planning?

We felt compelled to begin writing this book to expand upon our recently published Corwin Press book entitled *Co-Teaching for English Learners* (Dove & Honigsfeld, 2018) to address collaborative planning in greater depth. We wanted to produce a ready-to-use, reader-friendly guide for all teachers working with language learners. In this way, this book not only closely aligns with the essential concepts and practices presented in our previous books but also addresses how educators serving ELs/MLs in any context (whether co-teaching is feasible or not) can effectively develop curricula, plan units of study, write lesson sequences, or have other shared learning experiences together. We wish to offer a quick reference on all key aspects of collaborative approaches to planning while working with ELs/MLs.

Our goal is to offer a concise yet substantial publication that will serve as a must-have guidebook for all novice as well as more seasoned educators who are moving away from working in isolation. This book is for teachers who wish to work more collaboratively with their colleagues but might not know how to get started or wish to explore how to be more effective and impactful. This book is structured around critical information all teachers—K–5 classroom teachers, 6–12 core content area teachers, and ELD specialists (in some contexts referred to as ESL [English as a second language], ENL [English as a new language], or EAL [English as an additional language] teachers) as well as other instructional support personnel, including teaching assistants and paraprofessionals—need to have at their fingertips, with a special emphasis on content and language integration.

The knowledge base on inclusive practices for students with disabilities as well as for ELs/MLs has been expanding (Beninghof, 2020; Friend & Cook, 2012; Honigsfeld & Dove, 2010, 2012, 2015, 2019; Murawski & Lochner, 2017; Peery, 2019; Villa et al., 2013). Many researchers of inclusive education as well as practitioners in schools with collaborative cultures emphasize the need to engage in a cycle of collaboration, particularly when instruction for students is co-taught. We have been supporting school districts around the United States and internationally (having visited over 30 states to date) to help develop practices that support a collaborative, integrated service delivery model for ELs/MLs. We also train teachers in the collaborative instructional cycle, which consists of four interrelated phases: collaborative planning, instruction, assessment, and reflection (see Figure 1.1). We have found that all four phases together will maximize teacher effectiveness and impact on ELs'/MLs' language acquisition, literacy learning, and content attainment, yet we firmly believe that co-planning is critically important and, in many cases, may not be practiced enough or not done effectively or intentionally enough.

Neglecting any of the four elements disrupts the balance and continuity of the cycle and may negatively impact student learning. While co-teaching itself or other collaborative, integrated instructional practices might receive substantial attention, teachers need time and structured opportunities for the other three components of the collaborative instructional cycle, whether they co-teach or not, in order to

a. Collaborate to create multi-level, differentiated unit and lesson plans
b. Engage in collecting and analyzing formative and summative student data
c. Reflect on the teaching-learning process that took place in the class
d. Negotiate the taught curriculum so that it integrates English language and literacy development with content instruction
e. Collect and analyze data about effective instructional practices
f. Consider the needs, strengths, and challenges of collaborative partners

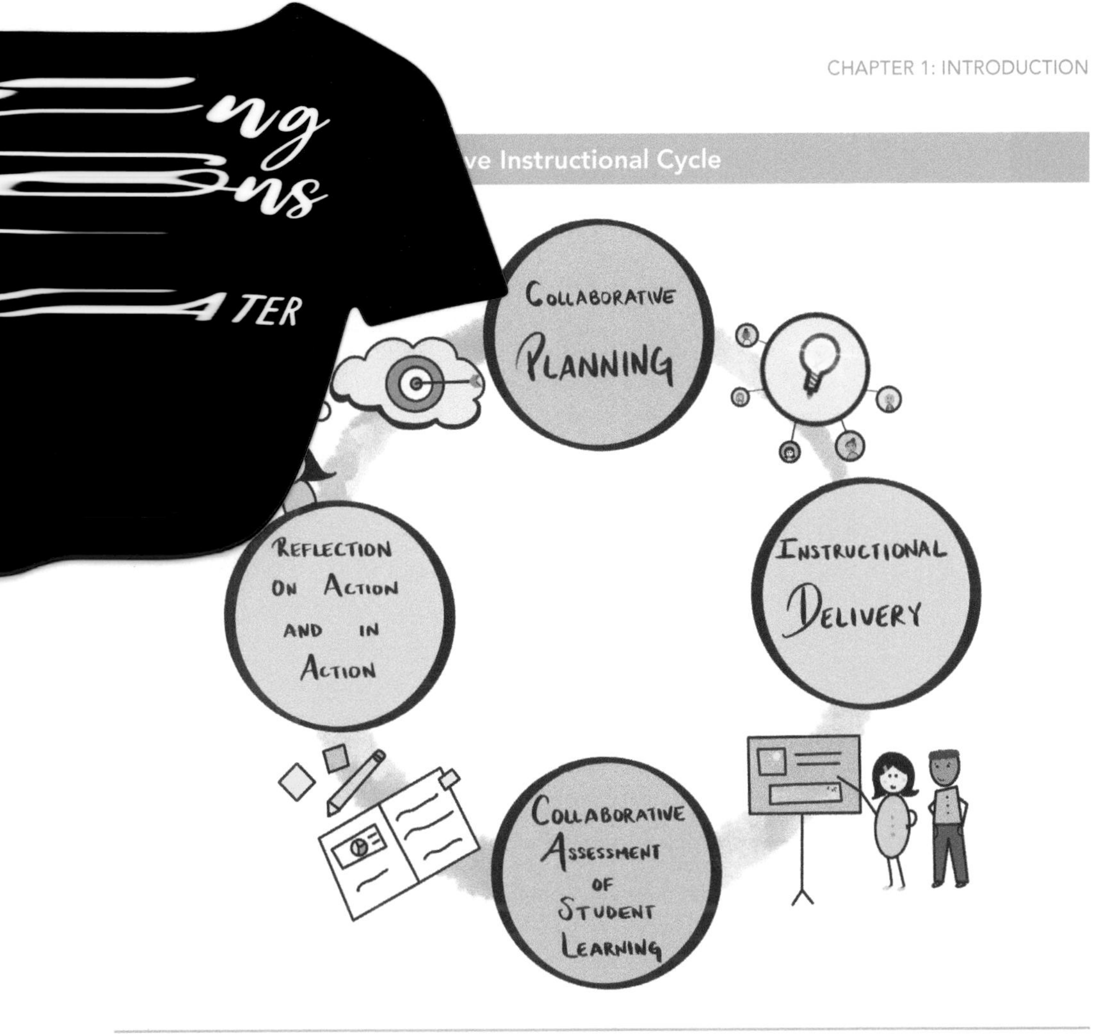

ve Instructional Cycle

What Is Collaborative Planning?

Co-planning is a process that supports the consistent, high-quality implementation of standards-aligned language, literacy, and core content curricula while allowing general education teachers and instructional specialists to coordinate and refine their plans for instruction and assessment. Creating the logistical support for collaborative planning must be a top priority: administrators must consider all the creative ways to provide opportunities for teachers to work together for a sustained amount of time, on a regular basis, with clear goals and agendas in place. For effective teacher collaboration, teachers must be prepared to share

- Expertise of content, knowledge of literacy and language development, and pedagogical skills
- Instructional resources, technology tools, and supplementary materials that are scaffolded and differentiated
- Instructional strategies that represent research-informed and evidence-based best practices

- Approaches to co-teaching—ways to co-deliver instruction and group students to optimize classroom space for student engagement
- Time, attention, and unwavering support for the practice of collaboration

BASIC TOOL KIT

- Essential tools and resources to support successful co-planning:
    - English language arts and content standards
    - ELD or English language proficiency (ELP) standards
    - Curriculum maps; scope and sequence charts
    - Content-area texts and teachers' guides
    - Knowledge and use of technology for co-planning and lesson delivery
    - Co-planning framework or action plan to accomplish co-planning tasks
    - Creativity, open-mindedness, and willingness to be flexible

Teachers must regularly engage in collaborative planning—spending at least one planning period a week in collaboration with another—to engage in a professional dialogue about the range of needs their students have as well as to investigate the academic complexities and linguistic demands of the learning standards in core content areas. During co-planning, teachers rely on each other's expertise and resources to accomplish the following:

- Review the target standards and core curricular goals
- Establish learning objectives and instructional procedures for reaching those objectives
- Target the academic language development of all learners, with special attention to ELs/MLs and other speakers of nonstandard English
- Integrate Individualized Education Program (IEP) goals into their lesson plans
- Determine appropriate modifications and adaptations that will offer the necessary support to students who need them
- Agree on formative assessment tools to be used to inform their instruction

A SNAPSHOT FROM THE FIELD

Gillian Skorka, Agata Majchrzak, and Hallie Sacca Lertora have formed a three-way partnership in PS 160, District 20, Brooklyn, New York, to serve English learners, some of whom are also classified with learning disabilities. Together they share about their collaborative partnership as follows:

> *Our routines and systems for co-teaching are centered around our grade's curriculum map, which specifies which lesson will be taught on which day. We check in with each other every morning to ensure that we are on schedule and adjust accordingly for the day/week. This check-in helps us in maintaining open communication and guarantees we are on the same page throughout the week.*
>
> *Since there are three teachers in this classroom and limited common planning time among the three of us, we have found Google Docs to be extremely useful when it comes to lesson ideas, writing lesson plans, and discussing overall logistics for all activities. Before school, during lunch, and after school, we are able to speak in person about any ideas we have or changes we have made to the lesson. We communicate via e-mail when it comes to distributing responsibilities for the creation of any and all lesson materials as well as delegating the various roles that each of us will take on during the lesson implementation. Since we are fortunate enough to have seven periods a week in which we co-teach together (one English as a new language (ENL), one special education, and one general education teacher), we find it important in our lesson plans to each write one teaching goal/objective (totaling three goals). It is easy for our roles to start to blend together during the moments when we are co-teaching, so writing down our personal goals helps each one of us to stay focused on a specific cohort of students (for example: the ENL teacher has a main focus of language while the special education teacher's goal is for the students to be able to use visuals to comprehend the passage). Our common goal, however, is always to find an appropriate balance between teaching towards our content objective while still equally providing support for the elements of a corresponding language objective.*

A SNAPSHOT FROM THE FIELD

See Figure 1.2 for a master schedule shared with us by Sergio González, principal of the Northwood Middle School. This is how he explains the work done at his school:

> *At Northwood Middle School, our daily mission is to be a unified community that proactively engages students, staff, and families in creating an environment that is supportive of the academic, emotional, and social success of all students. Our school's administration team, school leadership team, and members from our district office created a master schedule that emphasized co-planning and collaborative opportunities for all teachers. As you will see, Northwood's 2019–2020 schedule provided all teachers with common plan periods so they could co-plan and collaborate with one another. Our mission drives our decisions at Northwood, so in order to live our mission, we built a structure that allowed teachers and staff to learn and grow with one another for the success of all students.*

with colleagues and also determine when they have accomplished what they have set out to do. We have documented that collaborative planning time needs to be secured for the purpose of curriculum planning, such as curriculum mapping and alignment (Dove & Honigsfeld, 2018; Honigsfeld & Dove, 2015, 2019), for collaborative assessment practices (Calderón et al., 2020), and for building and participating in professional learning communities (also see DuFour & Eaker, 1998; Fisher et al., 2013; Roberts, 2020), in addition to routinely co-planning lessons and units of study. To ensure successful collaborations as well as enhance professional growth, teachers need to have some control over the purpose of their collaborative activities and also should be given the opportunity for engaging in self-directed professional learning (Fullan & Hargreaves, 2016). All in all, clarity is needed for what is to be expected from teacher collaboration, professional engagement, and personal development that, in turn, will ultimately affect student growth.

Figure 1.2 Master Schedule With Embedded Co-Planning Times

ADV	PERIOD 1	PERIOD 2	PERIOD 3	PERIOD 4	PERIOD 5 6th Grade Lunch	PERIOD 6 7th Grade Lunch	PERIOD 7 8th Grade Lunch	PERIOD 8	PERIOD 9
7th	SS 6	SS 6	**PLAN**	PLAN	SS 8	SS 8	Lunch	SS 8	SS 8
8th	8 Math w/ Yu (Room 121)	8 Intensive Math	**PLAN**	PLAN	8 Math w/ Bergman (Room 204)	Resource (IMC)	Lunch	8 Intensive Math (Room 101)	8 Math w/ Yu (Room 121)
8th	PE 7	PE 7	PE 8	PE 8	**PLAN**	Lunch	PLAN	PE 6	PE 6
7th	CMA 7	CMA 7	CMA 8	CMA 8	**PLAN**	Lunch	PLAN	CMA 6	CMA 6
8th	ELA 8 w/ ESL & SPED co/Cronin & Douglass	ELA 8 w/ ESL & SPED co/Cronin & Douglass	**PLAN**	PLAN	ACCL ELA 8	ACCL ELA 8	Lunch	ELA 8	ELA 8
6th	Math 8	Math 8th	**Plan**	Plan	Math 8 co w/Anaya	Math 8	Lunch	Adv Math 7	Adv Math 7
7th	PLAN	**PLAN**	ACCL ELA 7	ACCL ELA 7	ACCL ELA 7	Lunch	ACCL ELA 7	ELA 7 w/ SPED-Siegel	ELA 7 w/ SPED-Siegel
6th	PLAN	**PLAN**	ELA 7 w/ ESL-Rovner	ELA 7 w/ ESL-Rovner	Lunch	ELA 6 w/ ESL-Rovner	ELA 6 w/ ESL-Rovner	ELA 7 w/ ESL-Rovner	ELA 7 w/ ESL-Rovner
6th	ELA 6 w/ESL-Pomagier	ELA 6 w/ESL-Pomagier	ELA 6 w/ SPED & ESL-Pomagier & Schuman	ELA 6 w/ SPED & ESL-Pomagier & Schuman	Lunch	ELA 6 w/ SPED & ESL-Pomagier & Schuman	ELA 6 w/ SPED & ESL-Pomagier & Schuman	**PLAN**	PLAN
6th	Math 6	Math 6 co w/Kolze	Math 6 (co) w/Kolze	ADV Math 6	Lunch	ADV Math 6	Math 6 co w/Kolze	**PLAN**	PLAN
			PE 8	PE 8	Ravinia	Ravinia	Ravinia	Ravinia	Ravinia
7th	8 ELA co w/Benson (Room 118)	8 ELA co w/Benson (Room 118)	**PLAN**	PLAN	8 Intensive ELA	8 Intensive ELA w/ Ratner	Lunch	Resource (Room 111C)	Resource (Room 101)
8th	8 Sci - co/ Noveron	**PLAN**	**PLAN**	Sci 7	Sci 7 w/ Noveron	Lunch	Sci 7 w/ Noveron	Sci 8 co w/ Noveron	Sci 7 - co w/ Noveron

ADV	PERIOD 1	PERIOD 2	PERIOD 3	PERIOD 4	PERIOD 5 6th Grade Lunch	PERIOD 6 7th Grade Lunch	PERIOD 7 8th Grade Lunch	PERIOD 8	PERIOD 9
6th	DL Spanish 6	DL Spanish 6	DL Spanish 6	DL Spanish 7	DL Spanish 8	DL Spanish 6	Lunch	PLAN	PLAN
8th	7 Orchestra Tu/Fr	7 Band Tu/Fr	8 Orchestra Tu/Fr	8 Band Tu/Fr	**PLAN**	Lunch	PLAN	6 Band Tu/Fr	6 Orchestra Tu/Fr
8th	8 ELA co w/Benson (Room 118)	8 ELA co w/Benson (Room 118)	**PLAN**	PLAN	8 ELA w/ Kahn (Room 116)	8 ELA w/ Kahn	Lunch	8 ELA co w/ Kahn	8 ELA co w/ Kahn
(T&FR)	Chorus 7	Chorus 7	Chorus 8	Chorus 8	PLAN	Lunch	PLAN	Chorus 6	Chorus 6
7th	Sci 8 - co/ Petitte	Sci 8	**PLAN**	PLAN	Sci 8	Sci 8	Lunch	Sci 8	Sci 8
(W&TH)	Lessons	Lessons	Lessons	Lessons	PLAN	Lunch	PLAN	Lesson	Lessons
6th	PLAN	**PLAN**	Resource	7 Math co w/Rabb (Room 220)	7 Intensive ELA	Lunch	7 Intensive ELA w/ Ratner	7 Intensive Math w/ Stella	Math 7 co w/Raab (Room 220)
8th	Art 7	Art 7	Art 8	Art 8	**PLAN**	Lunch	PLAN	Art 6	Art 6
8th	DL SS 8	DL Spanish 8	**PLAN**	PLAN	DL SS 8	DL Spanish 8	Lunch	DL SS 8	DL SS 8
	IMC	IMC	IMC	IMC	PLAN	Lunch	PLAN	IMC	IMC
8th	6 ELA co w/Janzen (Room 203)	6 ELA co w/Janzen (Room 203)	6 Intensive ELA	6 Intensive ELA	Lunch	6 Intensive ELA	6 Intensive ELA	**PLAN**	PLAN
6th	Reading PLUS	Reading PLUS	Reading PLUS	Reading PLUS	Reading Plus	Reading PLUS	Lunch	**PLAN**	PLAN
6th	ELA 6 w/ESL & SPED-Harris & Ratner	ELA 6 w/ESL & SPED-Harris & Ratner	ACCL ELA 6	ACCL ELA 6	Lunch	ACCL ELA 6	ACCL ELA 6	**PLAN**	PLAN

(Continued)

(Continued)

ADV	PERIOD 1	PERIOD 2	PERIOD 3	PERIOD 4	PERIOD 5 6th Grade Lunch	PERIOD 6 7th Grade Lunch	PERIOD 7 8th Grade Lunch	PERIOD 8	PERIOD 9
7th	ACCL ELA 8	ACCL ELA 8	**PLAN**	PLAN	ELA 8 w/ESL & SPED- Petitte & Douglass	ELA 8 w/ESL & SPED- Petitte & Douglass	Lunch	ELA 8 w/ESL & SPED- Petitte & Douglass	ELA 8 w/ESL & SPED- Petitte & Douglass
6th	6 Intensive Math	6 Math w/ Cohn (Room 206)	6 Math w/ Cohn (Room 206)	6 SCI w/ Middendorf (Room 217)	Lunch	6 SCI w/ Middendorf (Room 217)	6 Math w/ Cohn (Room 206)	**PLAN**	PLAN
6th	Music 7	Music 7	Music 8	Music 8	**PLAN**	Lunch	PLAN	Music 6	6 Music
7th	SS 6	**PLAN**	**PLAN**	SS 6	SS 7	Lunch	SS 7	SS 7	SS 7
7th	PLAN	**PLAN**	ELA 7 w/ESL & SPED- Siegel & Schwarz	ELA 7 w/ESL & SPED- Siegel & Schwarz	ELA 7 w/ESL & SPED- Siegel & Schwarz	Lunch	ELA 7 w/ESL & SPED- Siegel & Schwarz	ACCL ELA 7	ACCL ELA 7
7th	Sci 6	Sci 6	Sci 6	Sci 6 co w/ Kolze	Lunch	Sci 6 (co) w/ Kolze	Sci 6	**PLAN**	PLAN
6th	Sci 8 w/ Cunningham (Room 200)	**PLAN**	**PLAN**	Resource	Sci 7 w/ Cunningham (Room 200)	Lunch	Sci 7 w/ Cunningham (Room 200)	Sci 8 w/ Cunningham (Room 200)	Sci 7 w/ Cunningham (Room 200)
6th	Math PLUS	Plan	Math Plus	Math PLUS	Math PLUS	Math PLUS	Lunch	**PLAN**	Math PLUS
	PE 7	GB/BR	GB/BR	GB/BR	GB/BR	GB/BR	GB/BR	GB/BR	GB/BR
8th	DL SS 6	DL SS 6	DL SS 6	DL SS 6	Lunch	DL SP 6	DL SS 6	**PLAN**	PLAN
7th	Sci 8 w/ Fiore (Room 202)	Resource (Room 111C)	**PLAN**	PLAN	8 ELA co w/ Kahn (Room 116)	8 ELA co w/ Kahn (Room 116)	Lunch	8 ELA co w/ Kahn (Room 116)	8 ELA co w/ Kahn (Room 116)
6th	ELA 6 w/ Cochrane (Room 205)	ELA 6 w/ Cochrane (Room 205)	ELA 6 w/ Cochrane (Room 205)	ELA 6 w/ Cochrane (Room 205)	Lunch	ELA 6 w/ Cochrane (Room 205)	ELA 6 w/ Cochrane (Room 205)	**PLAN**	PLAN
7th	ACCL Math 6	**PLAN**	Math 7	Math 7 co w/Gore	Math 7	Lunch	Math 7	PLAN	Math 7 co w/Gore

ADV	PERIOD 1	PERIOD 2	PERIOD 3	PERIOD 4	PERIOD 5 6th Grade Lunch	PERIOD 6 7th Grade Lunch	PERIOD 7 8th Grade Lunch	PERIOD 8	PERIOD 9
6th	Math 6 w/ Cohn (Room 206)	Sci 6 w/ Middendorf (Room 217)	Sci 7 w/Wolf (Room 219)	Math 7 co w/Raab (Room 220)	Math 8 co w/Bergman (Room 201)	Sci 8 w/Fiore (Room 202)	Lunch	**PLAN**	Plan
8th	Spanish A	French A	Spanish A	PLAN	**PLAN**	Lunch	Spanish A	French B	French C
6th	6 ELA 6 w/Janzen (Room 203)	6 ELA 6 w/Janzen (Room 203)	Newcomers (Room 203A)	Newcomers (Room 203A)	Lunch	Intensive ELA with Cronin	Intensive ELA with Gore	**PLAN**	PLAN
6th	PLAN	**PLAN**	ELA 7 w/ Blanks (Room 215)	ELA 7 w/ Blanks (Room 215)	Lunch	ELA 6 w/ Blanks (Room 215)	ELA 6 w/ Blanks (Room 215)	ELA 7 w/ Blanks (Room 215)	ELA 7 w/ Blanks (Room 215)
8th	PE 7	PE 7	PE 8	PE 8	**PLAN**	Lunch	PLAN	PE 6	PE 6
7th	Spanish C	Spanish C	Spanish B	PLAN	**PLAN**	Lunch	Spanish B	Spanish C	Spanish B
8th	Resource (Room 111C)	Resource (Room 111C)	6 ELA co w/Cochran (Room 205)	6 ELA co w/Cochran (Room 205)	Lunch	6 ELA co w/Cochran (Room 205)	6 ELA co w/Cochran (Room 205)	**PLAN**	PLAN
6th	PLAN	**PLAN**	7 ELA co w/Marvin (Room 213)	7 ELA co w/Marvin (Room 213)	7 ELA co w/Marvin (Room 213)	Lunch	7 ELA co w/Marvin (Room 213)	Newcomers (Room 203A)	Newcomers (Room 203A)
7th	PLAN	**PLAN**	7 ELA co w/Marvin (Room 213)	7 ELA co w/Marvin (Room 213)	7 ELA co w/Marvin (Room 213)	Lunch	7 ELA co w/Marvin (Room 213)	7 ELA co/ Bingham (Room 211)	7 ELA co/ Bingham (Room 211)
7th	PLAN	**PLAN**	DL SS 7	DL SS 7	DL SP 7	Lunch	DL SS 7	DL SP 7	DL SS 7
7th	STEM 7	STEM 7	STEM 8	STEM 8	**PLAN**	Lunch	PLAN	STEM 6	STEM 6
8th	PE 7	PE 7	PE 8	PE 8	**PLAN**	Lunch	PLAN	PE 6	PE 6
6th	Reading PLUS	**PLAN**	Reading Plus	Reading Plus	Reading Plus	Lunch	PLAN	Reading Plus	Reading Plus
8th	Sci 6	**PLAN**	Sci 7	Sci 6	Sci 7	Lunch	Sci 7	Science 7	PLAN
7th	Math 8 co w/Anaya	ADV Math 8	**PLAN**	PLAN	ACCL 7th	Adv Math 8	Lunch	8 GEO	Math 8 co w/Anaya

4. **Consistency**

When working with ELs/MLs, we need to recognize that instructional standards and learning targets should be the same for all learners, even if the pathway to achievement requires some students to have a different amount of instructional time or types of support, such as scaffolds and differentiation, to meet with success. In addition, instruction in support of English language and literacy development needs to be consistently integrated with content instruction in every classroom where ELs/MLs are being taught. When co-teaching is not the targeted model for instruction, co-planning ensures that ELD teachers avoid a fragmented, disjointed service delivery that may lead to discontinuous instruction in their stand-alone ELD classes—confusing the very students who need the most consistency of all (Honigsfeld & Dove, 2010, 2019).

5. **Continuity**

Instructional continuity is consequential to favorable outcomes for ELs/MLs. It ensures that they are learning in programs that provide cohesive instruction, incorporate grade-level curricula, and are measured by appropriate standards-based assessments and benchmarks for content, language, and literacy development. Continuity rejects any disjointed, fragmented, skills-based, or happenstance curricula that are sometimes used in stand-alone or co-taught ELD programs, inasmuch as they contain no true integration of grade-level content and language learning and separate ELs/MLs from either the subject matter or direct language instruction needed to excel in school. To enhance instructional continuity, co-planning must be in place to support standards-aligned, integrated curricula while encouraging general education teachers and instructional specialists to coordinate and refine their plans for continuous instruction and assessment. Our work is informed by the Council of the Great City Schools (2017) framework that firmly claims that academic language development must take place within the context of grade-level core instruction. Such an integrated approach to teaching recognizes that

- Language is inseparable from the content and vice versa: content informs what language may be targeted and needed, and language is systematically embedded in the content.
- Content instruction always includes both challenges and opportunities for language and literacy learning.
- Academic language better develops when high-impact, cross-cutting, cross-disciplinary strategies are utilized.
- Intentional focus on language development unique to each content area as well as disciplinary literacy will benefit all students.

6. **Communication**

Changes that occur in education continually bring new challenges to teachers and their attempts to collaborate with one another. Lack of time and proximity to one another have sometimes resulted in the formation of techniques and skills for exchanging information and ideas that do not promote effective communication. In turn, this lack of clarity can place in jeopardy the development of common understandings, the ability to come to consensus, and the accuracy of intentions, all of which can create situations in which miscommunication thrives.

In order to offer some tips for successful collaborative interactions, we gleaned the following from Taylor's (2015) effective communication strategies:

- **Actively listen.** Withhold judgment, advice, or the need to speak.
- **Ask clarifying questions.** Demonstrate your interest and willingness to engage in conversation.
- **Be clear and succinct.** Respect each other's time as well as allow sufficient opportunities for discussion.
- **Paraphrase and summarize.** Reflect back on what you have heard to ensure the correct information and ideas were exchanged.
- **Practice empathy.** Share your feelings with one another to promote understanding and trust.
- **Provide feedback.** Support an exchange of ideas by giving and receiving feedback from one another.
- **Be present.** Avoid distractions, focus on the matter at hand, and fully enjoy your shared time together.

A SNAPSHOT FROM THE FIELD

Kristina Robertson, English learner (EL) program administrator in Roseville Public Schools, shared with us how a unique form of collaboration had emerged during COVID-19 conditions.

In Roseville Public Schools near Saint Paul, Minnesota, educators created a Collaborative Academic Response Education (CARE) team model to provide support to EL/MLs during the pandemic. The CARE teams, a collaborative group of teachers, paraprofessionals, social workers, cultural liaisons, counselors, and administrators embody the six elements of successful co-planning. CARE team members are identified based on EL/ML student needs, whether they are academic, attendance-based, or social-emotional support. CARE team members meet regularly, usually once a week

(Continued)

(Continued)

to discuss student progress and how the team can provide targeted support to help the students reach their goals. In this model, the students and families know who the CARE team members are and how to connect for additional support. Each CARE team member knows the students' unique needs and which team member can best support them. This collaborative model has been instrumental in creating a proactive approach to student struggles in the pandemic and developing trust with families who find school systems confusing or have barriers to accessing support for their child. Each student and family receive a welcome document with CARE team members' names, titles, and contact information, so communication can be a two-way street to support student success. CARE team members complete the Online Learning Success Plan document (see Figure 1.3) to track evidence of additional supports for EL/ML success. EL/ML students and families have benefited from a dedicated team of professionals collaborating for their success!

Figure 1.3 Online Learning Success Plan

- **Expectations**
- **Organization**
- **Engagement**
- **Responsibility**

CARE team members will complete this form for English learners who need additional support and collaboration to be successful. It is to be completed with evidence provided of staff attempts offering additional support and collaboration to the student and family.

Think holistically: What learning must be accomplished in a week? Is it realistic given the student's limited language and distance learning abilities? Then, imagine how supports might be designed to suit those parameters and ensure success with a collaborative team and parents.

Date:	**Time period (dates from-to):**	**Content:**

EXPECTATIONS	DEMONSTRATE LEARNING *Provide steps for completing the task and specify requirements.*	EVIDENCE AND DATE *Link to documents showing evidence.*
	❑ Learning Objective CLEAR	❑
	❑ Explanation WRITTEN AND VERBAL	❑
	❑ MODELING of tasks	❑

ENGAGEMENT AND ACCESS	ACCESSIBLE LEARNING *Describe student access and how tasks and requirements were modified for student engagement and success.*	EVIDENCE AND DATE *Link to documents showing evidence.*
	1. Access:	
	2. Engagement strategies:	
	3. Modified tasks:	
	4. Paper assignments offered:	

ORGANIZATION	MANAGE TIME AND TASK *Provide a checklist and familiar format to help students submit work meeting the expectations.*	EVIDENCE AND DATE *Link to documents showing evidence.*
	❑ Weekly lesson format is CONSISTENT	❑
	❑ Student receives a CHECKLIST of tasks	❑
	❑ COLOR-CODING or NUMBERING is used as a guide	❑

RESPONSIBILITY	CONNECTION WITH MULTIPLE SUPPORT PEOPLE *Action steps and collaborative partners on student success.*	EVIDENCE AND DATE *Specify dates and times of contact and link documentation of action steps. There should be multiple attempts to contact and work with families.*
	1. Parent support	**Action plan:**
	2. Counselor support	**Action plan:**
	3. Cultural liaison support	**Action plan:**

Icons: istock.com/PCH-Vector

What Is in This Book?

Based on our research over more than a decade and several decades of practical experience related to teacher collaboration in support of ELs'/MLs' content, language, and literacy development, we hope to make a compelling case for why all teachers should engage in collaborative planning to support all students in their academic and linguistic growth. We also wish to share with you how to do it!

In the next five chapters, we describe five essential components (see Figure 1.4) for effective collaborative planning for the sake of ELs/MLs and other culturally and linguistically diverse (CLD) student populations as follows:

- Curriculum development, mapping, and alignment (Chapter 2)
- Data-informed planning and evidence-based instructional decision making (Chapter 3)
- Co-planning frameworks, routines, and protocols (Chapter 4)
- Planning for integrated language and literacy development (Chapter 5)
- Multidimensional scaffolding for rigor, relevance, relationships, and research-informed instructional practices (Chapter 6)

Figure 1.4 Five Essential Components of Collaborative Planning

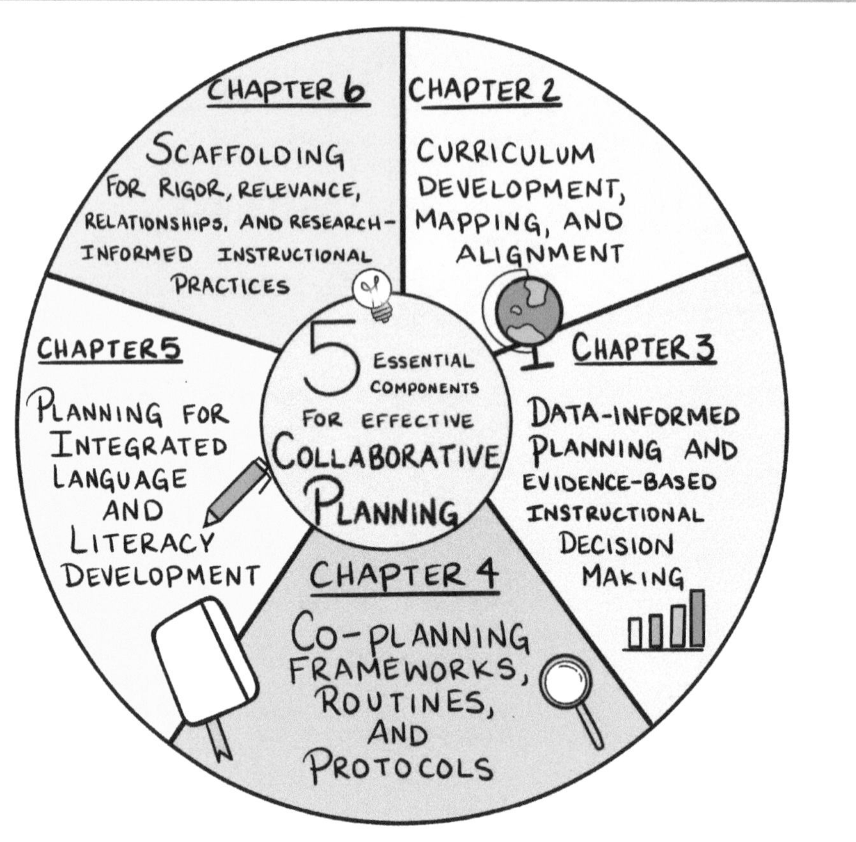

Here is a brief summary of what each chapter will reveal:

Chapter 2: Curriculum Development, Mapping, and Alignment for Integrated Instruction

In this chapter, we explore the dimensions of an integrated curriculum—one that encompasses language and content standards, learning objectives, and assessment measures.

We distinguish between curriculum mapping (the goal of which is to engage in documenting the taught or planned curriculum utilizing backward and forward mapping) and curriculum alignment (the goal of which is to address the academic demand and linguistic demand of the core curriculum). In addition, we unpack curriculum design features that pay close attention to developing curricula with ELs/MLs in mind. In this way, we help our readers design culturally relevant and sustaining educational programs that integrate students' funds of knowledge, funds of identity, and language proficiency levels as well as core content instruction in English language arts, mathematics, science, and/or social studies with explicit focus on English language development in classes that contain both emergent and fluent English-speaking students. We acknowledge the challenges of designing and implementing an integrated curriculum and offer practical suggestions on how to address them.

Chapter 3: Data-Informed Planning and Evidence-Based Instructional Decision Making

In this chapter, we recognize the role that careful analysis of formative and summative assessment data play in collaborative planning. We promote an asset-based philosophy to student assessment and data collection and offer clear guidance on how to collect and analyze meaningful data about student learning (related to both content attainment and language and literacy development) and plan instruction based on the information gained from the data.

We present learner portraits and review the five language proficiency levels as well as realistic expectations for each. We identify the roles and responsibilities of collaborating teachers and share tools for progress monitoring, formative assessment, summative assessment, and benchmarks that are meaningful and authentic and that yield valid and reliable information.

Chapter 4: Co-Planning Frameworks, Routines, and Protocols

In this chapter, we note that collaborative planning requires time commitment and careful design as well as agreed-upon structures and routines, which create a strong basis for collaborative practices to yield desired outcomes. We support our readers to make decisions about planning language instruction through the use of pedagogical frameworks, some of which are tried-and-true models of instruction for ELs/MLs. We showcase collaborative routines for co-planning and instructional routines that support the co-planning process. To accomplish this complex task, we invite our readers to apply multiple lenses (that is, cognitive, linguistic, and social-emotional) to their collaborative lesson planning. Planning protocols, templates, and tools will be included as well as tips for virtual planning.

Chapter 5: Planning for Integrated Language and Literacy Development

In this chapter, we present the power of collaborative work teachers engage in developing language- and literacy-rich learning opportunities and environments where core content and academic practices as well as students' social-emotional development are integrated with English language development. Later in the chapter, we narrow our focus on how to plan for academic language using a three-dimensional framework addressing collaborative planning for word-level, sentence-level, and discourse-level language development. Further, we examine planning for oracy and literacy across developmental levels and core content areas.

Chapter 6: Multidimensional Scaffolding: Rigor, Relevance, Relationships, and Research Informed (4 Rs)

In the final chapter, we offer several frameworks for collaborative planning, within the context of which scaffolding will be highlighted. The classic strategy of scaffolding is redefined and richly illustrated as we make a case for using four guiding principles (rigor, relevance, relationships, and research-informed best practices) and provide guidance on how to select from nine types of scaffolds to be included in every lesson (instructional, linguistic, multi-modal, multi-sensory, digital, graphic, collaborative, social-emotional, and environmental).

STOP AND PROCESS

iStock.com/bombuscreative

Based on your professional knowledge and teaching experience, which of these statements are best aligned with your beliefs about and experiences with collaboration?

1. Teacher collaboration cannot be mandated, yet leadership support is essential to secure logistical support for it.
2. You can co-plan without co-teaching, but you cannot co-teach without co-planning.
3. The most frequently cited obstacle to teacher collaboration is time.
4. Collaborative planning can be successful as a grassroots effort: one teacher team can be a catalyst for change.
5. General education and ELD teachers are both responsible for content and language learning and benefit from sharing their expertise in co-planning.

How Is This Book Organized?

While every chapter follows a unique internal organization determined by the topic, there are some recurring features in each. We introduce each chapter with a sketch note by Claribel González to offer a visual overview of what is coming. At the beginning of each chapter, we "Zoom In" on a scenario involving a student and present a short vignette that depicts the topic of the chapter from the student's perspective—what the student does and experiences when the ideas presented in the chapter are enacted. After zooming in, we "Zoom Out" to analyze what was happening in the vignette from a bird's eye view or in the larger context and why it matters. Topic exploration comes next, with a structure and headings unique to each chapter.

Some recurring features in each chapter are as follows:

- **Chapter opening quotes from educators around the United States and beyond** to set the tone for each chapter.
- **What Research Says** is peppered throughout the chapters to provide brief, seminal or current information in support of specific ideas and practices.
- **Sound Bites** are brief quotes with thought-provoking questions that serve as food for thought as well as possible sounding boards for professional dialogue.

- **Summary tables and sketch note diagrams** offer step-by-step suggestions on getting started and sustaining each of the five components for effective collaborative planning.
- **Stop and Process** statements invite you to consider your own beliefs, prior knowledge, and experiences regarding the topic of the chapter.
- **Pause for a Moment** inserts ask you to do just that . . . pause and consider a reflective question that is being discussed in the chapter.
- **Snapshots From the Field** reveal promising practices and authentic examples from around the United States and beyond.
- **The Tools of the Trade** present ideas for technology tools and/or digital or print-based resources that are relevant to the chapter topic.
- **Celebrations** furnish evidence of successful collaborative planning by showcasing the authentic achievements of collaborative teams from around the United States and beyond.
- **Collaborative Reflection Questions** are suitable for individual learning or collaborative book studies.
- **End-of-chapter QR codes** reveal interviews with us, the authors of the book, in which we provide answers to frequently asked questions about collaborative planning.
- **Collaborative Action Steps** end each chapter with some guidance for implementation.

Pause for a moment and jot down what positive experiences you have already had with co-planning. What evidence do you have from your own practice or from the professional literature in support of collaborative planning?

____

____

____

____

Where Is the Evidence for Collaborative Planning?

We emphasize the value of collaborative planning and support our claims with research coming from Leana's (2011), Hargreaves and Fullan's (2012), and Hattie's (2015, 2018) work on (a) human capital and social capital, (b) professional capital,

(c) collaborative expertise, and (d) collective teacher efficacy. We are inspired by Fullan and Quinn (2016), who suggest that "deep collaborative experiences that are tied to daily work, spent designing and assessing learning, and built on teacher choice and input can dramatically energize teachers and increase results" (p. 63). We position co-planning within the integrated, collaborative instructional cycle and affirm that collaborative planning ensures clarity, curricular continuity, and pedagogically sound program design and instructional implementation for culturally and linguistically diverse students. The most compelling evidence in support of teacher collaboration has emerged from the work of Hattie (2018), who has documented a groundbreaking discovery of the importance of collaborative expertise as well as recognized the power of collective efficacy. He also claims that the greatest barrier to students' academic achievement is within-school variability. For this reason, meaningful teacher collaboration—sharing successful instructional strategies, examining student data, reflecting on effective teaching practices, and so on—must be prioritized. When teachers collaborate and form high-functioning teams, the whole is greater than the sum of its parts, and their collective efficacy—their belief in their collaborative effectiveness—is increased (Donohoo et al., 2018). Donohoo (2017) concluded that certain enabling conditions contribute to higher collective teacher efficacy. When transferred to the context of working with multilingual learners, teachers' collective efficacy indicates the shared belief—a new frame of reference—that together they can achieve success with ELs/MLs. This belief is exemplified by so many teacher teams we have worked with across the United States and internationally, one of which is the Ready Set Coteach team, John Cox, Ashley Blackley, and Allyson Caudill, all NBCT educators featured in Figure 1.5. Each grade-level co-teaching partnership (Allyson and John—third grade, and Allyson and Ashley—second grade) co-plans at least once a week, and they collaborate as a triad at least once per month to vertically align their curriculum and instruction. Co-planning how they integrate language and content promotes shared ownership of lessons and also allows them to reach all students.

Figure 1.5 The "Ready Set Coteach" Team of the Wake County Public School System Collaboratively Planning

What Research Says

There is growing research-based evidence (Dove & Honigsfeld, 2014; Greenberg Motamedi et al., 2019; Honigsfeld & Dove, 2017; Peercy et al., 2017), practitioner documentation (Foltos, 2018; Norton, 2016), and state and local policy initiatives (DESE, 2019; NYSED, 2018) to support teacher collaboration and integrated services for ELs/MLs. We have found four major themes emerging from the research:

1. Teacher learning and capacity building (such as the body of work developed by Martin-Beltrán & Madigan Peercy, 2014; and others)
2. Teacher relationship and trust building (Honigsfeld & Dove, 2017; Pawan & Ortloff, 2011)
3. Shifts in instructional practices and role definition due to collaborative and co-teaching approaches to serving ELs/MLs (Davison, 2006; Martin-Beltrán & Madigan Peercy, 2012; Peercy et al., 2017)
4. Equity in education and culturally responsive teaching (Compton, 2018; Scanlan et al., 2012; Theoharis & O'Toole, 2011)

While research on teacher collaboration and co-teaching is expanding (Kuusisaari, 2014), "the long-standing culture of teacher isolation and individualism, together with teachers' preference to preserve their individual autonomy, may hinder deep-level collaboration to occur" (Vangrieken et al., 2015, p. 36).

Words of Caution

Our decade-long work with collaborative teams (as well as our own on-going collaboration) taught us to avoid painting a rosy picture here; instead, we must acknowledge the challenges as well as the complexities of bringing differences of personal and professional knowledge and opinions together during the collaborative process. Avila (2015) also cautions that "respectfully working through places of discomfort and congeniality can lead to a rich weaving of expertise and experiences from each teacher that ultimately benefit our ELLs. . . . [And] teachers of ELL students must accept and create a complex view of collaboration, one that includes space for disagreement and difference" (p. 39). Let's be mindful of who is included and who is excluded from collaborative planning opportunities. Let's go beyond classroom teachers and ELD teachers forming teams and working in collaboration to co-plan instruction and consider all other key contributors to a child's language, literacy, academic, and social-emotional development. Is there space created for building collaborative expertise among social workers, guidance counselors, literacy specialists, librarians, special subject teachers, teaching assistants, and so on?

Collaborative planning thrives when differences in professional experience and expertise are honored and disagreements turn into dynamic, constructive discussions around not just what works best but what works best for whom, when, and why? There is no easy answer, no cookie-cutter response, or silver bullet. The magic is in the hard work of building professional relationships and collaborating with intention and integrity, and within the realm of research-informed practices.

COLLABORATIVE REFLECTION QUESTIONS

1. Assess your current workplace practice with teacher collaboration. Which collaborative activities do most teachers participate in? Who is most often included or excluded from collaborative conversations?
2. What structures and resources are already in place to support collaborative planning in your school? What structures and resources need to be developed or acquired?
3. What successes have you experienced with collaborative planning? What do you see as the main challenges?
4. What are the general concerns teachers have about collaborative planning? How comfortable are teachers with sharing their ideas or misgivings?
5. To what degree do you think consistent collaborative planning is possible? What types of collaboration are needed between teachers and administrators to foster the practice?

Watch Andrea and Maria discussing some highlights of Chapter 1. In what ways do you think this book is going to meet your professional learning needs? What questions are going on in your mind as you begin this exploration with us?

COLLABORATIVE ACTION STEPS

Consider the overarching goal of the book and your own goals as you embark on this journey with us.

1. Develop a set of questions that you hope the book will answer.
2. Identify your own and your colleagues' learning needs.
3. Set short-term and long-term learning goals related to collaborative planning for ELs/MLs.

2 Curriculum Development, Mapping, and Alignment for Integrated Instruction

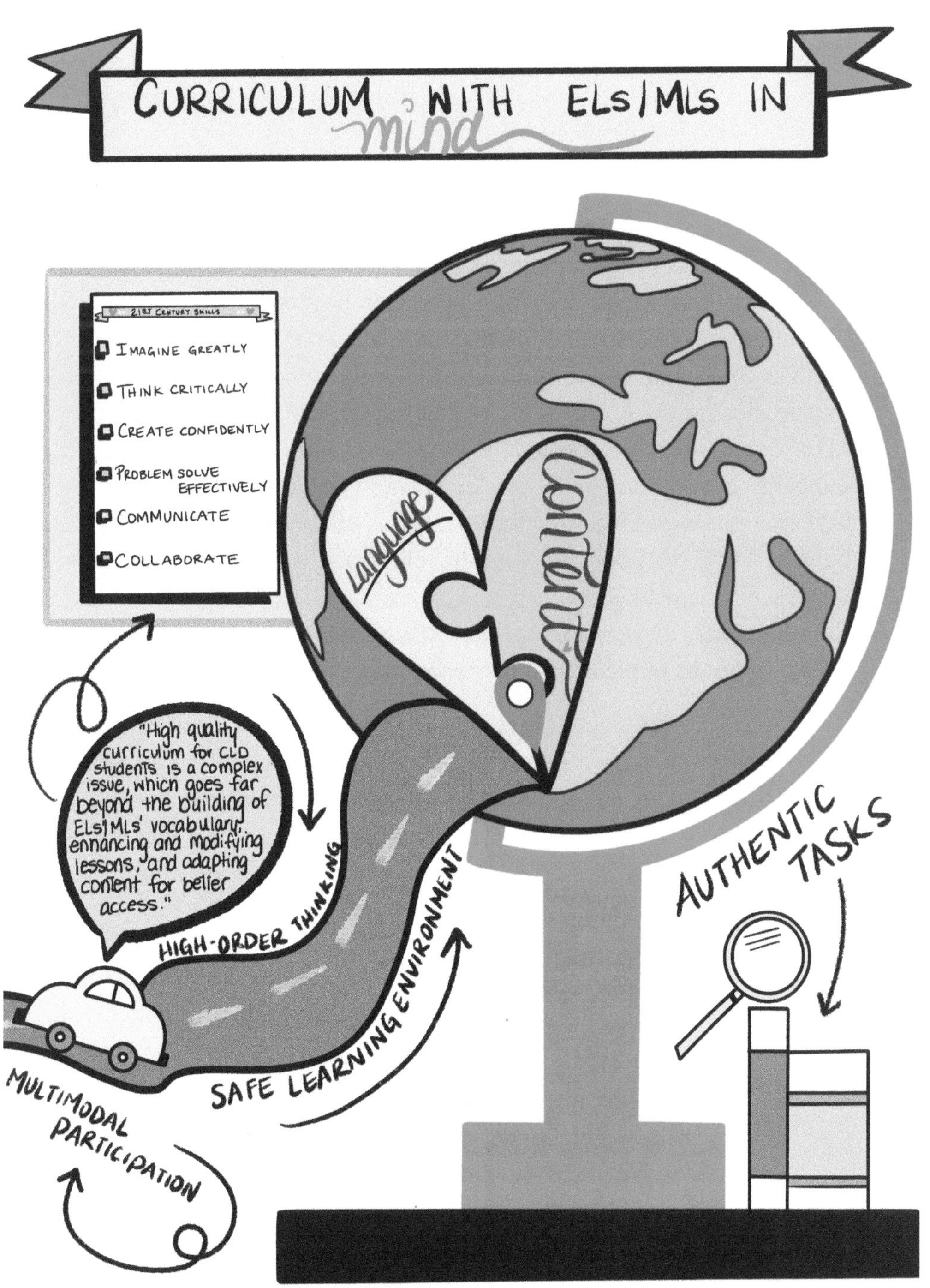

"You have to value our expertise, but not label us by our expertise."

—Lisa Ballenger-Petitte, eighth-grade special education teacher
Northwood Junior High School, Illinois

"Sustained collaboration strengthens teachers' pedagogical approaches to co-planning and co-teaching, English learner strategies and supports, and language and literacy development. As a result, they provide highly effective, robust instruction by focusing on developing teacher efficacy on teaching the writing process, integrating the curriculum, developing high-quality content and language objectives, determining domains-based goals for English learners, and using rubrics and criteria to develop agency and independence in all learners."

—Marybeth O'Brien, principal
Gilmore Elementary School, Brockton, Massachusetts

What is curriculum? And maybe more important to ask for our purposes, what does the most viable, culturally and linguistically responsive curriculum for English learners/multilingual learners (ELs/MLs) look like? Apart from textbook definitions and different perspectives of the meaning of curriculum, educators generally differ on their conceptual understandings of the subject, and they may be even more in disagreement when it comes to considering curricula for programs that serve ELs/MLs. School systems commonly produce written curricula, which incorporate standards and learning goals, implementation guides, and scope-and-sequences, as well as required and recommended texts, materials, digital media, and assessments. Nonetheless, it does not automatically follow that the written curriculum is the one that teachers actually use to plan and deliver instruction (Glatthorn et al., 2019). By the same token, curricula devised for the language and literacy development of ELs/MLs may not be implemented in the way they were intended either.

From our abundance of informal and formal conversations with teachers and school leaders, we have confirmed that many English language development (ELD) programs are either devoid of specialized written curricula for English language learning or have incorporated purchased curriculum materials, programs, and texts that may or may not be used with fidelity. In addition, we have also noted earlier,

> The practice of compartmentalized curricula may be detrimental to the learning of all students in that it does not foster students' abilities to draw on previously learned information across the disciplines or make complex, meaningful connections between content classes. This division of subject matter particularly impacts the success of diverse learners, who with their special learning needs, are not only trying to make sense of academic content but also in some cases must navigate a mainstream American

> school culture due to ethnic, social, and language differences. (Honigsfeld & Dove, 2013, p. 3)

In this chapter, we explore the importance of identifying and documenting the taught curriculum for ELs/MLs, how integrating content-area curriculum with ELD program objectives is critical, and how curriculum frameworks and instructional and co-planning routines are the essential foundations for successful teacher collaboration.

Zoom In

In a sixth-grade English language arts class in a large urban middle school, ELs/MLs with various levels of English language proficiency and former ELs/MLs are reading the novel *Bud, Not Buddy* alongside their homegrown English-speaking peers. With these children is a girl who is not yet fluent in English; she's a newcomer who can hardly express herself in class. Yet this student, Delfina, feels at ease because the instruction in this class not only supports her access to content-area curriculum but also encourages her continual growth in English while welcoming her use of her home language skills.

What makes Delfina feel so confident and secure is easy to see. The walls of the brightly lit room are filled with colorful student work samples, targeted word walls, enlarged photographs reflective of student diversity, and a plethora of posters, timelines, and charts in multiple languages. Along with the other students, Delfina avails herself of the multimedia equipment and the latest technology in the room. She enjoys the movable desks and chairs that easily allow her to be a part of different student groups. In a closer look at the curriculum devised for this class, it is simple to understand how students like Delfina feel safeguarded, supported, and confident to take the necessary risks in order to learn.

Zoom Out

How does the curriculum for this class make a difference? Thanks to a purposeful collaboration among a team of educators—ELD, grade-level, and content teachers—the English language arts (ELA) curriculum was devised to have multiple access points for Delfina and her fellow sixth graders to learn the content being presented along with planned multisensory and multimodal activities and differentiated assessments for practice and identification of both students' successes and possible learning gaps. Additionally, formal and systematic instruction of English language and literacy skills was woven into the curriculum so that the development of fluency and competencies in English are not just a happenstance. For example, for newcomers like Delfina, instruction for the novel *Bud, Not Buddy* focuses on the novel's broad themes, such as hope (esperanza), perseverance (perseverancia), and the importance of family (la importancia de la familia) using visual representations, home language supports, and brief text summaries as well as carefully selected sentences and paragraphs from the original text to deeply analyze. The curriculum specifies appropriate YouTube video clips that not only bring the novel to life but also establish the setting of the book and frame the era of the Great Depression. The novel is also available for Delfina in her home language.

This curriculum unit provides for integrated content and language instruction supported by the standards, aligned with appropriate subject and ELD goals, and routinely scaffolded using research-informed instructional strategies that foster the success of student learning. The aforementioned team of teachers devised this carefully planned unit of study, among others, and incorporated it into one entire sixth-grade ELA curriculum map. Some of the most important and unique features of this ELA curriculum include (a) full integration of instruction for ELs/MLs within the main body of the document and (b) creation of a cycle of increasingly challenging tasks that "apprentice students to language use appropriate for the academic contexts" (de Oliveira, 2019, p. 2). Information for teaching ELs/MLs and ELD is not added onto the curriculum or placed in a separate framework or addendum as other school districts may do. Placing the importance of ELD for ELs/MLs front and center in the curriculum map sends the message that all teachers are teachers of ELs/MLs and collaboration is not merely an option or a unique opportunity but a nonnegotiable professional commitment.

Curriculum Perspectives

Definitions of curriculum generally involve explanations of the purpose of education and the nature of schooling accompanied by broad descriptions of standards, learning objectives, instructional delivery methods, and assessment plans developed within the scope of a particular area of study. It might be considered a tool in the hands of educators to navigate the broader aspects of acquiring knowledge, to assure positive learning experiences for children, or even to shape future society. Taking a different perspective, Schiro (2013) examines the nature of curriculum by considering the issues that underlie an overall vision for learning and how ideologies or philosophies of education inform the frameworks on which curricula are based, which include

- The importance of academic disciplines and accumulated knowledge
- The needs of society and the training of youth to meet those needs
- The development and growth of individual potential
- The promotion of societal norms that support justice, fairness, and equality for all people

In similar fashion, we too must ask what is the nature of curriculum, and what is our vision for curriculum development when we focus on the education of ELs/MLs.

The Challenges of a Standards-Based Curriculum

A standards-based curriculum generally places value on learning standards, core content (English language arts and mathematics), standardized assessments, and the data that they furnish. Some educators have been proponents of a standards-based curriculum, believing it provides all students with access to learning mainstream content, holds all students accountable to meet the same benchmarks, and ultimately promises to yield more equitable outcomes. Standards, as such, are commonly believed to be "a common yardstick used by educators and researchers as a powerful framework for conceptualizing teaching and measuring learner success" (Cox et al., 2018, p. 104). Providing ELs/MLs with the opportunity to access the same content as their English-fluent peers is one of the unmistakable reasons why we also favored a standards-based curriculum and the promise it held to assure an equitable pathway for academic success for all learners. Unfortunately, the way that standards-based curriculum instruction has been implemented has left much to be desired.

A SOUND BITE

"Teachers are designers. An essential act of our profession is the crafting of our curriculum and learning experiences to meet specific purposes. We are also designers of assessments to diagnose student needs to guide our teaching and to enable us, our students, and others (parents and administrators) to determine whether we have achieved our goals" (Wiggins & McTighe, 2005, p. 13).

Many teachers believe that the choice of curriculum is not within their power to change.

How do you view teachers in relation to their impact on the curriculum? What can teachers in your context do to assure that ELs/MLs have a culturally and linguistically responsive curriculum that meets their learning needs?

Icon: iStock.com/Vectorig

The adoption of standards-based curricula has produced mixed reviews. In a recent study concerning Louisiana's adoption of standards-based curriculum policies, "Black and Hispanic students, and those receiving free or reduced-price lunch (FRL), underperformed on standardized assessments compared with their non-FRL, white, and Asian counterparts, and the gap between these groups may be widening" (Kaufman et al., 2019, para. 8). Many educators have complained that standards-based educational reforms have successfully narrowed the curriculum to the degree that, for example, students in Grades K–5 are immersed most often in developing their math and literacy skills with little room for other subjects such as science, social studies, health, music, and art. Froehle (2017) expresses several reasons why the standards-based movement has gone wrong:

> As for academic standards, we made this all too hard. We organized curricula based on content and skills when we should have focused on what people do with that content. What do humans need to survive in a world undergoing rapid, continuous change? They must creatively generate, connect, organize, communicate, and act upon ideas. Perhaps most importantly of all, they must integrate new information to change their ideas. (para. 9)

From the onset of standards-based curriculum, instituted over a decade ago, teachers have had little time to adjust to the reality of standards-based instruction, and the consequence has been that implementation has often been challenging, lacking, or even flawed. According to Fullan (2016), "partly because of physical isolation and partly because of norms of not sharing, observing, or discussing one another's work, teachers do not develop a common technical culture" (p. 100). Yet, how can teachers rely on collaborative practices to support them when the curricular sands are constantly shifting? Most certainly, the initial institution of common statewide standards, and the revision of those standards since their inception in many states, has left school administrators time and again, with the support of their faculty, to align them with local curricula. While time is being spent adjusting what is being taught, little attention may have been paid to how instruction is delivered, particularly to include all ELs/MLs.

With high-stakes standardized tests connected to teachers' overall performance evaluations, many teachers have taken it upon themselves or have been directed by their administrators to teach only what is being tested as well as engage in hours of standardized test preparation (Menken, 2008). There is little doubt that the implementation of standards-based curriculum went awry when the stakes became so high and curriculum instruction was narrowed to include only the small portion that was being assessed. The dangers of these trends cannot be underestimated. Many educators believe that collecting math and reading data is purposeful because they have been indoctrinated to do so. However, the overzealous reliance on collecting data from standardized tests may not only be irrelevant to ELs'/MLs' academic and linguistic development but also bring about the use of inaccurate data that can have significant consequences and a detrimental impact on the way in which ELs/MLs are taught and learn. In order to promote a boost in standardized test scores, this shift in curricular focus has been even more devastating in lower-performing schools where the consequences of failure have been met with the prospect of state oversight or district takeovers.

A SOUND BITE

Kibler and colleagues (2014) recognize that "despite these critiques, as well as the contradictions of yet another monolingual reform movement in an increasingly multilingual country, the current situation nonetheless offers a unique opportunity for researchers and practitioners to re-examine educational practices and assumptions about second language development, teaching and learning, and assessment for students who are both learning and demonstrating their knowledge of new standards-based curricula through an additional language" (p. 433).

What are your experiences with how standards-based instruction has impacted ELs/MLs? Which aspect(s) of this statement might need special attention in your context to better support ELs/MLs? How might teachers better examine their standards-based practices?

Icon: iStock.com/Vectorig

As we look at the current challenges of core-content curricula, we might question "the wisdom of standardizing what everyone teaches and learns" (Sleeter & Carmona, 2017, p. 10). Consider how until only recently, school curriculum was generally "Eurocentric and male-centric, both in content and perspective, virtually ignoring the history, stories, perspectives, literature, and accomplishments of women and people of color" (Gorski, 2020, para. 4). Yet by far, curriculum is now more inclusive of multicultural literature, history, art, and music even though remnants of the past still remain. Nonetheless, we still must contemplate how to best serve culturally and linguistically diverse students within the framework of a standards-based curriculum.

When we develop a curriculum, we must consider its purpose, content for instruction, process for lesson delivery, and the evaluation used to determine its effectiveness. For the purpose of developing a framework for this work, we look to Sleeter and Carmona's (2017) four guiding questions to consider as follows:

1. What purposes should the curriculum serve?
2. How should knowledge be selected, who decides what knowledge is most worth teaching and learning, and what is the relationship between the teacher and the knowledge-selection process?
3. What is the nature of students and the learning process, and how does it suggest teachers should organize learning experiences and relationships?
4. How should a curriculum be evaluated? How should learning be evaluated? To whom is curriculum evaluation accountable? (pp. 10–11)

In the following section, we will use these questions with ELs/MLs in mind as a framework for exploring how to create effective curricula to determine, promote, and support the language and content learning of ELs/MLs.

Developing Curriculum With ELs/MLs in Mind

When documenting a general curriculum plan, units of study might be specified along with time frames for their completion; specific aspects of literacy development might also be addressed, such as appropriate concepts or strategies for developing reading comprehension or particular writing skills within the scope of the content. Some curricula might include general guiding questions, key content and skills aligned with the standards, critical vocabulary, and a list of materials and resources. These are the mechanics and methods behind creating a curricular document. However, let us consider the ideology and purpose behind curricula developed with culturally and linguistically diverse students in mind using the previously stated four central questions from Sleeter and Carmona (2017) adapted for our specific purposes of curriculum development for ELs/MLs (see Figure 2.1).

1. **What purposes should the curriculum serve for ELs/MLs?** To start, we uphold the premise that a curriculum for ELs/MLs must be rigorous, grade-level appropriate, and culturally inclusive; it must provide both basic and discipline-specific language and literacy development along with content-area knowledge. Therefore, all curricula must be written with culturally and linguistically diverse students in mind. No students—ELs/MLs, students with disabilities, emerging readers and writers, and so on—should be afterthoughts when it comes to providing access to core curricula, and their pathways for success should not just be consigned to curricular addenda. To serve all students, directions for reaching

Figure 2.1 Key Questions for Curriculum Development for ELs/MLs

specific learning needs must be integrated into the curriculum. All students need 21st century skills to ready them for higher education learning and employment. They all must develop literacy skills—basic literacy (reading and writing), disciplinary literacy, digital literacy, numerical literacy, financial literacy, media literacy, cultural literacy, emotional literacy, native-language literacy, and so on. They all need to know how to do the following:

- Imagine greatly
- Think critically
- Create confidently
- Problem solve effectively
- Communicate—verbally, visually, and in writing—with clarity and in multiple languages
- Collaborate successfully with diverse groups of people

How do we achieve this? With a rigorous curriculum that thoughtfully considers students' explicit learning needs and "genuinely values all learners and fosters integrated learning opportunities for all students to thrive" (Dove et al., 2015, p. 4). It is critical for all students to have access to the necessary preparation and learning that is provided by content-area experts—the regular classroom and core-subject teachers—and for everyone to have opportunities to be taught the same curriculum. We must remember and affirm that we are not just teaching content—we are teaching students. Therefore, we must keep in mind all ELs'/MLs' inherent potential for learning and cultivate relationships with them that affect their engagement and ultimately their overall performance.

What Research Says

Murphy and Torff (2019) note that "teachers support less rigorous curriculum for English language learners (ELLs) than for general-education (GE) students" (p. 90). In their study, Murphy and Torff surveyed over 200 teachers who work in urban districts with large populations of English learners. They concluded that teachers' beliefs about the lack of abilities of English learners resulted in these students receiving a less rigorous curriculum, which subsequently decreased their overall academic performance.

2. **Who decides what is most important to teach, and what role do the diverse cultural identities of ELs/MLs have in the knowledge-selection process?** When it comes to who decides what to teach, *the heart of the matter lies with what educators generally believe about the abilities of ELs/MLs.* If those decision makers act with a deficit-based point of view—focused on what ELs/MLs can't do, their determinations shape not only what is being taught ELs/MLs but also how it is being taught, where it is being taught, and with whom it is being taught, as well as the rigor or intensity with which it is being taught. The results of deficit thinking often culminate in a watered-down curriculum, and the culturally and linguistically diverse students immersed in such curricula invariably receive the not-so-subtle message that they are not capable, resulting in an achievement gap for ELs/MLs (Murphy & Torff, 2019). However, when ELs/MLs are exposed to and engage with rich and rigorous curricula, they perform better overall.

What content is included in the curriculum? It is essential for those who control or influence what is taught to collaborate with those who represent various facets of the community so that all students' lives and cultures are thoroughly integrated into the curriculum. Consider as well that the curriculum does not have to identify one set of knowledge or essential information for all students to know; it can also offer variations or selections for what is to be taught in order to include "diverse funds of knowledge and arenas for research, debate, and dialogue" (Sleeter & Carmona, 2017, p. 17). Students must see themselves, their experiences, and their cultural heritage included in the curriculum.

3. **What is the nature of ELs/MLs and the learning process, and how does it suggest that teachers should organize learning experiences?** ELs/MLs are a heterogeneous population of students that have different strengths, abilities, and challenges, with one sure thing in common—they all have varying levels of

English language proficiency and similarly, differing abilities and experiences with their complex linguistic repertoires. When we examine the variations in each of our ELs'/MLs' learning portraits, we must consider the different aspects of the learning process and how instruction might differ for students who need to develop content, language, and literacy knowledge in English at the same time. Consider how we might do the following:

- Draw the attention of ELs/MLs to authentic tasks of learning
- Enhance ELs'/MLs' memory and retrieval of information
- Support the development of ELs'/MLs' receptive and expressive language and literacy skills during general class instruction
- Coordinate ELs'/MLs' acquisition of strategies and skills to support and motivate them to learn
- Engage ELs/MLs in high-order thinking
- Allay ELs'/MLs' fears and create safe learning environments where multilingual, multimodal participation is not only allowed but valued and encouraged

When we remain ever mindful of the multi-faceted nature of teaching ELs/MLs, we can further examine how we organize learning experiences for them so that lessons are accessible and meaningful and are in step with what is being taught in the core curriculum.

4. **How should the learning of ELs/MLs be evaluated?** The problem with standardized tests is that they measure a small portion of student learning, and research suggests that they focus on surface-level understandings and provide only partial evidence of what students have achieved (Harris et al., 2012). Concerning ELs/MLs, it is important to note that the available data school districts have on students' levels of language proficiency "are at best approximations—and at worst distortions—of what students are capable of doing" (Bunch & Walqui, 2019, p. 12). It is certain that the complicated realities of assessing ELs/MLs are often placed at odds with the methods of annual standardized core content assessments prescribed by state and local mandates. These assessments too often result in invalid and unusable data when attempting to address the needs of ELs/MLs. It is critical that the "means of evaluating student learning be fair and broad enough to capture the full measure of what children know and can do" (Sleeter & Carmona, 2017, p. 18). (See Chapter 3 for more specifics about assessment practices with ELs/MLs.)

Ultimately, it is these four questions that need to be collaboratively explored by school communities before considering the development of any curriculum with ELs/MLs in mind. School leaders, teachers, parents, students, and members of the community should have the opportunity to probe these overarching issues in order to create meaningful curricula for culturally and linguistically diverse pupils.

A SNAPSHOT FROM THE FIELD

Lora Tittiger, English language development teacher, Harrisburg School District, Harrisburg, Pennsylvania, shared her department's work with us as follows:

> *A unique opportunity for aligning curriculum with students' needs opened up when our district leadership encouraged English language development/English as a second language (ELD/ESL) teachers to be included on content curriculum writing teams. At first, there was some resistance on both sides. Content teachers did not want the subject areas watered down, and on the other hand, ELD/ESL teachers felt unsure how the content could be adjusted for all ELP (English language proficiency) levels. Gradually, multi-disciplinary teams formed and began to work across grade-level strands, in addition to specific content areas. This collaboration enabled ELD/ESL teachers to understand the subject areas more deeply, based on the statewide standards, to better support our colleagues and students in the content classroom. Conversely, the content teachers at different grade-level strands on the teams became more aware of the needs of students at specific ELP levels. The outcome was the creation of content curriculum ESL overlays, complete with suggested supports for levels 1–4 ELP levels, for any content area, based on WIDA descriptors and Pennsylvania's ELD standards.*

STOP AND PROCESS

iStock.com/bombuscreative

Based on your professional knowledge and teaching experience, which of these statements are best aligned with your beliefs about and experiences with curriculum for ELs/MLs?

1. Curriculum mapping is an effective procedure for collecting data about the taught curriculum for ELs/MLs.
2. Our curriculum maps reveal four types of information: the content (essential knowledge taught), the processes and skills used to teach the content, the assessment tools, and key resources used.
3. Without curriculum alignment, ELD services may become fragmented, the content delivered in each class disjointed, and the skills introduced and practiced confusing for ELs/MLs.

(Continued)

(Continued)

4. Curricula for ELs/MLs should be amplified rather than simplified.
5. The curriculum offers consistent scaffolded supports and opportunities for students to demonstrate their language, literacy, and content knowledge.
6. The curriculum includes culturally relevant topics, texts, resources, and materials to engage ELs/MLs.

Quality Curriculum for ELs/MLs

We already have noted the importance of rigorous instruction for ELs/MLs and how it is essential to immerse culturally and linguistically diverse students in culturally and linguistically responsive core curricula to close the achievement gap. But all too often, we have observed that the "lack of consistency, lack of rigor, and lack of relevance and coherence of the planned and taught curriculum within a district or school result in teachers being left to their own devices to decide *what* to teach" (Dove et al., 2014, p. 36). When teachers are overly engaged in *what* to teach, they inevitably do not have adequate time to focus on *how* to teach; the results are often teachers' fragmented pursuits of curricular resources.

> Instead of a haphazard compilation of lessons downloaded from websites that so eagerly pop up on teachers' computer screens, what teachers need are rigorous yet appropriate curricular resources: curriculum maps, curricular frameworks, scope and sequence documents, pacing guides, and assessment tools that consider the needs of diverse learners every step of the way. (Dove et al., 2014, p. 37)

What, then, determines a quality curriculum for ELs/MLs? What critical factors should frame the design and development of relevant instruction for culturally and linguistically diverse students? Bunch and Walqui (2019) focus on five key tenets that define quality learning for ELs/MLs that include the importance of social interaction, scaffolding of instruction, rigorous student participation in safe learning spaces, the simultaneous development of language and content, and language learning opportunities anchored in context. Inspired by the work of Bunch and Walqui, we have expanded their list to include key aspects of a quality curriculum for ELs/MLs as follows (also see Figure 2.2 for a preview).

- **Clarity.** Teacher clarity is vital for students to focus on selected learning targets and to participate in and complete corresponding activities to demonstrate their success. It is essential for teachers of ELs/MLs not only to clearly identify what students need to learn (learning intentions) and

Figure 2.2 Key Aspects of a Quality Curriculum for ELs/MLs

how students will know they have learned it (success criteria) but also to establish the supports that will be provided for learning to take place using a step-by-step approach (learning progressions). Almarode and Vandas (2018) emphasize that "the effect of students achieving clarity can more than triple the rate of learning" (p. 6); they identify the essential components to achieve clarity, including the co-construction of learning targets and success criteria with students, the collection of ongoing data through formative assessment, the ability to provide "effective feedback on and for learning" (p. 6), and the importance of conferencing with students about their progress.

- **Asset-based approach.** To achieve equity and to value the potential of all learners, educators focus on an asset-based approach to learning that emphasizes students' strengths. In this way, students "are valued for what they bring to the classroom rather than being characterized by what they may need to work on or lack" (NYU Steinhardt, 2018, para. 2). With this type of positive approach, teachers turn the tables on assumptions that are sometimes made about students' abilities, often propagated by summative or "standardized" test scores, and instead make decisions based on a more holistic view of a student's skills and facility with academics and language learning as well as their interests and talents that go beyond those that are assessed in school.
- **Discrete versus integrated instruction.** Language learning is not a linear process. Although foundational, step-by-step skill building is essential for students to develop language and literacy competencies, a complete focus

on discrete language skill sets, such as isolated phonics lessons, grammar worksheets, pronunciation drills, and vocabulary exercises, without exposure to actual meaningful text and opportunities for students to think critically will not result in student mastery. In contrast, integrated approaches to language learning incorporate language and literacy building along with students' development of content-area knowledge as well as mechanisms for students to practice speaking and writing (productive skills) and reading and listening (receptive skills).

- **Culturally responsive teaching.** Understanding and making meaningful connections to students' culture and community can enhance students' sense of belonging and support student success through relating what they learn in school to their lived experiences outside of school. These types of connections can support students to access rigorous curriculum and develop essential academic skills. To support the development of learning experiences that are student-centered and culturally inclusive, and that promote positive academic outcomes for all students, we would like to highlight four key aspects of this type of teaching adapted from the New York State Education Department's Culturally Sustaining-Responsive Framework (2019):

    - A welcoming and affirming environment for the whole school community, which includes relationship building with students and their families as well as materials and resources that reflect students' identities
    - An inclusive curriculum and assessment plan, which encourages students to be co-creators of the curriculum as well as the integration of readings, materials, and resources that reflect student diversity
    - High expectations and rigorous instruction for students, which incorporates the examination of social justice issues and provides opportunities for civic engagement and student leadership
    - Ongoing professional learning for educators, which supports the examination of one's beliefs and assumptions about diversity, the alignment of curriculum to integrate marginalized voices, and the development of guidelines on how to respond to contemporary world events that deal with diversity issues

High-quality curriculum for culturally and linguistically diverse students is a complex issue, which goes far beyond the building of ELs'/MLs' vocabulary, enhancing and modifying lessons, and adapting content for better access. Although in the next section of this chapter, we do consider the different types of ELD programs in place in various schools and the tailoring of ELD curricula associated with each of them, we strongly advocate for the inclusion of the components of a high-quality curriculum—the most important issues to consider—listed in the summary chart/checklist in Figure 2.3 no matter which ELD program a school has chosen to employ.

Figure 2.3 Checklist for a High-Quality Curriculum for ELs/MLs

YES	NO	COMPONENTS OF A HIGH-QUALITY CURRICULUM FOR ELS/MLS
		Learning targets and success criteria that are clearly established for language development and content learning as well as aligned to state and local standards
		Learning activities and assessments that are aligned to language- and content-learning targets
		Instruction that is rigorous, relevant, meaningful, and comprehensible for all students
		Instruction that taps into students' prior learning and background knowledge
		Topics of diversity and marginalized voices that are integrated into the curriculum in contrast to token learning opportunities
		Units of study that are carefully crafted to include differentiated and scaffolded instruction and authentic assessment practices according to levels of language and literacy proficiency
		The teaching of language and academic skills simultaneously and language learning that occurs within academic contexts appropriate to students' age and/or grade level
		Opportunities for critical collaborative interactions among peers that are distinctly designed to develop language and literacy skills
		Curricular themes that foster diversity learning, including acceptance, respect, empathy, advocacy, and social justice
		Multiple meaningful opportunities for students to practice speaking and writing (productive skills) and reading and listening (receptive skills)
		An asset-based approach to learning that incorporates student diversity in thought, culture, and positive personal capital
		Students as co-creators of the curriculum that cultivates students' active engagement, interests, and lived experiences
		Opportunities for civic engagement and leadership by culturally and linguistically diverse students
		Appropriate materials and resources that reflect student diversity and various viewpoints

online resources Available for download at **resources.corwin.com/CoPlanningforELs**

A SNAPSHOT FROM THE FIELD

In Boise Public Schools, the co-teaching team of Mrs. Emilie Eisenberger, ELD co-teacher, and Mrs. Aurora Dickinson, second-grade teacher, meets with the other members of the second-grade team to evaluate their yearlong plan and consider how content and language will be integrated. The following anecdote is how they describe their work:

> *We use district- and curriculum-supplied instructional maps to generate a yearlong outline for instructing math for an academic year. These maps allow us to envision the content we will be teaching along with the particular time we want to spend on each of the units. The use of these maps is helpful to ensure all of our content standards are being addressed, along with integrating assessment and review time. When the content has been addressed, we focus on specific academic language and resources that we will need for each of the units. Before the beginning of each unit, the grade-level team meets during a professional learning committee (PLC) to lay out more specific weekly foci during the unit. These focal points revolve around the mathematical structure of the content we are teaching (Geometry: Week 1 attributes, Week 2 composing, Week 3 decomposing). Their identification allows the co-teaching team to plan very specifically around the content and language objectives for each week of a unit. The co-teaching team uses a shared drive where all weekly plans and resources reside. Even though only Mrs. Dickinson and Mrs. Eisenberger co-teach together, all members of the second-grade team have access to the plans and resources in the drive.*

Types of Programs and Related Curricula

Different types of ELD programs commonly influence the curriculum selected or developed for language and literacy instruction. Yet, "the *intentionality* and *cohesion* of the planned curriculum are nonnegotiable" (Dove et al., 2014, p. 36) in that the lesson objectives, content, instructional delivery, learning activities, and formative and summative assessment plans must align in some way with the general core curriculum in order for ELs/MLs to be on a learning trajectory leading toward successful completion of their academic coursework. Still, in order for a curriculum to meet the language development needs of ELs/MLs, we must also consider the makeup of the ELD program in which the written curriculum will guide instruction. However, we must take into account that there are "50 departments of education, one for each state, overseeing some 16,000 school districts . . . in more than 100,000 schools . . . each school district has latitude for shaping education policy" (Eisner, 2017b, p. 313), which makes it difficult to detail all the possible programs established for ELs/MLs. For the purposes of our discussion of quality curricula for ELs/MLs, we have broadly described various ELD programs and the general curricula most often associated with each of them in Figure 2.4.

Figure 2.4 ELD Programs for ELs/MLs

PROGRAMS	DESCRIPTION	TYPICAL CURRICULUM
Stand-Alone ELD Programs	• Classes are separate from general education courses • Student population is segregated (only ELs/MLs) • Classes may include multi-grade-level students to accommodate the instruction of ELs/MLs • Instruction may or may not contain academic content similar to students' grade level • Classes may be organized according to ELs'/MLs' level of language proficiency or grade level	• Curriculum is developed separately from the core school curricula. • Instruction generally focuses on the four skill areas of language development—listening, speaking, reading, and writing. • Some programs incorporate language arts and content-area instruction using specific instructional strategies.
Support ELD Programs	• Programs primarily support ELs/MLs to comprehend the core curricula subject matter to achieve success in grade-level/content-area classes • Classes are either stand alone or within general grade-level/content classes • Student population may be segregated (only ELs/MLs) or integrated	• Support ELD programs generally are without any set curricula. • ELD specialists' primary responsibility is to support completion of students' content-area work. • English language development is mostly individualized and dependent on the support each student needs.
Transitional Bilingual Education (TBE) Programs	• TBE promotes academic skills in ELs'/MLs' primary language while developing language, literacy, and academic skills in English	• Core education curriculum is delivered bilingually.

(Continued)

(Continued)

PROGRAMS	DESCRIPTION	TYPICAL CURRICULUM
	• TBE facilitates the transition of ELs to an all-English instructional program • Student population is segregated (only ELs/MLs who speak the same primary language)	• ELD is integrated into instruction. • The challenge for TBE programs is to balance lessons bilingually and implement instruction uniformly in all bilingual classes.
Dual-Language or Two-Way Immersion Programs	• The goal is for students to develop language proficiency and academic skills in two languages • The student population is generally half English speakers and half speakers of another language	• Core education curriculum is delivered bilingually. • Students acquire an additional language through content-area instruction. • Lessons are balanced bilingually.
Commercially Developed Programs	• These programs are sometimes adopted as curricula for ELD • Literacy or content-based approaches to learning English are the basis for these programs • Student population may be segregated (only ELs/MLs) or integrated	• They are touted to accelerate the development of ELs' language and literacy skills to support success in grade-level classes. • Programs may be scripted, not developed for ELD, or meet the complex learning needs of ELs/MLs.
Integrated ELD	• These programs are designed to teach all students in general education classes • Student populations are integrated • Student support services are integrated • Classes may be co-taught or instructed by a dually certified/endorsed teacher of ELs/MLs • Teacher collaboration is an essential practice	• Curriculum integrates ELD and academic content development. • Students have multiple, meaningful opportunities to speak, write, read, and listen in class as they engage in academic practices. • Whole class and small-group instruction are identified to support students' varied learning needs.

Integrated Curricula for ELs/MLs

We have detailed in Figure 2.4 the different aspects of ELD curricula with their corresponding programs and recognize the challenges and, in some cases, the difficulties of some ELD programs to offer robust support for the academic learning needs of ELs/MLs. Yet we are ever mindful of the jointly released guidance by the U.S. Department of Education's Office for Civil Rights (OCR) and the U.S. Department of Justice (DOJ) "reminding states, school districts, and schools of their obligations under federal law to ensure that English learners (ELs) have equal access to a high-quality education and the opportunity to achieve their full academic potential" (U.S. Department of Education and the National Center for English Language Acquisition, 2016, p. iii). When we consider the opportunities ELs/MLs may have to learn from quality curricula that will support their overall learning success, we ultimately direct our attention to integrated ELD programs and curricula for ELs/MLs.

What, might you ask, constitutes an integrated curriculum? Among many others, Gibbons (2015) suggests that "in a well-planned integrated curriculum where there is a dual focus on both content and language, students have many opportunities to develop subject knowledge and relevant academic language simultaneously" (p. 93). Drake and Burns (2004) define it as follows: "In its simplest conception, it is about making connections" (p. 2). They further posit questions such as "What kind of connections? Across disciplines? To real life? Are the connections skill-based or knowledge-based?" (p. 2). In this section of the chapter, we will respond to these questions and others as we explore the meaning and the mission of integrated curricula for the sake of ELs/MLs.

A SOUND BITE

Mike Schmoker (2019) affirms the power of locally developed curricula when he cautions educators as follows: "Don't be duped by those who claim that curriculum can only be provided by some prominently endorsed (but unproven) commercial program [. . .]. The most notable successes occur in schools and districts whose teachers build their own admittedly imperfect curriculum. [. . .] Good homegrown curriculum respects teacher time and expertise, as well as state and local contexts, and it *doesn't* succumb to the exigencies of market forces" (p. 31).

Which aspect(s) of Schmoker's statements ring true in your particular context? What has been your experience with commercially developed program curricula? What has been your experience with teacher-developed or homegrown curricula? How might these statements relate to your experience with curricula developed for ELs/MLs?

Icon: iStock.com/Vectorig

Defining Integrated Instruction for ELs/MLs

Integrated ELD classes generally combine core content instruction in English language arts, mathematics, science, and/or social studies with explicit English language development in classes that contain both emergent and fluent English-speaking students. Integrated ELD classes are often co-taught by a content-area teacher and an ELD teacher or are taught by a teacher certified in the content area and certified or endorsed to teach ELD classes. Lee (2019) proposes that "since ELP [English Language Proficiency] standards must align with content standards (and not the other way around), content areas must be the point of departure for ensuring alignment." She further emphasizes "that alignment of ELP standards with content standards is a shared opportunity and responsibility that calls on the expertise of educators across EL education and content areas" (p. 536). In addition, integrated courses or classes frequently encourage the use of students' full linguistic repertoires (such as multiple languages or dialects) for meaning making, and they incorporate class routines, active student engagement, and differentiated instructional strategies to meet the needs of all learners.

Integrated instruction requires teaching teams—grade-level/content-area teachers, ELD teachers, literacy specialists, special educators, instructional coaches, and paraprofessionals, as well as others—to collaborate regularly in order to plan, assess, and reflect on instruction for the sake of ELs/MLs. It involves the coordination of student support services so that ELs/MLs are engaged in a coherent and cohesive program of instruction.

Designing Integrated Curricula for ELs/MLs

Curriculum design for ELs/MLs incorporates learning targets for developing language and content-area skills based on local and state learning standards as well as learning activities, resources, materials, texts, assignments, teaching strategies, and assessment plans. Walqui (2019a) further identifies how planning for instruction for ELs must be based on the abilities and needs of students in that lessons should be "uniquely and specially situated to satisfy particular goals with specific students, under specific situations in a class, school, and time . . . address the choice of texts, the architecture of lessons, and the role and sequence of tasks" (pp. 43–44). She elaborates on the nature of good lessons, an integral part of the curriculum, that contain the following:

- **Motivating learning targets and active student engagement.** Lessons must be situated in learning topics and activities that invite participation and involve students in meaningful interaction to develop skills and understandings.
- **Coherence across units of study.** All learning—content, activities, and outcomes—must be interrelated to provide meaningful pathways from simple to complex understandings and language learning.
- **Step-by-step progressions toward learning targets.** Students need to engage in structured tasks that not only help them to develop basic language and literacy skills but also lead them to build on what they have already learned to acquire essential academic skills to meet all learning targets.
- **Multiple assessment procedures.** In addition to teacher-initiated informal and formal assessments, include plans for students to self-evaluate and for peers to monitor each other's progress.

In addition to these broad-based guidelines for integrated ELD curriculum planning and instruction, we must also carefully consider and clearly plan *how* we incorporate explicit language and literacy instruction for ELs/MLs within integrated classes to include the following:

- **Language practices.** Authentic experiences of meaning making across all content areas
- **Language skills across domains.** All basic and academic forms of speaking, reading, writing, and listening
- **Conceptual development and vocabulary usage.** Basic vocabulary and general academic as well as subject-specific concepts
- **Grammar.** Simple and complex sentence structures
- **Language functions.** Language needed to describe, summarize, compare, predict, infer, sequence, persuade, evaluate, and so on (see also Figure 2.5)

Figure 2.5 Components of Explicit Language and Literacy Instruction for ELs/MLs

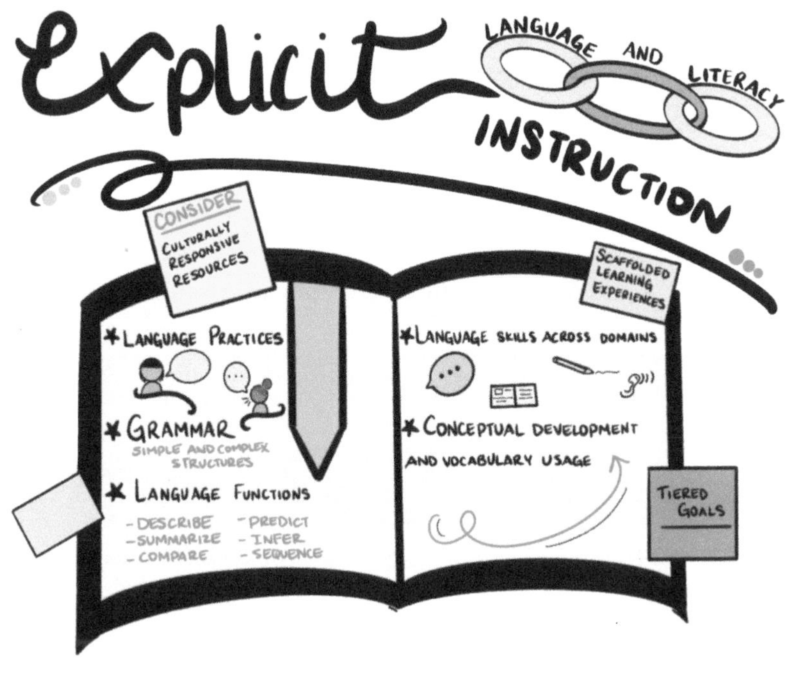

In designing an integrated curriculum for ELs/MLs, we must also consider the use of the following:

- **Culturally responsive resources.** In order for all students to better understand the world in which they live, "curriculum design must move beyond the token cultural holiday or historical person study from select ethnic groups and incorporate the lived experiences of students from the various cultural groups represented in the school. It is essential that students be able to see their lives reflected in what is being taught" (Honigsfeld & Dove, 2015, p. 46).
- **Tiered goals.** ELs/MLs must be viewed as a heterogeneous group of learners, each having attained various levels of proficiency and achievement in English language, literacy, and academics. "For this reason, supporting these students through the use of tiered goals can establish a pathway for each of them to meet academic benchmarks through intermittent steps developed for individual learners" (Honigsfeld & Dove, 2015, p. 46).
- **Scaffolded learning experiences.** Scaffolding provides students with different ways to access information and develop new skills using a variety of learning strategies and techniques. (See Chapter 6 for more information about ways to scaffold instruction.) Using scaffolding "maintains the intensity and rigor of instruction, yet provides smaller doses of information for students to examine, analyze, and acquire in a given time" (Honigsfeld & Dove, 2015, p. 46).

We recognize that educators might feel a bit overwhelmed by the complexity of an integrated curriculum that is devised for the sake of ELs/MLs. A truly integrated curriculum takes time, and it is often developed in phases possibly taking multiple school years to complete. Integrated curriculum design and development also can occur at various levels of a school district's organization—at the district, school, grade, content, or individual-class levels. In Figure 2.6, we give a brief synopsis of what might be accomplished at various levels when collaboratively developing integrated curricula for ELs/MLs.

No matter which level is involved, it is essential that all teachers who will be responsible for teaching the curriculum be intimately involved in designing, developing,

Figure 2.6 Planning Integrated Curricula

LEVEL OF THE ORGANIZATION	REASON FOR COLLABORATION	BENEFITS
Entire district	To establish common goals and a common curriculum framework from prekindergarten to high school graduation; the focus is on curriculum mandates, curriculum continuity, and meeting state standards and state regulations	• All stakeholders have input • Assures a common understanding of curricular frameworks for ELs/MLs • Able to provide needed resources • Assures consistency across schools
Whole school	To plan coordinated instruction based on locally defined, broad-based outcomes	• Supports the responsibility of all faculty in the instruction of ELs/MLs • Provides an opportunity for all administrators and teachers to have buy-in • Addresses local groups of ELs/MLs • Establishes need for professional development
Multiple grades	To plan a multigrade scope and sequence of target content area to meet established district and school goals and establish opportunities for curriculum acceleration	• Assures curricular continuity • Allows for forward and back mapping of curricular goals for ELs/MLs
Grade level	To plan learning experiences for a multi-class scope and sequence of the content	• Provides consistency of instruction • Supports grade-level collaborative conversations
Class or group	To establish learning targets and plan scaffolded and differentiated learning activities, resources, and assessment tools	• Targets small-group instruction • Makes best use of available resources
Individual students	To plan individualized instruction for students by accelerating and/or adapting curricula using appropriate accommodations and modifications	• Addresses the learning needs of individual students • Allows students to learn at an optimum pace

Source: Adapted from Honigsfeld and Dove (2015, p. 49).

and writing the curriculum; it is important for all educators' voices to be heard. Additionally, it is critical for all educators to recognize and value diverse funds of knowledge, allowing all students access to "intellectual resources of diverse communities, including those that have been historically silenced . . . [in order to] enable creative dialogue and work, out of which we might better address problems that seem intractable" (Sleeter & Carmona, 2017, p. 9).

A SNAPSHOT FROM THE FIELD

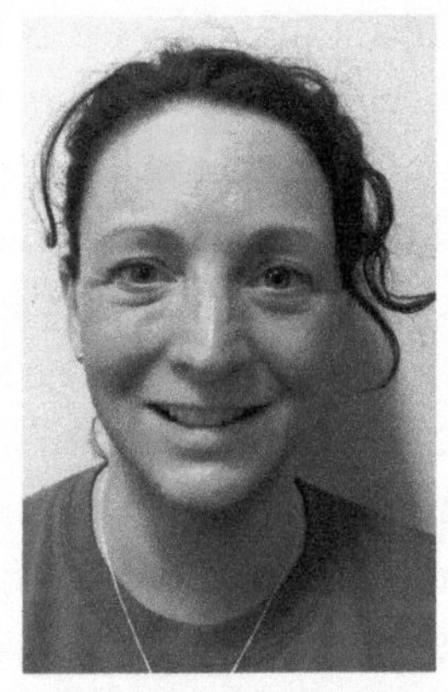

Amanda Wyatt, EL teacher from Mehlville School District—St. Louis, Missouri, shared with us how curriculum planning evolved in her school in collaboration with two of her colleagues, Sarah Fahrner and Jamie Williams.

In 2018, I heard Andrea Honigsfeld and Maria Dove speak about the importance of supporting our ELs when planning curriculum at the district level. This inspired me to reach out to our elementary curriculum director. When an email came out requesting teacher support for the social studies planning committee, I quickly responded, suggesting a new approach for EL teachers where we could provide support through training and co-planning with content teachers.

Beginning steps have been made in this direction. The elementary curriculum director, Sarah Fahrner, our EL instructional coach, Jamie Williams, and I met and discussed ideas for content-based language objectives, tiered vocabulary, field trips, hands-on learning opportunities, and much more. The director was happy to see how these simple structures not only help EL students, but help all students learn. The biggest takeaway was the importance of content-based language objectives. Restructuring the content objectives this way helped strengthen the learning and assessment opportunities. We discussed how these provide enriched language opportunities as well as exact expectations for students and how teachers are collecting evidence of learning.

From this meeting, we concluded the need to have our EL department available to meet with content teachers on the committee to co-plan at the district level. We are looking forward to the adventure ahead. It is great to know while we do things well, there is always room for improvement through collaboration.

A SOUND BITE

"Curriculum, from the learner's standpoint, ordinarily represents little more than an arrangement of subjects, a structure of socially prescribed knowledge, or a complex system of meanings which may or may not fall within his grasp. Rarely does it signify possibility for him as an existing person, mainly concerned with making sense of his own life-world" (Greene, 2017, p. 147).

"Culturally relevant instruction is simply not about the heroes and holidays associated with a student's culture. Rather it represents the current culture lived by the student, all that it represents in terms of neighborhood, heritage, family, history, and sociopolitical issues. . . . When standards are taught in a culturally relevant way, students are more likely to learn the curriculum" (Linton, 2011, p. 63).

What is your viewpoint of culturally relevant instruction? How do students in your context view the curriculum? What is your experience with these practices? Which aspect(s) of these statements might need specific attention in your context?

Icon: iStock.com/Vectorig

A Deeper Dive Into Developing Integrated Curricula for ELs/MLs

We are often inspired by the writing of others in our field and would like to begin this section of the chapter with a short excerpt from the work of Jung et al. (2019), who write about the beliefs that drive inclusive education and equity as follows:

> The philosophy of the staff within a school directly and significantly affects the systems of support that are available for students. We have learned the hard way that meaningful improvements in what a school *does* only stick and have purpose when the adults in the school reevaluate what they know and come to a new understanding of the labels and language they use, how instruction and intervention should be delivered, where students are served, the roles of everyone in the school, and what their expectations are—for both their students and themselves. (p. 15)

Although these authors are describing their beliefs about special education practices, we concur that these fundamental ideas about equity—the need to reevaluate how teaching and learning occur, and for educators to better understand how all students are truly served—parallel our beliefs about how to approach the development of an integrated curriculum to serve ELs/MLs.

Prerequisites

Prerequisites are essential elements in an overall plan to organize the construction of a curriculum. When properly set, prerequisites create a systemic framework for the curriculum development to function more effectively. We strongly suggest before educators jump into the creative aspects of developing an integrated curriculum to consider the following factors to make the process run smoothly:

- **Culture of the district/school environment.** Begin by considering the extent to which teachers and administrators are prepared for the shift in practice from employing stand-alone ELD curricula to integrated ELD curricula. When the district/school culture does not embrace the notion of student inclusivity, teachers might feel unprepared for such change and harbor resistance. In this case, more emphasis should be placed on the development of teacher knowledge on language development as well as the benefits of an integrated curriculum and training to foster the implementation of an integrated ELD curriculum for ELs/MLs.

- **Leadership.** Recognize who will lead the charge to develop an integrated ELD curriculum. In some cases, the clear choice of a leader for such a project is an experienced ELD specialist. However, the institution of a strong co-leadership team composed of an ELD teacher and a content-area teacher might best support all teachers to have buy-in. In this way, the co-leaders would be better able to support, facilitate, direct, and promote peers to interact respective of each team member's expertise.
- **Collaboration.** Contemplate who should be involved in the team that develops the integrated ELD curriculum or decide if multiple teams must be established in order to tap into the expertise of teachers at different grade levels and in different content areas.
- **Goal setting.** Keep in mind what it is you want to accomplish in your quest to create an integrated ELD curriculum. What are your main objectives for your curriculum team to accomplish? Will you begin by using existing curricula as a guide, or will you start from scratch? Will you create a curriculum that encompasses an entire year, or will you develop it quarterly to assess its effectiveness? Goals are also contingent upon the amount of time teams have to complete identified tasks as well as the expectations set by administrators.
- **Communication and documentation.** Identify how team members will communicate with one another to share ideas, information, and assigned work apart from face-to-face meetings. Will team members contact one another via email or text messages? Will curriculum documents be a part of a shared folder via Google Docs or Dropbox? Establishing how teams coordinate and share their work at the onset allows everyone to have a say about their comfort level with using specific tools for collaboration.

Pause for a moment and jot down which of these prerequisites are in place in your context. Which ones might need to be improved?

____

____

____

____

Mapping the Curriculum

Curriculum maps are guideposts for what language, literacy, content knowledge, application, and skills should be taught in any particular course of study over a specified period of time. Although the curriculum-mapping process might appear to be quite cut-and-dried, beginning with clear and specific goals for each unit of study and ending with corresponding evaluation and assessment of students to determine the impact of instruction, Eisner (2017a) reminds us of the following:

> In large measure the construction of curriculums and the judgment of its consequences are artful tasks. The methods of curriculum development are in principle if not in practice, no different from the making of art—be it the art of painting or the art of science. The identification of the factors in the potentially useful educational activity and the organization and construction of sequence in curriculum are in principle amendable to an infinite number of combinations. (p. 134)

We concur with Eisner's (2017a) idea of curriculum organization having "an infinite number of combinations" requiring "artful blending for the educationally valuable to result" (p. 134), and we therefore hesitate to provide any particular step-by-step blueprint for developing an integrated ELD curriculum. However, what we will offer is a list of considerations for determining what an integrated ELD curriculum should specify as well as ideas for monitoring and revising a planned and taught curriculum. Accordingly, the following factors should be considered when developing and organizing an integrated ELD curriculum:

- **Units of study**—based on specific content topics including key concepts and information to be taught. Units for integrated curricula might focus on one of the following:
    - A discipline-specific curriculum, which follows the content of one subject, such as English language arts, algebra, U.S. history, biology, and so on
    - An interdisciplinary curriculum, which combines multiple subjects or is supported by broad-based themes—for example, courage, fairness, privilege, survival, and so on, for subject integration
    - A student-centered curriculum, which considers how students might make connections to their lived experiences and interests within a general content framework
- **Grade-level standards or learning targets**—including state content-learning standards, ELD standards, and building and district initiatives, and varied language-based expectations

- **Language and content objectives**—that are not only identified but equally assessed to determine the language and academic learning of ELs/MLs
- **Textbooks, materials, and resources**—that suitably represent diverse people, opinions, and perspectives
- **Instructional strategies**—that appropriately scaffold instruction to meet the different learning needs of all students
- **Activities for student engagement and interaction**—that provide students with opportunities to consistently engage in language and literacy practices across the four domains—speaking, writing, reading, and listening—as well as content-learning application
- **Pacing guides**—that uphold the notion that all students do not learn or make progress within the same time frame
- **Assessment practices**—including both formal and informal assessment strategies that are differentiated for all students to demonstrate their learning
- **Alignment**—in order to achieve coherence of instruction and provide students with rigorous academic and linguistic preparation relevant to core curricula and the opportunity to build new knowledge on what has been already learned. The dimensions to curriculum alignment include the following:
    - Appropriately sequenced and coordinated lessons across grade levels and subjects within the same discipline so that students build on what they have previously learned
    - Grade-level alignment so that all students in a particular grade are learning the same core curriculum from one class to the next
    - Assessments that are differentiated yet evaluate students' learning based on what has actually been taught
    - Coherence across grade-level subjects so that skills that are built in one subject area—for example, literacy and technology skills—are capitalized on and further supported and developed in other subjects as well.

One example of curricular coherence is illustrated in Figure 2.7, a template that supports the alignment of grade-level learning targets with levels of ELP. Note how both content and language learning goals are featured.

Figure 2.7 Planning Template for Curriculum Coherence

		ENGLISH LANGUAGE PROFICIENCY LEVELS					
Grade-Level Goals		ELP LEVEL 1	ELP LEVEL 2	ELP LEVEL 3	ELP LEVEL 4	ELP LEVEL 5	PROFICIENT
	Content Knowledge and Application						
	Oracy						
	Literacy						
	Social-Emotional Development						

(See **Chapter 5 for more in-depth discussion on using a multi-lens approach to instructional design for ELs/MLs.)**

Available for download at **resources.corwin.com/CoPlanningforELs**

Review, Revise, and Repeat

After you have mapped the curriculum, it is important to remember that your task with examining and re-examining its contents and its impact is never complete. We often express how curriculum maps should be considered as living and breathing entities, continually scrutinized for their effectiveness and forever being edited for clarity, suitability, and the degree to which the improvement of student learning is addressed. Therefore, the ongoing development of curriculum maps should include the realignment of their basic contents with evidence-based, current research-informed practices in order to better incorporate more appropriate texts, materials, resources, learning activities, instructional strategies, assessment plans, and so on. Education is constantly changing. With each passing year, new state and local initiatives frequently are adopted. For this reason and many others, the content, framework, and effectiveness of the curriculum should be evaluated and revised to meet the most current needs of your ELs/MLs.

Tools of the Trade

The following are resources that will provide curriculum creators with support for the design of an integrated curriculum for ELs/MLs:

- **Policies that govern the education of ELs/MLs.** The U.S. Departments of Education and Justice have issued fact sheets and other guidance related to the education and services to be provided for ELs/MLs. These guidance documents can help support the development of integrated ELD curricula. Find these and other supportive resources at https://www.colorincolorado.org/ell-basics/ell-policy-research/ell-laws-regulations.
- **Teacher-inspired curriculum mapping with Google Docs.** Teachers often find Google Docs as their go-to online tool for sharing information, and for curriculum mapping, it seems to be a popular choice as well. We have come across many examples of teachers developing both simple and intricate curriculum-mapping templates or using already established ones in Google Docs for teams to co-create and edit together. With Google Docs, multiple people can work in a single document at the same time making remote development of curricula accessible and uncomplicated.
- **Internet applications for curriculum mapping**. Another way to support the process of curriculum writing is to employ online software for documentation. The following are some examples of products that are available:
    - Rubicon's Atlas is designed to include each step in the process of curriculum development to support schools. It can be customized to incorporate a school's pedagogy, selected standards, and the general demands of curricular planning (https://it.lhric.org/rubicon_atlas).
    - Curriculum Mapper® allows teachers to create curricula aligned to standards and school initiatives. It reportedly identifies gaps and redundancies by generating reports that analyze your curricula (https://knowwhatyoutaught.com/software).
    - BuildYourOwnCurriculum (BYOC) is a software product that is described as easy to use, readily assessable, and able to align curricula districtwide. It supports the management of the continual assessment and improvement of curricula (http://schoolsoftwaregroup.com/).
- **English Learner Tool Kit.** This publication is intended to help educators provide equal access to curricular and extracurricular programs and resources: https://www2.ed.gov/about/offices/list/oela/english-learner-toolkit/chap4.pdf.

- **English as a second language (ESL) Model Curriculum Units (MCUs).** Massachusetts Next Generation ESL Project produced a series of videos that showcase lesson excerpts from their ESL MCUs being implemented in ESL classrooms: https://www.doe.mass.edu/ele/instruction/mcu/.

Celebrations

Portland Public Schools have been working on creating integrated science units that take English language development into careful consideration. This fourth-grade earth science/social studies/English language development unit entitled Our Ever-Changing Earth exemplifies a carefully constructed curriculum that skillfully integrates the development of language and content. The unit's interactive curriculum map delineates each of the 13 lessons along with overarching questions, lesson overviews, conclusions students will draw from each lesson, and end questions that lead students to the next steps to take in their inquiry of learning. There are links to individual lessons that offer outstanding detail to execute instruction that well supports ELs/MLs to meet content standards and develop English language proficiency. In this way, all teachers are prepared with the tools and techniques to support the needs of culturally and linguistically diverse learners. The curriculum unit also identifies the ELP standards as they relate to each lesson (see Figure 2.8).

Figure 2.8 Our Ever-Changing Earth ELP Standards Alignment

There are 10 ELP standards that are consistent across Grades K–12. The lessons in this unit address the following:

		LESSON												
		1	2	3	4	5	6	7	8	9	10	11	12	13
ELP Standards	1 – construct meaning					x		x	x	x		x	x	x
	2 – participate	x	x			x		x	x	x	x	x	x	
	3 – speak and write	x				x		x		x	x	x	x	x
	4 – construct claims		x			x		x	x	x	x	x		x
	5 – conduct research			x	x	x	x			x			x	x
	6 – analyze claims			x	x	x	x				x			
	7 – adapt language	x		x	x	x					x			x
	8* – determine meaning													
	9* – create clear speech and text													
	10* – standard English													

*ELP standards 8, 9, and 10 ongoing in every lesson.

Figure created by Portland Public Schools. Used with permission.

ELP Standards

1. Construct meaning from oral presentations and literary and informational text through grade-appropriate listening, reading, and viewing
2. Participate in grade-appropriate oral and written exchanges of information, ideas, and analyses, responding to peer, audience, or reader comments and questions
3. Speak and write about grade-appropriate complex literary and informational texts and topics
4. Construct grade-appropriate oral and written claims and support them with reasoning and evidence
5. Conduct research and evaluate and communicate findings to answer questions or solve problems
6. Analyze and critique the arguments of others orally and in writing
7. Adapt language choices to purpose, task, and audience when speaking and writing
8. Determine the meaning of words and phrases in oral presentations and literary and informational text
9. Create clear and coherent grade-appropriate speech and text
10. Make accurate use of standard English to communicate in grade-appropriate speech and writing

The unit further integrates the following science and social studies standards along with science and engineering practices and crosscutting concepts (see Figure 2.9).

Figure 2.9 Content Standards, Practices, and Concepts

NEXT GENERATION SCIENCE STANDARDS ALIGNMENT	SOCIAL STUDIES STANDARDS	SCIENCE AND ENGINEERING PRACTICES	CROSSCUTTING CONCEPTS
Performance Expectations (PEs) 4-ESS1-1 Identify evidence from patterns in rock formations and fossils in rock layers to support an explanation for changes in a landscape over time.	4.7 Explain the interactions between the Pacific Northwest physical systems and human systems, with a focus on Native Americans in that region.	Planning and Carrying Out Investigations • Make observations and/or measurements to produce data to serve as the basis for evidence for an explanation of a phenomenon.	Cause and Effect • Cause and effect relationships are routinely identified, tested, and used to explain change.

(Continued)

(Continued)

NEXT GENERATION SCIENCE STANDARDS ALIGNMENT	SOCIAL STUDIES STANDARDS	SCIENCE AND ENGINEERING PRACTICES	CROSSCUTTING CONCEPTS
4-ESS2-1 Make observations and/or measurements to provide evidence of the effects of weathering or the rate of erosion by water, ice, wind, or vegetation. 4-ESS2-2 Analyze and interpret data from maps to describe patterns of Earth's features. 4-ESS3-2 Generate and compare multiple solutions to reduce the impacts of natural Earth processes on humans.	4.8 Compare and contrast varying patterns of settlements in Oregon, considering, past, present, and future trends. 4.20 Construct explanations using reasoning, correct sequence, examples and details with relevant information and data. 4.21 Analyze historical accounts related to Oregon to understand cause-and-effect.	Analyzing and Interpreting Data • Analyze and interpret data to make sense of phenomena using logical reasoning. Constructing Explanations and Designing Solutions • Generate and compare multiple solutions to a problem based on how well they meet the criteria and constraints of the design solution. • Identify the evidence that supports particular points in an explanation.	Patterns • Patterns can be used as evidence to support an explanation.

Figure created by Portland Public Schools. Used with permission.

Additionally, the unit plan supports the integration of language and content objectives through the use of language routines that are specified for each lesson (see Figure 2.10). In the actual unit plan that the teachers can access, each of these routines is hyperlinked to clear and simple descriptions about how to use each of these routines.

Another important piece contained in this curricular unit is an assessment map (Figure 2.11) that offers formative and summative assessments for teachers to use to monitor student progress in meeting the targeted content and language benchmarks. Specific attention is paid to the four skill areas of language development, including students' oral language skills. The use of language-recording sheets and rubrics provides data for instructional adjustments to be made and also provides evidence of ELs'/MLs' overall progress in attaining English language proficiency. All students benefit from the attention that is paid to the development of language and literacy alongside the content.

Acknowledgment: This project was made possible with funding from the Gray Family Foundation for Geography Education.

Figure 2.10 Language and Interaction Routines

LESSON	LANGUAGE ROUTINES	LESSON	LANGUAGE ROUTINES
1	Gallery Walk Numbered Heads Together Think-Pair-Share	8	Gallery Walk
2	Think-Pair-Share Stand Up, Hand Up, Pair Up	9	Mix and Mingle Lines of Communication
3	Numbered Heads Together Think-Pair-Share	10	Supported Discussion (Accountable Talk bookmark)
4	Think-Pair-Share Quiz, Quiz, Trade	11	Think-Pair-Share (Grouping-pairs and quads)
5	Think-Pair-Share Round Robin Gallery Walk	12	Discussion Diamond
6	Quiz, Quiz, Trade Round Robin Numbered Heads Together Bees and Flowers	13	Think-Pair-Share Numbered Heads Together Lines of Communication Collaborative Poster or similar
7	Partner work		

Figure created by Portland Public Schools. Used with permission.

Figure 2.11 Assessment Map

LESSON	NGSS	ELD	ASSESSMENT
1: Observing Patterns	Begin to identify patterns	Communicate questions and wonderings	Gallery Walk language observation (ELD)
2: Phenomenon	Create a model to explain phenomenon of the Scablands	Explain cause and effect relationships present in model	Student Model Sheet (NGSS) Stand Up, Hand Up, Pair Up (ELD)
3: Stream Tables as Models	Carry out investigation and share results in board meeting	Engage in scientific talk about results of stream table investigation	Board meeting (NGSS/ELD)
4: Stream Table Investigations	Plan an investigation and collect data	Share the results of an investigation and engage in scientific discourse	Investigation planning sheets, boards (NGSS) Board meeting (ELD)

(Continued)

(Continued)

LESSON	NGSS	ELD	ASSESSMENT
5: Impact of Floods	Design model to mitigate impact of floods	Explain model and engage in revision process with peers	Whiteboard models (NGSS) Board meeting (ELD & NGSS) Exit Ticket (ELD & NGSS)
6: Mitigating Flooding	Design solution to flood impact	Explain solution and ask clarifying questions	Design, build test (NGSS) Gallery Walk (ELD)
7: Revising Solutions (Engineering)	Design solution	Explain solution	Engineering Design Assessment (NGSS & ELD)
8: What Do Rock Layers Tell Us?	Make observations and explain pattern	Ask questions, explain thinking	Gallery Walk observations and questions (oral), note pages (written) (NGSS & ELD) Written explanations on probe (NGSS & ELD)
9: Observing Patterns in Rock Layers	Model rock layers	Communicate thinking about patterns Express relative time	Student models (NGSS) Lines of communication (ELD, oral) Exit Ticket (NGSS & ELD - written)
10: Sharing and Recording Our Thinking	Explain patterns in rock layers	Participate in academic discussion	Rock layers probe (NGSS) Class discussion (ELD)
11: Cause and Effect	Explain cause and effect including evidence	Explain cause and effect including evidence	Exit Ticket (NGSS & ELD)
12: People and the Land	I can use maps to identify patterns	I can use maps to identify patterns	Exit Ticket (NGSS) Discussion Diamond (ELD)
13: Where, oh Where, Should I Live?	Determine patterns Make claim and support it with evidence	Make a claim and support it with evidence	Where, oh Where Should I Live student sheet (NGSS) Recommendation letter (ELD)

Three PPS administrators shared with us their perspectives on this integrated work:

Dr. Susan Holveck, PPS science program administrator:

> This was a collaborative effort that included a design process of deconstructing standards, creating an anchoring phenomenon to drive the unit, writing lessons, piloting units, revising based on teacher feedback, and finalizing. The work included classroom and ESL teachers in every part of the process. The collaboration was between classroom and ESL teachers, ESL TOSAs,* and Science TOSAs.* I am so proud of their work and the high level of collaboration that happened.
>
> *TOSA = teacher on special assignment

Veronica Magallanes, PPS ESL director:

> The unit exemplifies the degree of collaboration between content and our ELD educators that is possible and necessary. The work centered on creating an equitable written, taught, and assessed curriculum that benefited all of our students, especially our linguistically diverse emergent bilinguals. Since our work amplifies hands-on science, it provides the motivation for students attending to language in meaningful and purposeful ways. The integrated language work is reaching all of our dual-language programs.

Jennifer Hernandez, PPS ESL assistant director:

> Bringing in ESL teachers as co-teachers of science has been a game changer! While we knew this project was best for our students, the unintentional consequences have been amazing. Organically, collaboration between classroom teachers and ESL teachers occurred, both teachers found themselves as both the content and language teacher, and building principals saw the need to have more collaboration and professional development with their entire staff. Our desired outcome was to change how English language development instruction is delivered and the actual outcome was even more: ELD instruction was integrated with core content, students were no longer siloed in a pullout method, pedagogy and educational philosophies switched, and emergent bilingual (EB) students received a robust, equitable learning experience that created academic success, and that is a win!

The PPS Leadership Team would like to acknowledge PPS ELD/Science Curriculum Writing Team of TOSAs:

- *ELD TOSA—Leslie Lauretti, Rebecca Levison, Kate Yocum, and Anna Davis*
- *Science TOSAs—Geoff Stonecipher, Jen Scherzinger, Jennifer Mayo, and Kristin Moon*
- *Teachers who helped co-create Ever Changing Earth Unit—Laura Bullard, Katia Fleischman, Holly Henning, Alicia Nicholl, Janelle Hutchinson, Sheree LeDoux-Leos, and Randy Webster*

COLLABORATIVE REFLECTION QUESTIONS

1. The chapter-opening vignettes highlight the real impact of inclusive, integrated curricula for ELs/MLs. What has been your experience with various curricula for ELs/MLs? What are your thoughts about how effective integrated curricula might be with your students?
2. Sleeter and Carmona (2017) question what they call "the wisdom of standardizing what everyone teaches and learns" (p. 10). Identify what you think are the benefits and challenges of employing a standards-based curriculum. Justify your response by sharing examples from your own practice.
3. Consider the various aspects of a high-quality curriculum for ELs/MLs discussed in this chapter—for example, teacher clarity, an asset-based approach, culturally responsive teaching, and so on. Which aspect of a high-quality curriculum do you think is most important and why? What might you add to the list of components that assure high-quality curriculum for ELs/MLs that may not have been addressed in this chapter?
4. Examine the prerequisites for writing an integrated curriculum for ELs/MLs. Which prerequisites do you believe are within the control of teachers? Which prerequisites require more support from administration?

Watch Andrea and Maria discussing some highlights of Chapter 2. What resonates with you, and how would you take these ideas back into your context?

COLLABORATIVE ACTION STEPS

Consider what you have uncovered while reading this chapter and the new insights you may have gained. Identify how this chapter has shaped your thinking about curriculum planning and alignment in support of collaborative planning.

1. What has affirmed your knowledge and understanding of the chapter topic?
2. What did you read that has challenged your personal and professional ideas?
3. What next steps do you need to take to hone your co-planning skills and strategies?
4. As a result of the information presented in this chapter, what would you recommend be incorporated into your co-planning teamwork?

Data-Informed Planning and Evidence-Based Instructional Decision Making

SOCIOCULTURAL
ACADEMIC
COGNITIVE
LINGUISTIC

WHAT ASSESSMENT TOOLS AND MEASURES CAN WE USE THAT ARE:
FAIR?
MEANINGFUL?
EQUITABLE?

DATA
TOOL BOX

WHAT IS ACCURATE?

SUCCESS CRITERIA
CONTENT FOCUS
LANGUAGE FOCUS

INTEGRATED CONTENT AND LANGUAGE LEARNING INTENTIONS

WHAT IS MEANINGFUL?

WHAT IS ACTIONABLE?

FORMATIVE ASSESSMENT

Where am I now?
How can I close the gap?
Where am I going?

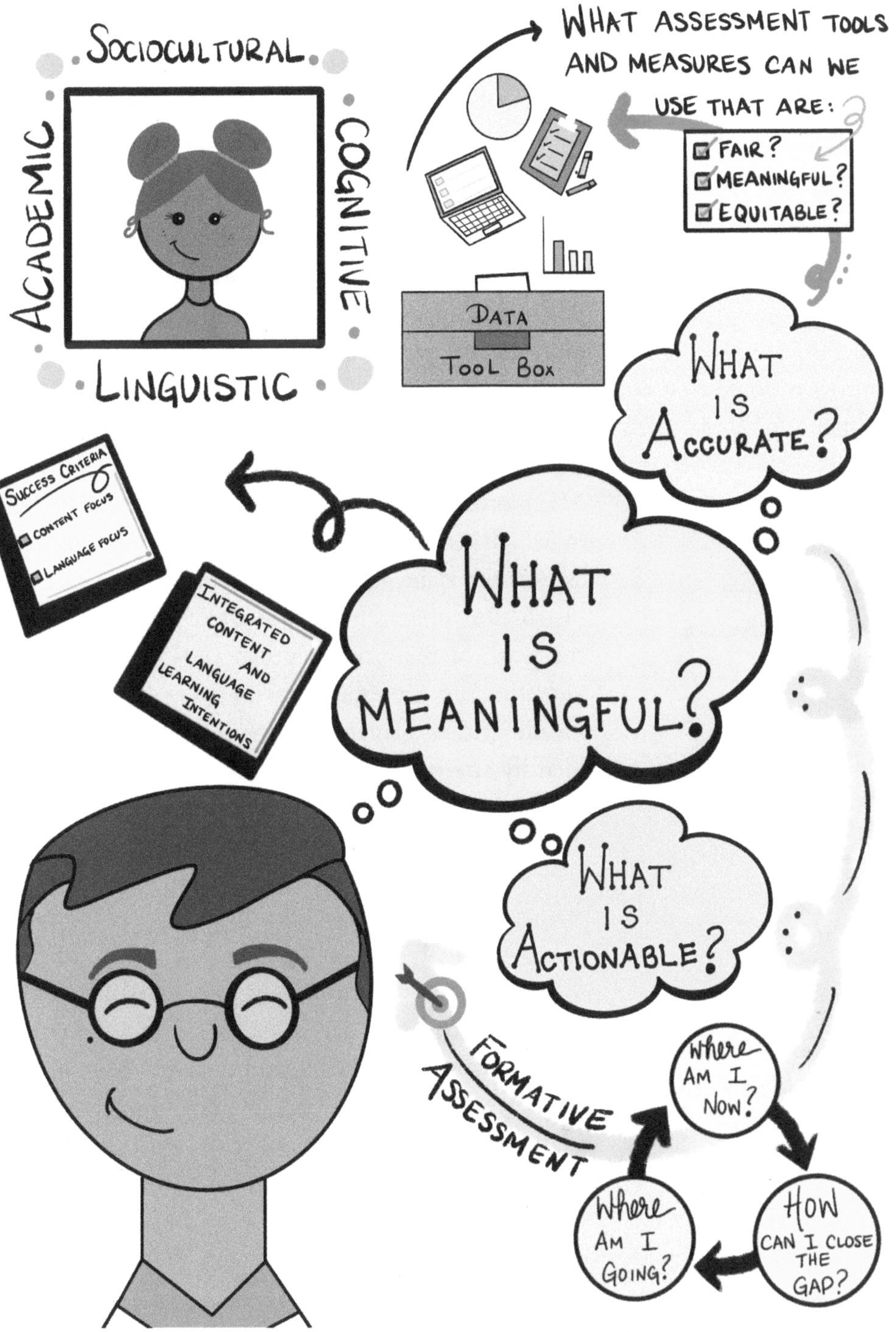

"Co-planning is a collaborative process that helps both educators and students of all abilities and ages. Teachers today can use co-planning as a way to improve instruction for the entire classroom by analyzing data, reflecting on it, and using the outcomes to make decisions together."

—Angélica Infante-Green, commissioner
Rhode Island Department of Education

"As teachers get to know each other and trust each other, they are able to talk through how they assess students and create rubrics that help guide how they look at student work. Content teachers need to have that trust in their EL Specialist to share the evaluating of student work. This then leads to stronger co-planning and co-teaching."

—Jill Ayabei, EL coordinator/coach
Nampa School District, Idaho

When you hear the words *data, assessment, grading,* and *accountability,* how do you react? Do you get perked up and excited to have access to, analyze, and make informed decisions based on student data? Do you wonder if another initiative is coming, requiring lock-step student evaluation and possible consequences for not demonstrating student growth? In this chapter, our intention is to support collaborative planning teams' reflective and thoughtful practices to use assessment data to make planning instruction with English learners/multilingual learners (ELs/MLs) in mind more meaningful. We intend to offer ways in which teams can organize and purposefully examine assessment data and make informed decisions for the instruction of ELs/MLs. For these reasons, we look to the work of Bambrick-Santoyo (2019), who offers four key principles for collecting and using data: (1) creating a meaningful assessment system; (2) examining the data to identify strengths and needs accurately; (3) turning data into action via more effective teaching; and (4) building a culture in which data are used to inform instruction.

A SOUND BITE

Gottlieb and Honigsfeld (2020) advocate that "linguistically and culturally sustainable classroom assessment, where teachers and students co-plan and co-construct performance tasks, use mutually-agreed upon criteria for success, and provide evidence *for* and *as* learning, represents equitable practices for multilingual learners" (p. 135).

Do you agree? What is your experience with assessment for learning (providing formative assessment data) and assessment as learning (giving students opportunities to self-assess and set goals for themselves)? How can changing assessment practices create more equity for ELs/MLs?

Icon: iStock.com/Vectorig

We wish to recognize that many educators are experts in collecting, analyzing, and responding to data. Day-to-day formative assessment practices and adjusting instruction based on students' needs are well-established practices across classrooms, schools, and districts. As you read this chapter, we invite you to take this opportunity to re-examine your assessment practices with the lens of language and literacy support and equity for ELs/MLs. Our hope is that it will also support your efforts to use data innovatively, creatively, and purposefully during collaborative planning for academic content, language, and literacy development of ELs/MLs (and academic language learners [ALLs], for that matter)!

Zoom In

Let's zoom in and meet some English learners:

> Javier is an active, eager-to-learn kindergartener; he's always ready to turn and talk, cooperate with other students during learning-center time, and participate in whole-class activities. His home language survey indicates that there are three languages spoken in his home, and he seems to be very fast to pick up conversational English. Javier has yet to make progress in sound-letter identification and tends to shy away from reading-skill tasks, yet he loves flipping through nonfiction picture books, drawing his own storybooks, and answering questions during story time.
>
> Aida is a third grader who was adopted by her maternal aunt. Her parents had to leave the country due to deportation. Aida was born in the United States and has strong communicative and reading skills in both English and Spanish. More recently, she seems not to attend to lessons during class, which has impeded her academic progress. When her parents left, she moved into her aunt's house, which she shares with many extended family members. Aida enjoys singing and dancing and has an extensive sticker collection, mementos from her many family vacation trips.
>
> Ahmed is a student in fifth grade. After spending over a year and a half in various refugee camps in Turkey, he has finally settled with his family in a large midwestern city in the United States. He speaks Arabic and has also developed some fluency in Turkish. Ahmed is eager to learn, but due to the political turmoil that has raged in his home country almost since his birth, his access to formal schooling has been sporadic. He enjoys competitive video games, watching and playing soccer, and building complex Lego sets.
>
> Kamlai is a reserved, quiet student, recently arrived from Thailand and enrolled in eighth grade. Though a recent arrival, she is quite proficient in reading and writing in English, but she rarely speaks in class because she is very self-conscious of her accent. Kamlai is having some difficulty adjusting to her new school life and making new friends. She thinks American students aren't serious enough about their learning. She loves the vast amount of resources—computers, materials, school supplies, and so on—that her new school provides, and she spends much of her free time reading.
>
> Nahjela is enrolled in eleventh grade in an urban high school. She attended a small, privately run school in Haiti and appears a bit overwhelmed by the over 3,000 students in her new school. Nahjela speaks little English but has the strong support of English-speaking family members who have

been living in the United States for many years. She approaches each of her school assignments with great care, and an older cousin supports her learning after school on a daily basis. Nahjela is a talented pianist and hopes to play someday at Carnegie Hall.

Zoom Out

Examining these five abbreviated learner portraits reaffirms our commitment to seeing multilingual learners as individuals with rich cultural and individual assets, complex needs, and endless potentials! We invite you to do the same. The shared approach to collecting, analyzing, and using data for collaborative planning must match this intention to see ELs/MLs as unique individuals with unlimited potential. Knips (2019) also urges educators to consider students' identities and backgrounds for equitable outcomes: "Ignoring students' diversity markers means pretending that their identity doesn't matter. In order to close gaps in student outcomes, we must name equity as an essential component to data analysis" (para. 3). Later in this chapter, we will further discuss how knowing and understanding students' backgrounds and strengths will support an asset-based approach to assessment rather than a deficit-based one.

Learner Portraits

Generating rich learner portraits and updating them regularly form an important part of gaining an overall picture of how to best support students. In order to do so, consider the following:

- Begin the process formally through enrollment and intake data collection forms based on your state and district mandates.
- Capture standardized data drawn from screening tests and annual assessments documenting students' level of proficiency, academic achievement, and unique learning needs.
- Make sure all educators working with ELs/MLs have access to such data and understand their implications for teaching.
- Remember to go beyond traditional assessment measures and tools (such as ELA and math annual state assessment data) that are frequently normed with English-proficient students.
- Seek a range of additional pieces of information that allow you to paint a rich portrait of each student.

Heineke and McTighe (2018) suggest a holistic portrait consisting of at least the following four dimensions: sociocultural, cognitive, linguistic, and academic. We adapted this framework for our purposes in Figure 3.1.

Figure 3.1 Multidimensional Student Portraits

<table>
<tr><th>DIMENSIONS OF IDENTITY</th><th>HELPFUL INFORMATION</th><th>DATA SOURCES</th></tr>
<tr><td>Sociocultural</td><td>Biographical data (age, grade, time in the U.S.)
Home experiences and family dynamics
Values and traditions</td><td rowspan="4">Student records
Home language surveys
Intake questionnaires
Student interviews
Caretaker interviews
Classroom observations
Student observations
Formal evaluations
Student writing</td></tr>
<tr><td>Cognitive</td><td>Exceptional needs
Giftedness</td></tr>
<tr><td>Linguistic</td><td>Home language and literacy practices
Language and literacy proficiency level
Language and literacy preferences</td></tr>
<tr><td>Academic</td><td>Prior schooling experiences
Academic levels of achievement in the core content areas</td></tr>
</table>

WIDA Can Do student portraits are also multidimensional and include information about each student's "educational background, languages, family, interests—in addition to what the student can do in English with information from the WIDA Can Do Descriptors and Proficiency Level Descriptors" (WIDA, 2020c, para. 1). Students may also significantly contribute to their own portraits and offer insights into their cultural and linguistic backgrounds and experiences and their favorite subject matters and topics of interest. They may also share work samples or even audio and video recordings revealing their knowledge and skills. "I've had teachers who start the year with this project and post the portraits around the room. They are fabulous for building community and sharing student strengths as a group" (K. Robertson, personal communication, January 18, 2021).

We appreciate seeing examples of student portraits that are electronically available to the entire faculty, can be shared and updated regularly, and also include sentence starters or language frames that reflect an asset-based, bias-reduced approach to capturing information about the student. Unconscious and implicit biases may impact how students are perceived. Thus, statements that include what the student has already accomplished academically, is passionate about, or is determined to do or what ambitions he or she has are critical. See Figure 3.2, developed by Carla Obenshain, an ESOL teacher, and Joanna Benporat, a fourth-grade RELA (Reading Language Arts) teacher at Langley Park McCormick Elementary School in Prince George County, and adapted by Claribel González for this book. Carla uses student portraits to get to know her new students online and to collaborate with her colleagues to better respond to their needs.

Figure 3.2 Student Portrait Template

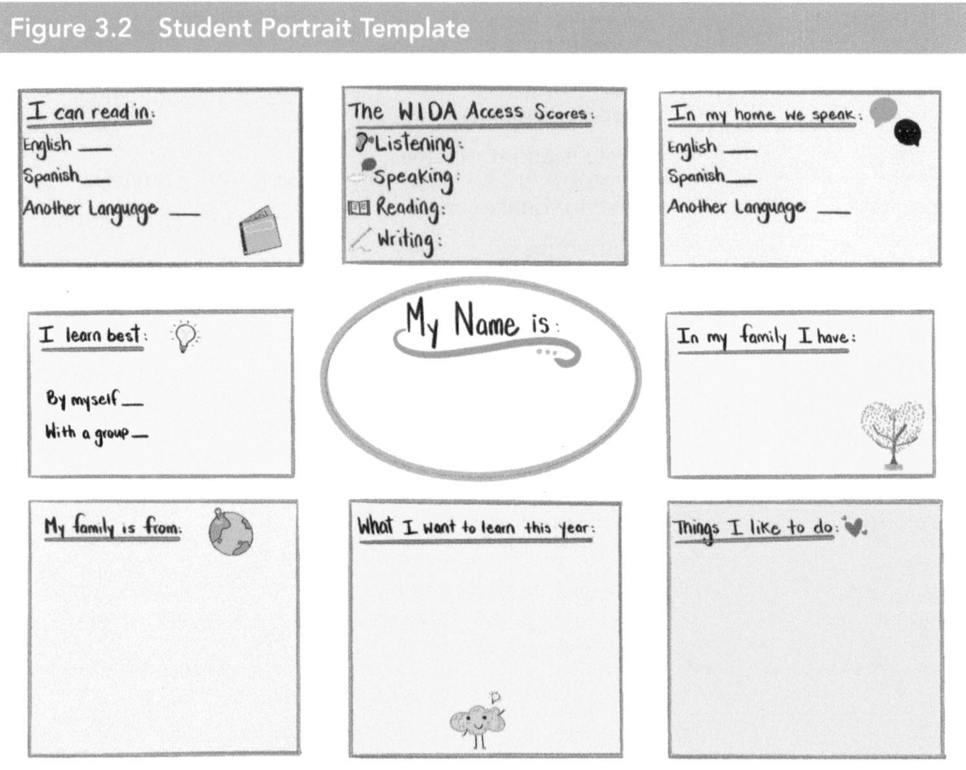

Figure created by Carla Obenshain and Joanna Benporat. Adapted by Claribel González. Used with permission.

See Figure 3.3 for a different English Learner Portrait Template designed by Alycia Owen, EAL (English as an additional language) teacher at American International School of Guangzhou (AISG) China and completed by all of her students.

Creating, reviewing, and periodically updating learner portraits may be a key step to initiating data-informed, evidence-based collaborative planning. Rivera (2020) suggests using learner portraits strategically throughout the year as a tool for collaboration:

1. Start the year with reviewing what your students can do.
2. Begin each new unit with reviewing what special interests, unique experiences, and relevant talents your students have. This activity will also help to gauge how to build or activate background knowledge, how to utilize students' existing expertise, and how to plan for appropriate scaffolding.
3. At the end of the year, highlight students' growth and assets to help transition them into a new grade level.

In addition, the learner portraits may be digitized and combined into a portfolio over a student's academic career to see how they change over time. You might

Figure 3.3 A Student-Completed Learner Portrait

I lived in Korea until I was 14 and then I move to Guangzhou, China. AISG is my first international school in my life!	NAME I'm a new student!	**My family:** my parents and I are in Guangzhou and my sister lives in Korea. She is a university student.
My first language is Korean. I also speak Chinese and English. I speak Korean at home.	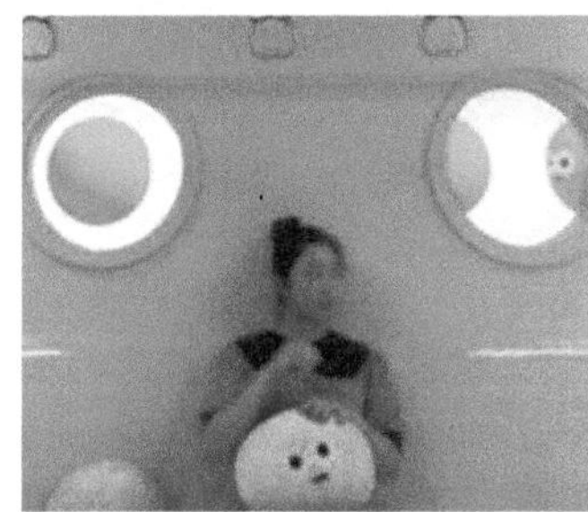	**My most challenging classes are** Social Studies & Science **My favorite class** is Math
My strength is working with others.		**Classes and activities outside of school:** I have Chinese and English classes. I still need some improvement on languages.
My hobbies and interests are listening to music and watching K-dramas.	**I would like my teachers to know:** I need some time to adapt to new changes. And I also want to improve my English skills at AISG! :)	**WIDA Scores** Speaking: 2 Writing: 2 Reading: 4 Listening: 4

Figure created by Alycia Owen and completed by Chaeyun (Jenny) Kim. Used with permission.

wonder what else can be done to integrate evidence about student learning into planning and instruction meaningfully. Let's visualize available data as a timeline that has three broad-brush points to help depict temporal relationships among data sources originating in the past, present, and future in relation to planning for integrating content and language instruction. (See Figure 3.4 to help think of how data supports planning on a continuum.) Please notice that some items that may originally be listed under the past or present will extend into the next time frame, recognizing that data and evidence about student growth is a dynamic process rather than a fixed piece of information.

Past data sources. Data generated at intake will have important information about students based on their home language surveys, their entry test, and annual standardized assessments that measure growth within a year as well as help place students or reclassify them. When considering day-to-day planning and instruction, these data may be considered to capture a moment in the past and may offer more static information.

Present data sources. Ongoing formative assessment that happens both formally and informally to capture information about the moment the data were collected or about the present. Through a series of daily (or frequent) snapshots, we capture dynamic data about students and are able to monitor their progress and intermediate,

Figure 3.4 Data Continuum to Inform Planning

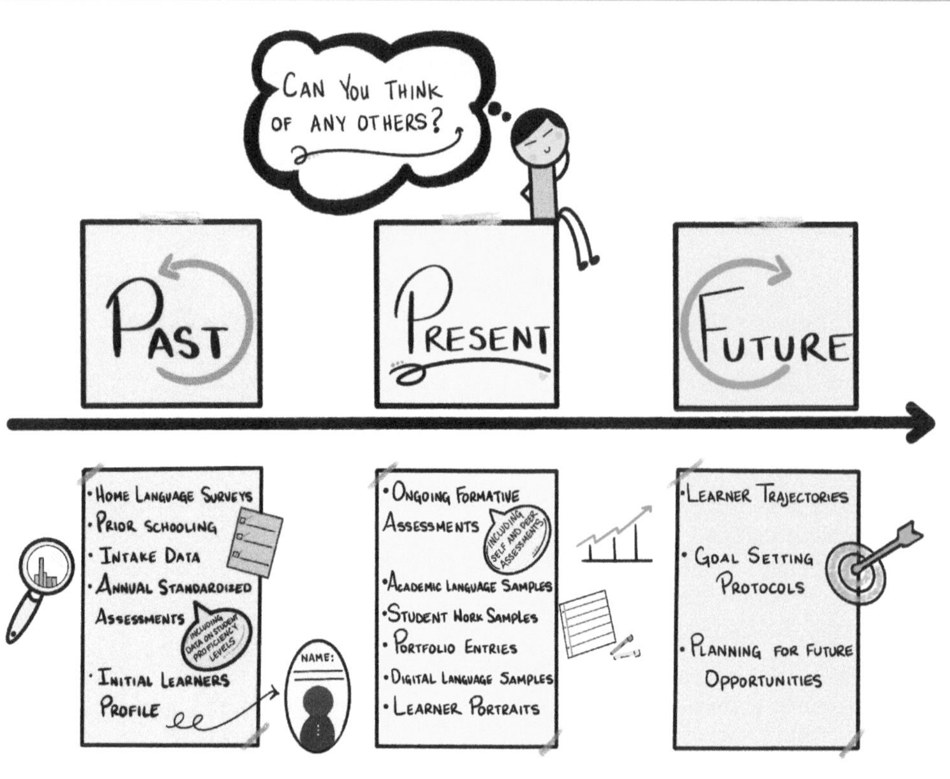

short-term, and long-term growth. We need to thoroughly understand where the students are in their learning at a given time and where they are heading next, which takes us to the "future."

Future data sources. Based on a comprehensive look at students' past and present indicators of language and literacy development, we may also consider their learning trajectory; as such, we are able to gauge the future by anticipating immediate and long-term needs of our ELs/MLs. In other words, let's plan instruction more proactively—knowing which student will need what, who might need some backmapping or foundational skill building, and who might need sustained interventions due to identified learning disabilities, and so on. Planning for the future includes short-term and long-term goal setting that help us identify learning targets based on all available data. With this mindset, we will have more clarity on how to provide additional support to move all students forward to meet expectations and to enhance or accelerate their learning.

Figure 3.5 is a goal-setting template that invites students to consider what learning processes or study habits they should develop and what their learning outcomes or goals may be. A similar template can be created to invite students to plan for their future outside of the K–12 academic setting.

Figure 3.5 An Example of a Completed Student Goal-Setting Template

MY GOALS	LEARNING PROCESSES	LEARNING OUTCOMES
Social Studies	Improve text annotations and note-taking	Incorporate notes into essays with correctly citing sources
English Language Development	Outline essays using templates and supports	Use compare and contrast language features and transitional phrases to create an academic voice
SEL	Seek peer support	Give and receive feedback from peers

The ultimate goal is to periodically collect evidence about learning and examine student work to determine what progress has been made and how to make informed decisions about next steps in our instructional practices.

What Research Says

Of all the different types of assessments, summative assessment reveals progress toward mastery. However, formative assessment that captures students' needs in the moment has received considerable attention. It may be especially important when designing instruction for ELs/MLs because language and literacy development for these students is especially dynamic, and putting the right type and amount of scaffolds in place is necessary (see more on this in Chapter 6).

Hattie (2012) cautions that "feedback is most effective when students do not have proficiency or mastery—and thus it thrives when there is error or incomplete knowing and understanding . . . Errors invite opportunities . . . They should not be seen as embarrassment, signs of failure, or something to be avoided . . . They are exciting, because they indicate a tension between what we now know and what we could know; they are signs of opportunities to learn and they are to be embraced" (p. 124).

Fisher and Frey (2014) recommend a systematic approach to formative assessment consisting of the following phases: (1) Feed-up: Clarifying the purpose, (2) Feedback: Responding to student work, and (3) Feed-forward: Modifying instruction (pp. 2–3).

We adapted Chappuis's (2015) seven strategies for formative assessment clustered around three key questions for co-planning purposes (Figure 3.6).

Figure 3.6 Key Questions for Formative Assessment and Implications for ELs/MLs

KEY FORMATIVE ASSESSMENT QUESTIONS	IMPLICATIONS FOR ELS/MLS
Where Are Our Students Heading? Strategy 1: Provide clear and understandable learning targets. Strategy 2: Use examples and models of work meeting, exceeding, and approaching the target.	ELs/MLs need to fully understand the learning target and must be given the opportunity to review multiple meaningful examples or models of work expected of them.
Where Are Our Students Now? Strategy 3: Offer regular descriptive feedback during the learning. Strategy 4: Teach students to self-assess and set goals for next steps.	ELs/MLs fare better when they are mentored, guided, and supported with the right amount and type of feed forward and feedback.
How Can We Close Any Learning Gaps? Strategy 5: Use evidence of student learning needs to determine next steps in teaching. Strategy 6: Design focused instruction, followed by practice with ongoing feedback. Strategy 7: Provide opportunities for students to track, reflect on, and share their learning progress with their peers, teachers, and family members.	ELs/MLs deserve (and must receive) challenging yet well-supported instruction to aid in their language, literacy, content, and social-emotional development as well as participate in learning activities that help them become self-directed, independent learners.

Source: Adapted from Chappuis (2015).

Most recently, Heritage and Wylie (2020) have suggested the following:

> Formative assessment is a planned ongoing process used by all students and teachers during learning and teaching to elicit and use evidence of student learning to improve student understanding of intended disciplinary learning outcomes and support students to become self-directed learners. (p. 14)

The Data-Informed Collaborative Planning Cycle

In a recent report, Villegas and Pompa (2020) caution that there are tremendous inconsistencies across state policies regarding criteria for EL/ML identification, reclassification, and inclusion into state accountability systems. While we wish to recognize this deep-rooted concern, it is beyond the scope of this book to address such complexities and challenges; however, we agree with Kristina Robertson, who suggests that "all students who have a home language other than English are developing their academic English skills whether they've been identified in the EL/ML program or not. All teachers need to be aware of student language development needs. Just because a student exits EL doesn't mean they no longer need further language development" (personal communication, January 18, 2021).

Our focus is on how to collect and meaningfully respond to the day-to-day data on ELs'/MLs' growth and needs to increase teacher impact on students' academic, linguistic, and social-emotional learning. Collaborative planning must start and end with our students. What do we know about ELs'/MLs' readiness to work with the upcoming concepts and skills? What do they already know, and what can they do independently or with support? We need to invest time into conducting collaborative inquiries into essential data about student needs and progress. Standards must be translated into developmentally appropriate units and lessons with clear learning intentions, success criteria, and learning progressions. Formative data gathered during learning experiences as well as summative data at the end of each unit of study will yield new data, and the cycle continues. See Figure 3.7 for a visual representation of the relationship between and among key phases of this cyclical process.

Figure 3.7 Phases of the Data-Informed Collaborative Planning Cycle

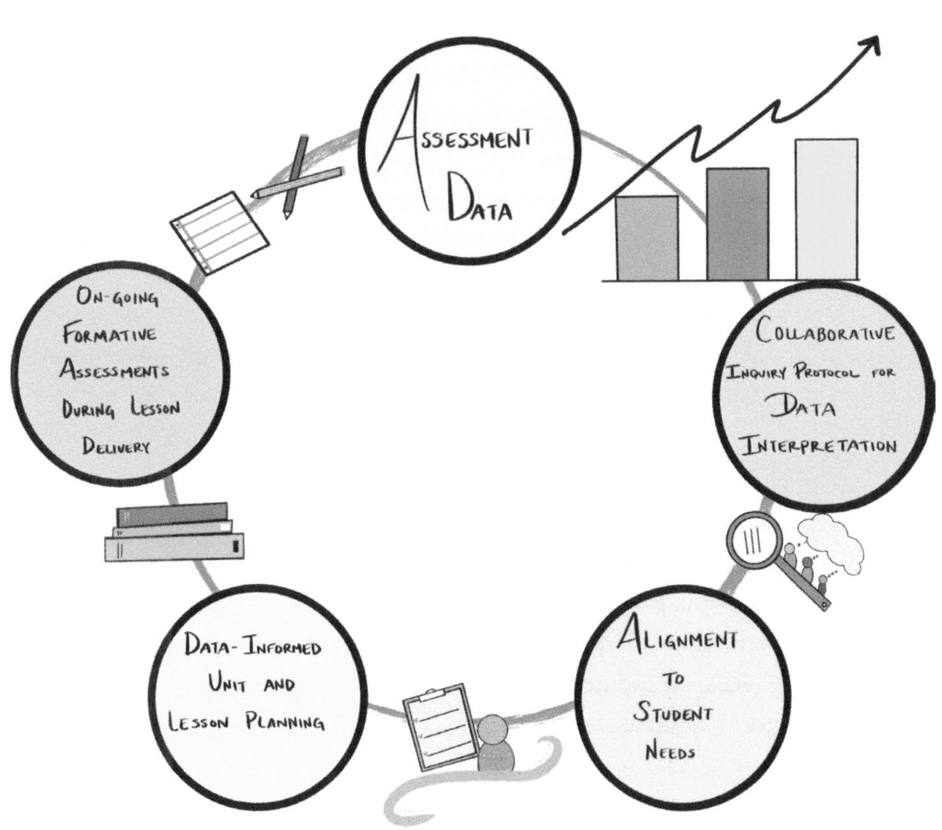

The Blueprint for Data-Informed Collaborative Planning

An issue frequently raised in educational circles is to decide what our educational prime directive is: Is the emphasis on teaching *the content* (to students) or teach *the students* in our care? In the collaborative planning cycle, examining the target standards, considering unit goals and developing lesson objectives (or learning intentions), establishing success criteria, and reviewing student data all happen both simultaneously and in a cyclical fashion. How and why would you wish to begin and end with assessment?

Step 1: Collect and Organize Data to Inform Planning

We have previously suggested that as collaborating teachers, you need *meaningful, accurate, and actionable* information about your ELs'/MLs' language development and content learning, so you "could plan more effective lessons, differentiate instruction more purposefully, and integrate content learning with language development opportunities across the four domains of listening, speaking, reading, and writing" (Honigsfeld & Dove, 2015, p. 70).

Pause for a moment and jot down what meaningful, accurate, and actionable information means for your practice or in your context.

____

____

____

____

Let's unpack these concepts here to enhance clarity and to support collaborative planning based on assessment data for the sake of ELs/MLs.

What Is Meaningful?

If we were to allow it, we could be overwhelmed by the flood of information available to us every day—anything from observational data, to anecdotal records, to attendance patterns, quiz grades, and standardized test scores. Instead of doing data collection (be careful not to slip into data hoarding with very little analysis and meaning-making), let's stay focused and intentional. For planning purposes, data about ELs/MLs will need to be (a) accessible to all teachers, (b) easy to interpret yet accurate (see more on that next), and (c) of high quality. When it is collected and shared in an organized fashion, all educators will be able to make sense of it and derive meaning from it. See Figure 3.8 for a quick review of what is and what is not meaningful!

Figure 3.8 What Is Meaningful and What Is Not . . .

WHAT IS MEANINGFUL . . .	WHAT IS NOT . . .
Academic language samples through which students can demonstrate what they know and can do	Asking students to interpret and respond to unnecessarily complex tasks or language embedded in the task
Authentic student work	Cookie-cutter, identical student products
Student ownership	Student responses in anticipation of what the teacher wants to hear/see
Genuine, student-authored writing from start to finish	Completing written grammar exercises or worksheets with predetermined writing topics

What Is Accurate?

Accuracy may be interpreted as assessments being valid and reliable. The information about our ELs/MLs is valid when we are collecting and interpreting the data *we intend to collect.* It is considered reliable when collaborating teachers agree on interpreting student information in the same way. See Figure 3.9 for a quick review about what accuracy is and what it looks, sounds, and feels like.

Figure 3.9 What Is Accuracy, and What Does It Look, Sound, and Feel Like?

WHAT IS ACCURACY?	WHAT DOES IT LOOK LIKE, SOUND LIKE, FEEL LIKE?
Success criteria are established.	Both teachers and students know what constitutes success.
Clarity of assessment task is ensured.	Both teachers and students understand what expectations are and how to show what students know and can do.
Rubrics are used consistently.	Rubrics are collaboratively developed with student input and review and reflect the different language ability levels and scaffolded supports students need to be successful.
Tasks are aligned to standards and unit learning outcomes.	A benchmark assessment or "part of a project," such as written, cohesive text prior to creating the final project of a travel brochure.

What Is Actionable?

To plan well for ELs'/MLs' content and language development along with social-emotional learning, we need information we can act upon. We need insights into what students can do and what they need support with to make progress toward goals and objectives. Collecting student test scores, checkmarks on exit slips, completed rubrics, and so on, results in data on top of data. The key idea here is to select data that will inform instruction and can be translated into teachable lessons. See Figure 3.10 for a quick review of what actionable means, what some examples from the classroom might be, and how to plan to respond to student needs.

Figure 3.10 What Is Actionable: Examples and Appropriate Responses

WHAT IS ACTIONABLE?	EXAMPLES FROM THE CLASSROOM	HOW TO PLAN TO RESPOND
Consistent examples of individual language use across different language samples	A student consistently uses regular and irregular past tense in narrative writing.	Plan to demonstrate correct past tense usage with the most common student errors. Demonstrate student growth as they make fewer errors.
Recurring patterns of language use for a group of ELs/MLs at a particular language proficiency level	Most students seem to string simple sentences together when asked to write at length. They do not seem to use compound or complex sentences for fear of making mistakes.	Plan for small group targeted instruction to model how to make compound sentences as a step toward more complex sentences.
Gaps in student content knowledge	Students may have little knowledge of U.S. historical events.	Plan for building background knowledge by including lesson activities that check for prior knowledge. Plan to provide instructional time to review key details of U.S. historical events.

Step 2: Engage in a Collaborative Inquiry Into Student Data

Building upon Singer's (2014) suggestion to establish problems of practice and inquiry questions, we encourage you and your colleagues to co-construct your collaborative planning and assessment practices by critically reflecting on and coming to a joint agreement regarding the following three key questions as well as their respective supporting questions:

1. **What are our shared goals for student learning?**
   a. Where are our students today, and where do we want them to go?
   b. How are we planning for content and language development?
   c. How do we measure student growth in both content and language development?

   d. How do we ensure sharing responsibility for student outcomes in both content and language development?

2. **How will all students, including ELs/MLs, on every level of proficiency demonstrate success?**
   a. What is our definition of success for ELs/MLs (and their English-proficient peers)?
   b. How do we differentiate instruction and assessment for all levels of ELs/MLs?
   c. How do we set attainable goals for all our students yet remain mindful of the grade-level benchmarks?
   d. What assessment tools and measures are we going to use that are fair, meaningful, and equitable?

3. **What instruction will we provide collaboratively to ensure success for all our students?**
   a. How do we integrate content and language instruction?
   b. How do we scaffold and support learning?
   c. How do we gradually increase student autonomy?
   d. How do we ensure active student engagement?

Engaging in structured conversations or collaborative protocols like this one enhances the effectiveness and outcomes of collaborations. As with all other tools, templates, and protocols, we encourage you to feel free to adapt this protocol to better align it to your own initiatives around assessment.

Step 3: Align Students' Learning Needs With Core Content Standards and Language (and Literacy)

Based on the scope and sequence of your core content curriculum, begin the alignment process by identifying the core content standards. As suggested by Fisher et al. (2019), closely examine the target standard(s) and highlight the key concepts students are expected to master and the essential skills they need to develop. During this conversation, pay also close attention to the academic or cognitive demands as well as the embedded language and literacy demands of the standards. To continue the alignment process, collaboratively analyze the language development standards that need to be addressed and align them to the language and literacy demands of the core content. Identify key language uses that will be addressed. Finally, based on the assessment data, highlight your students' essential learning needs in the areas of oracy and literacy. See Figure 3.11 for a completed planning template that helps capture key ideas during alignment work.

Figure 3.11 An Alignment Template Based on a Sixth-Grade ELA Unit

Core Content Standards (Next Generation)	English Language Development Standards (WIDA)	ELs'/MLs' Needs
6R3: In literary texts, describe how events unfold, as well as how characters respond or change as the plot moves toward a resolution. (RL) **6R6:** In literary texts, identify the point of view and explain how it is developed and conveys meaning. (RL) **6W2:** Write informative/explanatory texts to examine a topic and convey ideas, concepts, and information through the selection, organization, and analysis of relevant content. **6SL1:** Engage effectively in a range of collaborative discussions with diverse partners; express ideas clearly and persuasively, and build on those of other.	Standard 1: Social and instructional language Standard 2: Language of language arts	Building background knowledge Scaffolding to provide: • sensory support • graphic support • interactive support • digital support • socio-emotional support

CONCEPTS (NOUNS)	SKILLS (VERBS)	KEY ACADEMIC LANGUAGE USES	ORACY	LITERACY
Events Characters Plot Point of view Resolution	Describe Identify Explain Compare Contrast Express	English language learners communicate for social and instructional purposes within the school setting. English language learners communicate information, ideas, and concepts necessary for academic success in the content area of language arts.	Accountable talk stems and frames Group & Partner work	Adapted texts Differentiated texts Chunking texts Visuals Pre-taught vocabulary

Cognitive Demand

- I can analyze how dialogue or specific incidents reveal information about characters or move the plot forward.
- I can analyze how an author develops and contrasts the points of view of characters and narrators in a literary text.
- I can analyze the interactions between individuals, events, and ideas in a text.
- I can write an informative essay focusing on a specific topic and including relevant and interesting ideas and details.

Linguistic Demand

- I can make and orally describe inferences from the text.
- I can explain how the author develops different points of view.
- I can summarize the events and interaction of the text by using the "Somebody-Wanted-But-So-Then" strategy.
- I can utilize transition words and sentence frames.

Source: Adapted from Fisher et al. (2019). Completed example by Kelley Cordeiro and Erica Flores. Used with permission.

Step 4: Create Data-Informed Unit and Lesson Plans

Planning frameworks and instructional routines may support teachers as they engage in collaborative conversations about assessment data that will inform unit and lesson planning. According to Alber (2017), in order to be mindful of authentic student learning, teachers should not be "overly fixated on results from one test, from one day" (para. 1). Instead, teachers need to continuously collect formative and summative assessment data in order to select, review, and adjust what is being taught as well as plan for continuous ways of determining the needs and progress of students.

A SOUND BITE

Lee (2019) proposes that "content standards call for all students, including ELs, to engage in academically rigorous and language-intensive disciplinary practices, such as arguing from evidence and constructing explanations . . . To align with content standards, ELP standards must reflect the language learning opportunities and demands of content standards. Specifically, ELP standards must reflect the language needed to engage in disciplinary practices of content standards" (p. 537).

Do you agree? What is your experience with aligning language and literacy instruction with content standards? Which aspect(s) of this statement might need specific attention in your context?

Icon: iStock.com/Vectorig

First and foremost, unit-planning goals should be aligned with learning standards, and with ELs/MLs, both content and language standards need to be set as benchmarks as well as assessed. All too often, integrated instruction, defined for our purposes as the teaching of English language development (ELD) in combination with content instruction, includes the assessment of the content but not of language. Teachers need to collaboratively consider what types of formative and summative tools will be used to determine student success. Unit plans should reveal the learning path or learning progressions that students will make in both their core content attainment and their language and literacy development. Without such intentionality, language and literacy acquisition may at best become incidental.

Daily lesson plans should include learning intentions (or learning targets) that clearly identify what the expectations are when it comes to core content, academic language, and literacy development. According to Fisher and his colleagues (2019), "The success criteria provide a means for students and the teacher to gauge progress toward learning, thereby making learning visible to the teacher and the student" (p. 30). There are multiple ways to plan for meaningful learning intentions and success criteria with linguistically diverse students in mind, as shown in the two planning grids that follow. According to one approach, the learning intentions regarding the core content area and academic language and literacy development are treated as carefully aligned but separate entities with their own respective success criteria (see Figure 3.12 for an elementary integrated science/ELA example); whereas in the second approach, the learning intentions and/or the success criteria are viewed as fully integrated (see Figure 3.13 for a secondary integrated social studies/ELA example).

Figure 3.12 Completed Learning Intention Planning Grid 1

Learning intention in the core content area Today, we will use the words and pictures in an informational text to learn facts about owls.	**Success criteria with a content focus** 1. I can write a fact about owls. 2. I can identify whether I learned it from the picture or the text.
Learning intention in academic language and literacy At the end of the lesson, we will write at least two complete sentences to show our learning. We will explain our answers using the word *because*.	**Success criteria with a language and literacy focus** 1. I can write two complete sentences. Sentence frame: • I learned ______ from the ______. 2. I can use the word *because* to explain my answer. Sentence frame: • I know because in the ______ it says/shows ______.
Exemplars: I learned **owls can live in the rainforest** from the **text**. I know because in the **text** it says **owls live in rainforests and deserts**. I learned **owls build nests** from the **picture**. I know because in the **picture** it shows **an owl sitting in a nest**.	

Source: Adapted from Fisher et al. (2019). Completed example by Allyson Caudill, John Cox, and Ashley Blackley. Used with permission.

Figure 3.13 Learning Intention Planning Grid 2

GRADE 10 SOCIAL STUDIES	
Integrated content and language learning intentions: *I can explain the social, political, and economic factors that lead to Hitler's popularity after WWI* ***using a clear topic sentence and textual evidence.*** Green—language function Blue—content target Purple—language target	Success criteria with a content focus: Students' explanation will include details connected to – The U.S. stock market crash of 1929 – Scapegoating of the Jews – The embarrassment of having to follow the Treaty of Versailles
	Success criteria with a language and literacy focus: Students' explanation will include – A clear topic sentence that identifies their reason

GRADE 10 SOCIAL STUDIES	
	– Factual events using past tense verbs described with accuracy related to the stock market crash, scapegoating of the Jews, and the Treaty of Versailles – Connection established between these historical events and how they made Hitler popular among right-winged German nationalists using cause and effect terms such as, "prior to, leading to, in contrast, resulting in"

Source: Adapted from Fisher et al. (2019). Example completed by Tan Huyhn. Used with permission.

See Chapter 4 for further exploration of unit and lesson planning practices, frameworks, and protocols.

Step 5: Implement Continuous Assessment Practices During Lesson Delivery

Regardless of lesson delivery taking place in a stand-alone ELD class, a co-taught core content class, or a solo-taught class with no ELD specialist present, keep in mind that just about any task, learning activity, or student work sample or final product may provide valuable data on what your ELs/MLs can do. Figure 3.14 will highlight examples across the four core content areas of how assessing student performance from the perspective of content versus language will help better inform planning.

Figure 3.14 Continuous Assessment Practices for Content, Language, and Literacy

	EXAMPLES OF CONTINUOUS ASSESSMENT PRACTICES FOR CONTENT ATTAINMENT	EXAMPLES OF CONTINUOUS ASSESSMENT PRACTICES FOR LANGUAGE AND LITERACY DEVELOPMENT
Math	Students show how they solved equations	Students explain orally the steps taken to solve equations
Science	Students design an experiment	Students write a report at the completion of the experiment
ELA	Students read and analyze examples of a particular genre	Students use mentor texts to write in the genre required by the task
Social Studies	Students take a side regarding a controversial topic and provide evidence for their stance	Students use words, phrases, sentences, and/or paragraphs that are appropriate for arguing their point of view

A SNAPSHOT FROM THE FIELD

In Beth Harju and Jaymie Hogg's collaboratively taught classes, both teachers engage in ongoing assessment practices:

> *Teachers begin the lesson by explaining the day's objectives. The class continues to work on writing essays that compare and contrast renewable and nonrenewable resources with evidence from two sources. Students also revise and edit to improve their drafts. As they work through the writing process, students sign up on the whiteboard to conference with a teacher (classroom or ELL co-teacher) before they publish their final draft. While the conferencing teacher is working with students individually, the other teacher continues to support and monitor students in the class as needed. The conferencing teacher calls students one by one with their typed assignment opened. Each student reads his or her essay aloud while the conferencing teacher takes notes in a grading notebook noting his or her strengths, areas needing improvement, goals, and ideas for mini lessons. The teacher compliments the student on his or her strengths, for example, "I love the way you used sentence starters to show the language of comparing and contrasting. For example, in this sentence, you wrote, 'One major difference between renewable and nonrenewable resources is that renewable resources can be naturally replaced.'" The conferencing teacher asks if the student noticed anything while reading aloud that he or she would like to edit or set as a goal for their next writing assignment. After discussion with the teacher about verb tenses, the student notices that some of the draft is written in past tense and some in present tense. The student also had some difficulty with irregular past tense verbs (goed instead of went and runned instead of ran). The student makes the necessary corrections. The conferencing teacher shares the areas of improvement that were noted, and they work together to form a goal for the next conference. The student decides to set a goal of staying in the correct verb tense. The teacher makes a note to possibly teach a mini lesson on verb tenses for the class. The student is commended on completing the writing process. The conferencing teacher writes the goal that was agreed to on the student's page in the conferencing notebook and makes a note that this student might benefit from a lesson in past, present, and future verb tenses and irregular past tense verbs. The next student is called over for a conference.*

Based on your professional knowledge and teaching experience, which of these statements are best aligned with your beliefs about assessment?

STOP AND PROCESS

iStock.com/bombuscreative

1. Linguistically and culturally responsive and sustainable instructional and assessment practices lead to equitable education for ELs/MLs.
2. Teacher partnerships and shared decision making about ELs'/MLs' learning can enhance their academic, linguistic, and social-emotional outcomes.
3. A balanced approach to assessment includes all stakeholders (students, teachers, caregivers, and administrators).
4. Parents of ELs/MLs are regularly informed about their children's progress in ways that are fully accessible to them.
5. When teachers collaborate to design assessment measures, implement co-developed assessment tools, and interpret the assessment data jointly, they develop shared understanding of their students' assets and needs.
6. The primary role of formative assessment is to inform planning and instruction.
7. Classroom-based assessment data help shape personalized, differentiated, and authentic learning experiences for all.

A Tri-Part Approach to Assessment

One of our core beliefs is that everything we do in the classroom is driven by the relationships and interactions that take place in the classroom and school community. Assessment practices are no different. As suggested by Gottlieb and Honigsfeld (2020), "approaches to assessment are relationship driven, primarily among students (in assessment *as* learning), teachers (in assessment *for* learning), and school leaders (in assessment *of* learning)" (p. 143). These three types of assessments are summarized in Figure 3.15, with examples of what collaboratively planning educators do and what tools they use to collect and reflect on student data.

Figure 3.15 Summary of Types of Assessment With Associated Teacher Actions and Examples of Tools

TYPES OF ASSESSMENT	WHEN PLANNING COLLABORATIVELY, TEACHERS . . .	EXAMPLES OF TOOLS USED FOR DATA COLLECTION
Assessment *as* Learning	Consider student self-assessment data and goal setting Guide students to self-monitor their own learning Encourage students to take responsibility for their work and develop independence	Utilized by Students • Self- and peer assessment • Peer-editing checklists • Learning logs

(Continued)

(Continued)

TYPES OF ASSESSMENT	WHEN PLANNING COLLABORATIVELY, TEACHERS . . .	EXAMPLES OF TOOLS USED FOR DATA COLLECTION
	Help students document their growth and show evidence of their learning Create opportunities for self- and peer assessment and peer feedback Advance students' skills to advocate for themselves by explaining their own learning processes, strengths, and needs	• Interactive journals • Reflection tools
Assessment *for* Learning	Co-construct success criteria carefully aligned to learning intentions Co-create a menu of formative assessment tasks to encourage student choice Determine the formative assessment data collection methods Use data from previous formative assessment measures to plan instruction	Utilized by teachers and students • Graphic organizers • Checklists • Rubrics or project descriptors • Templates of criteria for success • Action research, along with reflection tools
Assessment *of* Learning	Review and update student portraits with summative data Review unit goals and desired outcomes Consider how standards and assessments are aligned	Utilized by administrators and school leaders, often with teachers • Communicated to parents and caregivers • Score reports from tests • Data from student portraits • School or district rubrics • School or district portfolios

Collaborative assessment as, for, and of learning ensures a multidimensional approach not only to assessment practices but also to collaborative planning. When teachers systematically examine what students can do and plan accordingly, they create a more equitable learning environment for all.

Tools of the Trade

You might wonder where to begin or how to accomplish all of what was presented in this chapter successfully. Let's share some essential tools and practices that will either support the initial steps of completing this work or allow you to enhance your existing practices. The *Tools of the Trade* section of this chapter will offer tools for data collection, data analysis, and collaboration with data interpretation in mind.

Tools for Data Collection

Use low-tech and high-tech tools for collecting actionable information about your students. Google Docs, Google Forms, and Google Sheets allow for not only the capture of essential information about students' progress but also its easy sharing.

Tools for Data Analysis

Large amounts of data documenting student progress in their core content areas as well as regarding their language and literacy development may be overwhelming and ineffective. Data charts that help visualize evidence for student learning as well as areas of gaps in student growth help teachers plan more effectively. For example, Santiago (2019), English learner coordinator for Ames Community School District in Iowa, cautions us to balance and humanize large-scale data with stories and narratives that help contextualize individual progress. Tools that support this approach include spreadsheets that yield charts and graphs and are supplemented with infographics and student portraits. Autocrat is a Google extension tool that helps merge data and create personalized documents from Google Sheets. Data visualizations complete with color coding of various levels of student growth and the use of protocols to analyze data in PLC discussions can help the team identify trends at the programmatic, grade, and individual student levels. See Figure 3.16 as an example Shaeley Santiago and her team generated and used to analyze data.

A SOUND BITE

While contemplating why teachers leave the profession and how to keep them from doing so, Rizga (2019) observed the following:

> When teachers plan classroom activities together, educators have a chance to implement improvements as a cohesive effort across the building, develop a shared vision and common language around learning goals, and learn how to detect outcomes using a broad range of data, including markers for key skills, such as resilience or collaboration, that can't be captured using standardized test scores. (para. 23)

Do you agree? What is your experience with improving cohesion of instruction while collaborating? How do you develop a shared vision and common language around learning goals for all students including ELs/MLs? Which aspect(s) of this statement might need specific attention in your context?

Icon: iStock.com/Vectorig

Tools for Collaboration

Collaborative Conversation Protocols about student data are helpful to structure discussions and make planning meetings that more specifically focus on student performance and progress more productive. We were inspired by Aguilar's (2013) work when we developed the following four-step protocol:

Step 1: Before the planning meeting, reflect on what your hopes and concerns are regarding student data and the information that will be examined:

What do you hope to see emerge from the data?

What are your predictions regarding the data?

What are some of your concerns that might transpire during the data discussion?

Figure 3.16 Data Visualization

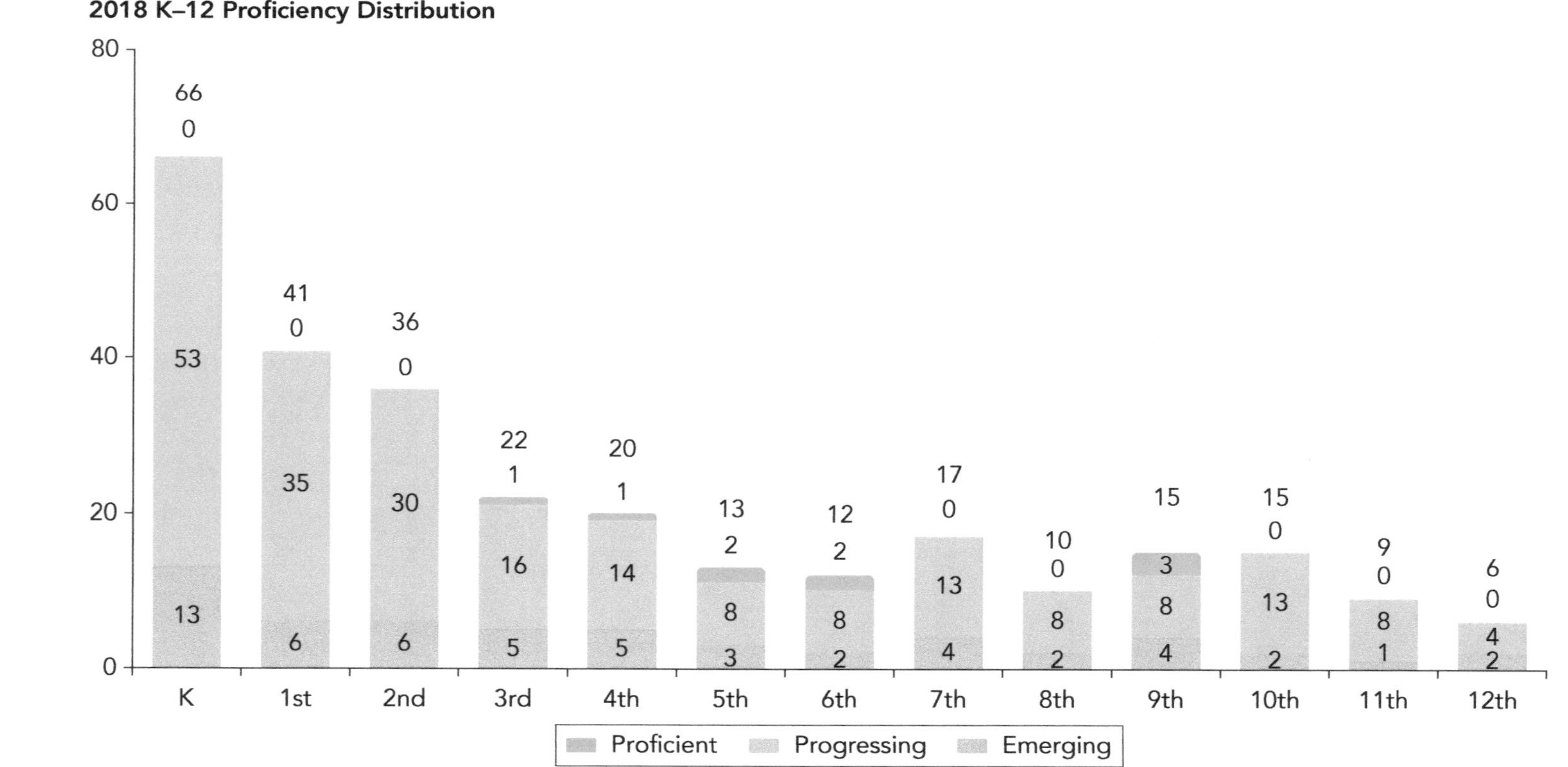

Figure created by Shaeley Santiago. Used with permission.

Step 2: Engage in a preliminary examination of the data and—withholding any judgment—make some observations using the Noticing and Wondering prompts that follow:

I noticed . . .

I wonder . . .

Allow everyone at the table to share their noticings and wonderings and offer each other some insights in a nonjudgmental, nonevaluative manner about what you are looking at.

Step 3: Cause and effect analysis

Revisit the patterns of data for a group of students (be it a cluster of students on the same proficiency level, a class, a grade level, etc.) or patterns of data and trajectory for individual students and identify possible explanations:

What do the data mean?

What are some plausible explanations?

What are the causes of certain patterns of student performance or linguistic behavior?

What are the implications for planning?

Step 4: Plan to respond to data

What reviews and reteaching needs to be planned and for whom?

What scaffolds and supports need to be planned and for whom?

What extensions and enrichments need to be planned and for whom?

We recognize that there are numerous other ways educators use student data and evidence of student learning.

Celebrations

Two members of the NCPA (Nansha College Preparatory Academy, Nansha, China) leadership team—Dr. Maria Domingues (current) and Patrick Kane (former)—introduced Harvard's Data Wise Improvement Process to their faculty. In addition, Aracelis Maldonado, acting head of school, and Emily (Roberts) Tewolde, English teacher, also participated in extensive training. They introduced a collaborative approach to examining student data utilizing the Data Wise norms and ACE Habits of Mind to help foster a positive, productive ethos addressing successful group dynamics needed to engage in collaborative work as well as the Meeting Wise protocol to structure and organize outcomes-based conversations.

DATA WISE NORMS

- Be here now
- Take an inquiry stance
- Ground statements in evidence
- Assume positive intentions and take responsibility for impact
- Stick to protocol to hear all voices
- Start and end on time

ACE HABITS OF MIND

A—Shared commitment to *Action*, *Assessment*, and *Adjustment*

C—Intentional *Collaboration*

E—A relentless focus on *Evidence*

Following is a snapshot of ongoing work begun during the 2019–2020 academic year concerning collaborative planning and assessment for English language learners (ELLs) (see Figure 3.17).

Figure 3.17 Meeting Wise Protocol Translated to Collaborative Planning for ELLs

STEP 1: ORGANIZE FOR COLLABORATIVE WORK.

PURPOSE OF THIS STEP: Establish structures and teams.

How to Connect It to Collaborative Planning for ELLs

- Identify co-teaching teams of teachers, English as an additional language (EAL) specialists, and teaching assistants to build their capacity to work together to support ELLs.
- Make time for collaborative inquiry work at least 2 hours per month.
- Define roles for each member in terms of how they will integrate their inquiry work to plan support for ELLs; use a protocol to acknowledge work style preferences.
- Co-teaching teams
    - Are coached to follow effective and structured meetings
    - Agree and know the norms for collaborative inquiry work and agree on the following: (1) using strategies to make colleagues accountable for following norms, (2) monitor norms on a regular basis, and (3) revisit and revise
    - Practice the ACE Habits of Mind
- The revised mission of the Data Wise Project states: "to support schools and systems in collaborative data inquiry leading to equitable and excellent outcomes for all children" (Harvard GSE, 2020, para. 4).
- Therefore, teams are expected to engage in activities that are related to equity so they can be prepared to fully engage in the improvement process.
- Specifically, educators take stock of how their own beliefs and assumptions impact their current experience and reduce their assumptions and biases about ELLs and colleagues that are different from them.
- Co-teacher teams share their WHYs.

STEP 2: BUILD ASSESSMENT LITERACY.

PURPOSE OF THIS STEP: Increase comfort with data.

How to Connect It to Collaborative Planning for ELLs

- Co-teaching teams
    - Review and discuss literacy skills students need to master
    - Study how results are reported (e.g., MAP, WIDA, SAT)
    - Learn principles of responsible data use and use a common language when discussing the inferences that can be made from different assessments. This knowledge will also be applied in Step 7 (Plan to assess progress) and in the design of assessments to measure student progress.
- Educators consider how assessments (e.g., MAP) are used to provide ELLs with a better language proficiency.

STEP 3: CREATE DATA OVERVIEW.

PURPOSE OF THIS STEP: Identify a priority question.

How to Connect It to Collaborative Planning for ELLs

- The leadership team narrows the scope of inquiry by identifying a focus area that best serves all their ELL students.
- The data overview tells the story of our student body as Chinese nationals in an immersion school and considers their language proficiency.

(Continued)

(Continued)

- The priority question is identified by all staff members of co-teaching teams, including EAL specialists and Chinese teaching assistants.
- Educators disaggregate data by different student subgroups according to their language proficiency.
- Educators discuss whose stories are told and not told as part of reviewing the charts.
- Connect back to the shared WHY (Step 1).

STEP 4: DIG INTO STUDENT DATA.

PURPOSE OF THIS STEP: Identify a learner-centered problem.

How to Connect It to Collaborative Planning for ELLs

- All members of the co-teaching team collaboratively select and examine a wide range of student data that is connected to the priority question identified in Step 3.
- Norms and protocols ensure that all team members contribute to the conversation in order to identify a learner-centered problem.
- Educators
  - Are aware of the assumptions they make about which students can meet standards
  - Identify the students that struggle the most and identify their strengths
  - Do not blame students and/or their families for poor student performance
  - Engage students in reflecting on their own learning
- Co-teaching teams collaborate with counselors and consider reviewing non-academic data.

STEP 5: EXAMINE INSTRUCTION.

PURPOSE OF THIS STEP: Identify a problem of practice.

How to Connect It to Collaborative Planning for ELLs

- Co-teaching teams
  - Collaboratively look at teacher-generated materials/resources
  - Observe teaching and learning in their classrooms
  - Understand that classroom observation is non-evaluative, cultivate norms, and use protocols to guide their process and conversations
  - Collaboratively look at instructional data to identify a problem of practice
- Educators
  - Discuss their vision for what equitable instruction should look like in classrooms
  - Discuss what patterns they see in how teachers interact with different students
  - Review how classroom resources align with all students' language proficiencies
  - Practice a growth mindset to avoid putting themselves on the defensive

STEP 6: DEVELOP AN ACTION PLAN.

PURPOSE OF THIS STEP: Create an action plan.

How to Connect It to Collaborative Planning for ELLs

- Co-teaching teams
  - Collaboratively select a research-based instructional strategy for addressing the problem of practice in teaching ALL ELLs
  - Collaboratively select indicators to describe how the instructional strategy will look in the classroom
  - Write an action plan that will include the list of tasks to be done, who will be responsible for each task, and by when they will be completed

- The strategies chosen
  - Take into consideration ALL ELLs
  - Include differentiation of students according to their different language proficiencies
  - Include actions such as giving more opportunities to demonstrate success and providing more individualized attention

STEP 7: PLAN TO ASSESS PROGRESS.

PURPOSE OF THIS STEP: Create a plan to assess progress.

How to Connect It to Collaborative Planning for ELLs

- Co-teaching teams consider multiple sources of data to measure student progress.
- Co-teaching teams specifically include student feedback as one of the sources of data.
- Educators plan to support students by assessing their own learning.
- Co-teaching teams plan to disaggregate data by students' subgroups.
- The assessment plan includes the following:
  - When each type of assessment data will be collected
  - Who will be responsible for collecting and keeping track of the data
  - How the data will be shared among faculty and administration
  - The goals for student improvement and proficiency
- Planning to assess progress includes the following:
  - **Short-term:** Collect data at regular intervals (e.g., students' classwork, students' reflections, classroom observation, conferences with students, focus groups, surveys)
  - **Medium-term:** Collect data several times over the year (e.g., open-ended assessments and rubrics)
  - **Long-term:** Collect once or twice a year (e.g., MAP, WIDA, AP, SAT)
- Co-teaching teams should plan their assessments in a way that they measure the same skills, be consistent from one version to the next, and are administered under standardized conditions.
- Educators agree collectively on test-administration procedures, and a consistent scoring system must be established.
- Educators calibrate teachers' scoring.

STEP 8: ACT AND ASSESS.

PURPOSE OF THIS STEP: Document improvements in teaching and learning and adjust as needed.

How to Connect It to Collaborative Planning for ELLs

- Co-teaching teams
  - Implement the action plan providing all students with the resources and support they need to succeed
  - Collaboratively assess their action plan in practice and reflect on how the team exhibited equitable practices
  - Collaboratively assess student learning and analyze whether their work has led to equitable outcomes
- Educators
  - Reflect on how external factors can affect performances of students
  - Adjust the action plan, if needed, based on evidence
  - Reflect on the extent to which the process addresses the shared WHY (Step 1)
- Teams celebrate success and document the journey.

Template adapted from Oberman and Boudett (2015).

The success story of NCPA continues to today! Many other schools we supported have similar successes with integrating collaborative planning with intentional planning and data-informed and evidence-based collaborative explorations. We hope that this chapter offered a multidimensional portrait of how collaborative assessment and planning fit together.

COLLABORATIVE REFLECTION QUESTIONS

1. Christina Torres (2019) reminds us that we can view assessment as an act of love. She reflects on her practice when she suggests that "data and assessments don't need to be cold-hearted tools that reduce my students to weaknesses and numbers. Instead, they can be another way I build deeper and more loving connections with students" (para. 8). How do your experiences with assessment relate to this claim? Is assessment an act of love in your context? Why or why not? How may assessing and giving feedback on language and literacy development become a sign of love?
2. How might collaborative teams ensure that the collection and analysis of language and content assessment data receive the time and attention they deserve? How might teams devise structures or routines to support regular collection of data and collaborative discourse that informs the planning of instruction for ELs/MLs?
3. What are the greatest obstacles in the collection and collaborative analysis of assessment data? How might these challenges be resolved? What tools might be in place to support the organization and analysis of assessment data?
4. In the chapter, we presented numerous research-informed principles and practices. How do you apply them to your own context? What is the role of formative assessment data in your collaborative planning? How does collaborative planning help you determine what language, literacy, and academic learning outcomes are expected? How do you design formative assessment practices and ensure all students get the feedback they need?
5. In her recent publication, Gottlieb (2021) suggests that collaborative planning and shared use of assessment data should not be just the teachers' responsibility; teachers can and should co-plan with their students, too:

   > It begins with co-planning when teachers and students co-construct learning goals and targets from language and content standards to match their essential questions. They then set criteria for success for those goals that are illustrated by models or examples of exemplary student work. Classroom assessment, an ongoing activity, is marked by interaction among students as well as between teachers and students with frequent actionable feedback to improve teaching and learning. (p. 181)

In what ways can you expand your collaborative assessment and planning practices to more fully include your students?

Watch Andrea and Maria discussing some highlights of Chapter 3. What would you add to their argument in favor of data-informed planning? In what ways did they affirm or challenge your thinking about this topic?

COLLABORATIVE ACTION STEPS

Consider the role of data and assessment practices in collaborative planning.

1. Determine who the key collaborators in your school or district are with whom you need to communicate, coordinate efforts, and collaborate.
2. Decide what key components of data-informed collaborative planning you are going to implement in your own context.
3. Identify assessment measures and practices that yield accurate, actionable, and meaningful data about ELs/MLs.
4. Examine how well assessment practices are aligned to instructional goals, objectives, or learning intentions.
5. Determine how information and evidence about your ELs'/MLs' learning will inform your instruction.

Co-Planning Routines, Frameworks, and Protocols 4

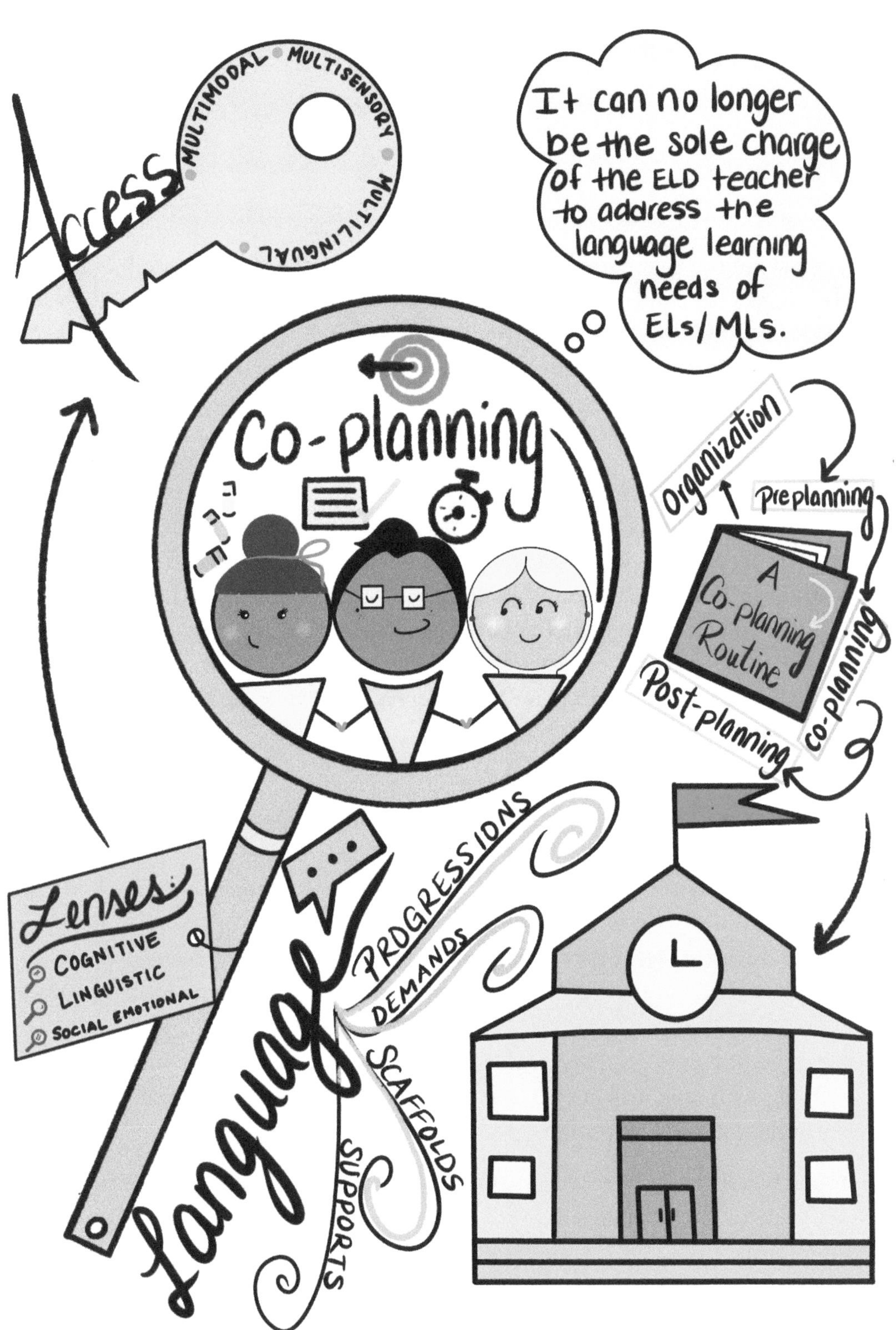

"Unit co-planning is more bang for the buck! I can only be WITH the class 30–45 min/week, but co-planning gets my effect (point of view, strategies, scaffolds, etc.) in the room ALL the time ^_^ "

—Sherry Liptak, itinerant ELL specialist
SD#33, Chilliwack, BC, Canada

"I've found that a week-at-a-glance which shows what will be covered in class and the assignment for each day helps not only the students but also the co-teachers be on the same page. My co-teachers and I develop these on Fridays before the upcoming week."

—Mark Yager, ESL teacher
Warren Central High School, Bowling Green, Kentucky

Co-planning often requires teachers to change not only what they do but also how they think. For co-planning to work, teachers must endeavor to share their beliefs, understandings, opinions, and convictions with fellow teachers and be open to incorporating unfamiliar ideas into their class instruction. Effective co-planning is markedly organized to energize teachers, and when workplace conditions are professionally and personally rewarding, the practice of collaborative instructional planning can thrive.

Co-planning involves, first and foremost, the commitment of teacher teams to work together to optimize learning experiences for students, and in particular, to devise instruction for English learners/multilingual learners (ELs/MLs). It requires shared goals for and beliefs in the abilities of ELs/MLs as well as a willingness to build trust, to take risks, and to forge new territory, often through leaps of faith. Co-planning also celebrates teacher autonomy and independence while championing the collective efforts of the team.

In this chapter, we identify the essential organizational elements involved in co-planning for ELs/MLs, and we showcase the different aspects of collaborative and instructional routines and frameworks for structured planning that make this practice sustainable long term. Moreover, we emphasize how collaborative planning involves so much more than lesson development. It is a tremendous opportunity for educators to share their ideas about teaching and learning pedagogy, devise appropriately integrated curricula for ELs/MLs to learn both language and content, coordinate the delivery of content, language, and literacy lessons, differentiate strategies and assignments according to students' abilities, remain mindful of students' social-emotional learning needs, and map out a course of action that effectively realizes the true potential of the collaborative planning process.

In our investigations, we have uncovered the efficacy of joint instructional planning and in particular, how it relates to the collaborative instructional cycle—co-planning, co-teaching, co-assessment, and reflection. We have noted the following:

> Productive co-teaching teams made time to consistently collaborate with one another whether or not collaboration time was a part of their teaching schedules. Although we found that many outstanding co-taught programs had regularly scheduled collaborative planning periods for grade-level or content-area teams as well as for co-teaching partnerships, we also noted that many teachers committed to working together outside of the school day whether or not they had common planning time. (Dove & Honigsfeld, 2020a, p. 68)

Although much of our research has focused on co-planning as it relates to co-teaching, there is much evidence for the practice whether or not co-instruction occurs. The various benefits that co-planning for the sake of ELs/MLs provides include increased teacher learning and capacity building (Martin-Beltrán & Madigan Peercy, 2014), positive shifts in instructional practices for ELs/MLs (Davison, 2006; Martin-Beltrán & Madigan Peercy, 2012), and the proliferation of equity education and culturally responsive teaching (Compton, 2018; Scanlan et al., 2012; Theoharis & O'Toole, 2011).

Zoom In

In an algebra class in a midsize high school in a suburban town, an English learner enters with a seemingly comfortable smile on his face. Hakeem, a new arrival from Egypt who has only been at the school for less than 6 weeks, notices the daily class routine has begun before the late bell rings. Hakeem, fluent in Arabic and French, is just beginning to develop his English language skills. Yet, he confidently sits in his assigned student group to begin the daily warm-up exercise.

The instructional routine that Hakeem's teacher has established puts him immediately at ease. He spends the first 10 minutes in a small group with fellow English learners for a teacher-led vocabulary lesson while other students, grouped either heterogeneously or homogeneously, are assigned tasks to complete according to their learning needs. Next, the teacher engages the whole class in direct instruction. She first identifies the learning targets and clearly communicates to her students what they should know and be able to do. Then, the teacher models her thinking as she solves the equation example, and she incorporates the vocabulary she taught earlier to her group of ELs/MLs to reinforce the use of the language and to clarify how it is used in similar ways in context. The lesson continues with students being grouped again for either guided practice directly with the teacher or collaborative practice with classmates.

Zoom Out

The routines in Hakeem's class not only provide him with a safe and secure learning environment but also frame the class period so that Hakeem knows what to expect from the moment he arrives to the time he leaves to change classes. Now what might happen if Hakeem's entire school engages in whole-school routines? How might these routines positively affect the quality of instruction and knowledge base of ELs/MLs?

Whole-school routines provide students with the ability to accomplish application and achievement tasks in different classes without learning an entirely new set of rules and procedures. Routines reduce the cognitive load of students when they know what to expect! When all classes adopt similar instructional routines and strategies, they in turn instill confidence in ELs/MLs about their learning abilities and also support students' transitions from class to class. They can particularly support learning so that ELs/MLs can do the following:

- Develop and maintain independence
- Build confidence in their abilities to learn successfully
- Experience smooth transitions from one class activity to the next
- Enjoy more positive learning experiences

We found one example of whole-school routines being used in a district in the suburbs of New York City. The schools in the district adopted the use of *The Daily Five* (Boushey & Moser, 2014), a literacy framework that supports a high level of engagement in reading and writing. The five components or tasks students complete include independent reading, working with words, daily writing, reading aloud, and listening to text read aloud. This literacy framework was adopted in each classroom. ELs/MLs as well as other students fared well using *The Daily Five* because its components created a routine that was consistently used across grade levels. In turn, students were well supported to analyze vocabulary and develop reading and writing fluency.

A SNAPSHOT FROM THE FIELD

Ingrid Corpuz, ESL teacher, shares her experience with the implementation of a schoolwide initiative that supported co-planning efforts.

Shamrock Gardens Elementary School (SGE), a Title I school in the Charlotte-Mecklenburg district in Charlotte, North Carolina, adopted Thinking Maps in 2016 as a tool to guide students' thinking processes. Thinking Maps™ is a set of techniques using "consistent visual patterns linked directly to eight specific thought processes" (Thinking Maps, 2018). The idea behind this implementation was the newly added Student Success by Design Plan, which provided our school-based committee (teachers,

facilitators, and administration) with increased flexibility with structuring our school and programs around student learning needs. One of the areas of need identified for a large percentage of our learners was the challenge to think critically and expand on their ideas. Therefore, we knew that it was time to do things differently. As we engaged in a schoolwide professional development series of Thinking Maps™ and got the opportunity to practice using these visual representations, we came to realize how incredibly useful this would be for our planning. We immediately began implementing Thinking Maps™ throughout our grade-level and vertical planning sessions to discuss unit plans, topics, activities, and assessments. Also, each teacher in the building had Thinking Maps™ posters and a table-size mat. These tools allowed students and teachers to discuss topics as a whole class and in small groups so that together they could determine the best plan of action, for example, when planning for writing or examining a text. Thinking Maps™ became a common language schoolwide for both teachers and students.

The process enhanced collaboration between classroom teachers and Special Education/ESL teachers. As the ESL teacher at SGE, Thinking Maps™ allowed me to co-plan with grade-level teams even though I did not attend the planning sessions or co-teach with grade-level teachers. For example, the first-grade level had a high concentration of English language learners (ELLs). They shared with me the Thinking Maps™ created during planning for ELA and Math, which provided me with a detailed overview of the upcoming lessons. They often used a circle map to brainstorm units and a tree map for lesson planning. My part was to identify key language objectives and vocabulary, suggest strategies to facilitate students' understanding, and recommend modifications to lessons, assignments, or assessments based on ELLs' needs they worked with. In addition to Thinking Maps™ used as a collaboration tool, I also found it to be extremely valuable for my planning. I often used a flow chart to display and share language objectives, critical steps within a lesson, resources I had selected to use, and vocabulary we would explore with our ELLs each class (see Figure 4.1). It served as a visual representation and guide to each lesson and a model to promote students' critical thinking. For the first few lessons, I listed the Thinking Maps™ we would use and explained my decision-making process. Eventually, I had a picture of a stick figure thinking as a representation of and call for students to decide which Thinking Map was most appropriate for each activity. The discussions became a natural part of each lesson. Students were comfortable with the process as Thinking Maps™ was a common visual language in our school.

(Continued)

(Continued)

Figure 4.1 Flow Chart Lesson Guide

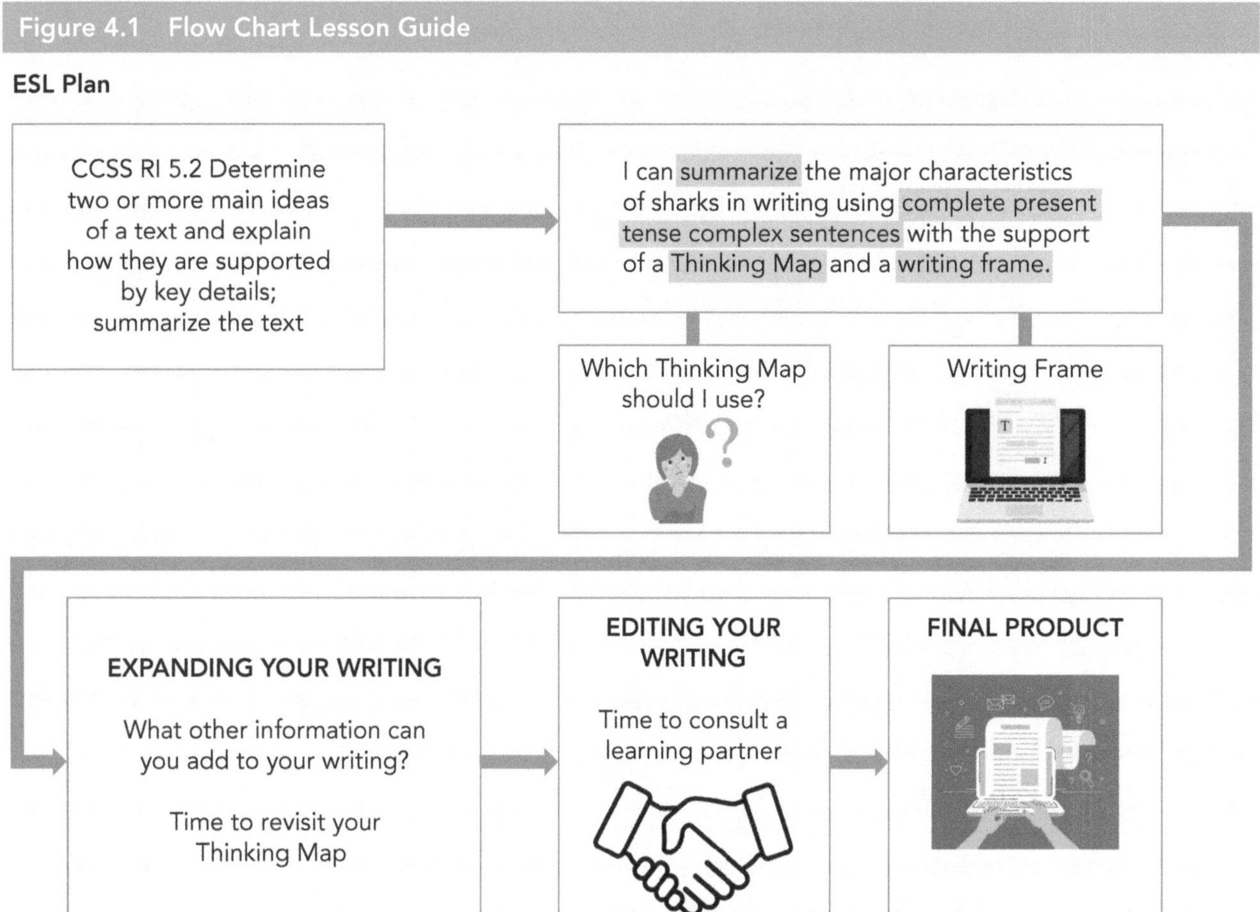

Figure created by Ingrid Corpuz. Image sources: istock.com/Barks_japan, istock.com/vladwel, istock.com/Warmworld, istock.com/vectorikart

Defining Routines and Frameworks

What is the purpose for establishing class routines and frameworks for instruction? Generally speaking, routines reduce the number of decisions that need to be made on a daily basis. They make instruction more efficient, they make students feel more confident and secure in their abilities to follow instruction, and they save time. Similarly, when class routines are in place, they support the process of co-planning. They create a structure for collaborative conversations, help teams prioritize their work, and often reduce the time needed for planning. Frameworks, on the other hand, are more like an organized collection of guideposts. They remind teachers of the specific elements that teaching routines must accomplish. For example, a framework might contain the learning standards or lesson objectives that need to be addressed, and a routine is the way in which those standards and targets are introduced and targeted during a lesson.

While teachers set routine procedures to manage their classes in order to take attendance, organize student activities, transition students from one task to the next, set criteria for behavior, and so on, our focus on routines in this chapter is set apart from the day-to-day demands of classroom management. Instead, we concentrate on instructional routines—detailed plans or step-by-step guidance for lesson delivery and how they can provide structures for teams to plan. We also examine how a variety of broad-based frameworks for instruction that have emerged from research findings in education can be the bedrock for collaborative conversations as well. To illustrate the use of a basic framework, consider a standard outline of a lesson as follows:

- Identifying benchmarks
- Setting learning attentions
- Drawing students into the lesson topic
- Modeling or demonstrating strategies and skills
- Providing opportunities for student practice
- Devising appropriate assessment

How might teaching teams co-plan by using this simple framework for collaborative discussions? Using a framework such as this can both guide professional dialogues about instruction and keep teams focused. It can help teachers to align the different parts of their lessons to assure continuity, alignment, and an inclusive, accessible lesson delivery. Yet sometimes, collaborative teams use more detailed frameworks that relate directly to the subject matter being addressed in their plans. These frameworks might contain the scope and sequence from commercial literacy and math programs, in-house developed content curricula, broad-based curriculum maps, state standard guides, on so on, which provide the structure for organized teamwork.

Some planning teams use models of instruction that are devoid of content but provide best-practice, research-informed models for lesson delivery. To illustrate, we offer some examples of general foundations for instruction later in this chapter that teachers use, such as Understanding by Design (Wiggins & McTighe, 2005), the gradual release of responsibility (Fisher & Fry, 2014; Pearson & Gallagher, 1983), Sheltered Instruction Observation Protocol (SIOP) (Echevarria et al., 2016), and so on. In addition, we also recognize how individual teachers as well as co-teaching teams establish their own routines, procedures, and protocols for instruction and offer how these might be used as frameworks for instructional planning. Most importantly, no matter which framework is selected to guide conversations, co-planning teams work together with this question in mind: What else do we need to do to best support the instruction of ELs/MLs?

In this section of the chapter, we will explore various frameworks and protocols for the instruction of ELs/MLs, emphasize how they are used to support teachers' joint planning efforts, and detail how teams plan with the language and literacy development of ELs/MLs in mind. Further into the chapter, we will explore co-planning routines—ways in which teaching teams use their limited time to accomplish joint planning tasks.

General Tenets in Planning for Language Instruction

The various aspects of planning language development instruction for ELs/MLs are complex and multileveled, particularly when it is conducted within the grade-level/

content-area class. With the demands placed on teachers for all students to meet grade-level benchmarks, **it can no longer be the sole charge of the English language development (ELD) teacher to address the language-learning needs of ELs/MLs.** Language and literacy development in conjunction with content-area learning must be incorporated into all lessons and in all classes for the sake of ELs/MLs. For this reason, Santos et al. (2012) offer this framework for determining how to respond to ELs'/MLs' needs by addressing the following:

1. **Language progressions**—How students learn language, both in terms of general language acquisition and in terms of the acquisition of discipline-specific academic language;
2. **Language demands**—What kinds of linguistic expectations are embedded within specific texts and tasks with which students are being asked to engage;
3. **Language scaffolds**—How specific representations and instructional strategies can be used to help students gain access to the concepts as well as to the language they need to learn; and
4. **Language supports**—How classrooms and schools can be organized to support students in continually building a deep understanding of language and content. (p. 4)

We need to make a fundamental point here. The above framework is critical to ensuring that attention is paid to the specific language and literacy development of ELs/MLs—moving them along a continuum to gain English language proficiency—and not just to support their learning of content knowledge and its application in their core classes. In order to apply these important considerations for language instruction, we have created a planning tool incorporating this critical framework that can be used when individually or jointly planning instruction for grade-level/content-area classes with ELs/MLs in mind (see Figure 4.2). It can also be used to analyze the strength of lesson and unit plans through the lens of working with English learners.

Figure 4.2 Language and Literacy Instruction in the Grade-Level/Content-Area Class

TYPE OF ATTENTION TO LANGUAGE	KEY QUESTIONS	PLANNING NOTES
Language Progressions	*What levels of language proficiency do these plans address?*	
	What content standards are being targeted and assessed?	
	What language-learning standards are being targeted and assessed?	

TYPE OF ATTENTION TO LANGUAGE	KEY QUESTIONS	PLANNING NOTES
Language Opportunities (Demands)	*What grade-level content, concepts, and texts are highlighted?*	
	What academic language—general and subject-specific—are featured?	
	What opportunities do students have to SWIRL (speak, write, interact, read, and listen)?	
Language Scaffolds	*What background knowledge is needed to be successful?*	
	What scaffolds are used to support the comprehension and application of language and content?	
Language Supports	*How do these plans foster schoolwide cross-disciplinary language development that all teachers embrace?*	
	What other systemic school supports do these plans incorporate?	

online resources Available for download at **resources.corwin.com/CoPlanningforELs**

Collaborative Planning Frameworks

People organize information in different ways. When we examined teachers who successfully engage in collaborative undertakings to improve their teaching practice for the sake of ELs/MLs, we found that they frequently use frameworks for planning instruction, establish their own systems and procedures for accomplishing recurrent collaborative tasks, and create lesson delivery routines in their classes that support their co-planning efforts. For this reason, we strongly recommend that co-planning teams select, adapt, or create a viable framework as a first step in the planning process.

Charlotte Danielson (2007) acclaims the benefits of establishing frameworks in that they have multiple dimensions to meet the needs of teachers with various skills and levels of expertise. They can be structured around common understandings, from day-to-day survival in the classroom to exploring ways to enhance instructional effectiveness. Kolko (2020), in his work as a designer, sees frameworks or models as a positive way to better understand the working of new ideas in order to streamline how basic information is presented; although they may only present a small part of the larger picture or scheme of things, frameworks can act as a guide to more fully examine the details. Therefore, we present frameworks for planning instruction as twofold—they meet a wide variety of teachers' needs to guide step-by-step as well as support teachers who think more globally, and they simplify the process of planning by more closely examining the specific aspects of lesson delivery.

Collaborative frameworks for planning instruction also help meet the challenges that teachers face at the various levels of their individual expertise. They can guide the brand-new teacher to more fully understand the expectations of teamwork, the responsibilities they have, and the roles they have to play. Frameworks support the busy schedules of even the most experienced teacher as well as bolster the work of curricular change or improvement. To simplify the process, we suggest that teaching teams not consume their time and effort to create brand-new frameworks for the purpose of planning instruction. Most often, we find that selecting and revising frameworks that are already in place can be most expediently used as guides for collaborative planning for the sake of ELs/MLs. In the next section, we will explore general instructional frameworks that are used for co-planning instruction. However, before we jump into reviewing specific instructional frameworks, let's consider a preparation framework to discern your team's readiness for a joint planning adventure.

In her books on collaborative teaching in elementary and secondary schools, Wendy Murawski (2009, 2010), well known for her work in the field of special education, suggests that co-planning teams identify their needs and challenges before they embark on the actual work of planning together. In Figure 4.3, we provide a list of questions, inspired by Murawski's work, that co-planning teams should consider as part of their initial discussions before beginning the work of designing instruction together for the sake of ELs/MLs.

Figure 4.3 Co-Planning Readiness Framework

GUIDING QUESTIONS	ADDITIONAL CONSIDERATIONS	NEEDED ACTION
Do we all know our roles and responsibilities in the co-planning process?	• How will we balance the input of team members? • How will we assure each member's contribution is valued?	
Do we have a set agenda for our co-planning sessions?	• What goals do we need to set for our co-planning? • What do we hope to accomplish? • What are our priorities?	

GUIDING QUESTIONS	ADDITIONAL CONSIDERATIONS	NEEDED ACTION
Do we have sufficient time to accomplish the tasks we have set?	• How often can and/or should we meet? • Is co-planning time built into our teaching schedule? • Are we able to make use of virtual meetings?	
Do we know the strengths and abilities of our ELs/MLs?	• Do we understand the process of acquiring an additional language? • Do we know what it takes for ELs/MLs to be academically successful?	
Do we all have the tools, technology, and materials we need for adapting, modifying, and differentiating instruction?	• How might we best accomplish and share the tasks of adapting, modifying, and differentiating instruction? • How might we support one another to use new tools, technology, and materials?	
Do we agree on best practices for informally and formally assessing ELs/MLs?	• How might we co-create assessment opportunities that support ELs/MLs to demonstrate their learning?	
Do we all feel comfortable with teaching the lesson content?	• How might we support one another to develop proficiency with the content?	
Do we all feel comfortable about developing the language and literacy skills of ELs/MLs?	• How can we support one another to understand best practices to develop the language and literacy skills of ELs/MLs?	

online resources Available for download at **resources.corwin.com/CoPlanningforELs**

What Research Says

There is much to consider in order to ensure collaborative planning is solid. Based on John Hattie's work, Fisher et al. (2019) suggest that *teacher clarity* plays a critical role in student learning. Based on Fendick's meta-analysis (1990), we also embrace the four dimensions of teacher clarity for ELs/MLs:

1. **Clarity of organization,** such that lesson tasks, assignments, and activities include links to the objectives and outcomes of learning.
2. **Clarity of explanation,** such that information is relevant, accurate, and comprehensible to students.
3. **Clarity of examples and guided practice,** such that the lesson includes information that is illustrative and illuminating as students gradually move to independence, making progress with less support from the teacher.
4. **Clarity of assessment of student learning,** such that the teacher is regularly seeking out and acting upon the feedback he or she receives from students, especially through their verbal and written responses. (p. xiv)

Teacher clarity contributes to determining the success of student learning—for both content and language development—in some critical ways. It supports creating standards-aligned learning experiences that include (a) establishing clear learning intentions, (b) identifying the success criteria based on the learning intentions, and (c) developing learning progressions that equip teachers with evidence-based instructional practices and equip students with opportunities for meaningful practice and independence. Teacher clarity also enhances assessment practices—both teachers and students need to know what is being taught and what the expectations and pathways are to learning to make sure assessment practices offer meaningful feedback and guidance (see Chapter 2 for more on curriculum design and Chapter 3 on assessment).

Instructional Frameworks

As we mentioned in the beginning of this chapter, for teachers to change their planning process, they must also change their thinking in addition to what they do. When structures are in place to support such changes, they can be the impetus for collaborative interactions and a productive co-planning process for teaching teams. The establishment of effective co-planning teams is critical not only for the development of instructional plans but also to the growth of teachers' professional learning. The frameworks offered here are research-informed models of instruction and presented as examples of how teachers adapt already established frameworks to plan instruction for ELs/MLs.

Understanding by Design

Wiggins and McTighe (2005) developed the Understanding by Design (UbD) framework for designing content units of study based on a *backward design* for planning, which recommends that teachers plan instruction with learning outcomes in mind. This framework had gained wide appeal when planning instruction in general, as well as more recently, with culturally and linguistically diverse (CLD) students in mind. The UbD framework supports teachers to use a three-stage process to consider the following: (a) overarching, long-term learning targets; (b) the development of authentic assessments; and (c) a course for learning to assure all students succeed. In addition to using this basic framework, Heineke and McTighe (2018) added the lens of working with CLD students to develop language and literacy skills alongside content-based learning. According to Heineke and McTighe, "the overarching goal of this framework is to provide equitable access to meaningful, authentic, and rigorous learning goals and experiences by tapping into students' rich and diverse backgrounds and supporting their language development" (p. 36) by combining the fundamentals of culturally and linguistically responsive teaching into the framework. Using this UbD framework with CLD students in mind, we offer the following planning tool for co-developing units of study for ELs/MLs (see Figure 4.4).

Figure 4.4 The UbD Planning Framework for ELs/MLs

STEP 1: ESTABLISH RIGOROUS CONTENT, LANGUAGE, AND LITERACY GOALS.

- *What are our big ideas for planning this unit with ELs/MLs in mind?*
- *What long-term goals are we targeting for language? Literacy? Content?*
- *What are the essential questions for students to explore?*
- *What scaffolds need to be in place to support the learning of ELs/MLs?*
- *What knowledge and skills are students expected to acquire?*

STEP 2: DEVELOP AUTHENTIC, CULTURALLY APPROPRIATE ASSESSMENTS.

- *What types of evidence will best determine whether or not students have met individual lesson goals? Overall unit goals?*
- *Which student performances and evaluations of tasks will best provide accurate evidence of student success?*
- *How might ELs/MLs make connections between their learning and their direct, daily experiences?*
- *How will we best know if ELs/MLs are able to transfer their learning to other contexts?*
- *If we use more traditional assessment practices, how might ELs/MLs be accommodated to demonstrate their knowledge, skills, and abilities?*

STEP 3: TEACHERS DEVELOP SCAFFOLDED LEARNING PLANS.

- *How will the unit of study be organized to assure participation from ELs/MLs?*
- *How does the learning plan support ELs/MLs to achieve the goals set in Step 1?*
- *How do lessons make use of ELs'/MLs' cultural and linguistic background knowledge?*
- *What scaffolded supports provide strategic language and literacy development for ELs/MLs?*
- *How will the learning sequence help students acquire new content knowledge and skills?*

The Gradual Release of Responsibility (GRoR)

Fisher and Frey (2014) interpreted and popularized the GRoR framework (Pearson & Gallagher, 1983) to include the planned, continuous reduction of teachers' use of direct instruction while providing increased opportunities for students to learn independently. According to Fisher et al. (2020), "the cognitive load should shift purposefully from teacher-as-model, to joint responsibility, to independent practice and application by the learner" (p. 12) (see Figure 4.5). The instructional parts of the GRoR framework that can be used to inform collaborative planning are as follows:

- **Focused instruction (teacher-as-model).** Teachers demonstrate and model skills, strategies, and tasks while thinking aloud so that students can better understand the thought process behind making predictions, problem solving, interpreting and applying new information, visualizing events, and so on. This component is generally completed with the whole class.
- **Guided instruction (teacher-to-student joint responsibility).** Some of the responsibility for learning is transferred to students as they practice the skills, strategies, and tasks together with the teacher's step-by-step guidance. Guided instruction may be differentiated; it can take place with the entire class or with small groups of students. This component of the framework works well for ELs/MLs who might need further guidance with language as well as content and a check for understanding.
- **Collaborative learning (student-to-student joint responsibility).** Students engage with one another in pairs or small groups to complete activities and tasks, often designed to encourage oral and written communication and to meet the learning targets set for the lesson. ELs/MLs often benefit from being included in heterogeneous groups of students who have varying degrees of English language and content proficiency. Tasks may be differentiated as well as include self and group checks for accountability.
- **Individual learning (independent practice and application).** Students work on their own to practice, extend, and apply what they have learned. Teachers often assign independent work to be completed outside of regular class time. Yet, Fisher et al. (2020) caution us to be mindful that, "although independent learning is the goal of education, students are often assigned independent tasks that they do not yet have the skills to complete alone" (p. 15). When additional time is needed to become ready for independent work, other components in the framework such as guided instruction or collaborative learning may be repeated.

Planning lessons using the GRoR framework gives diverse learners the needed support for developing new strategies and skills in stages before having to use them independently (Dove & Honigsfeld, 2018). Fisher et al. (2020) further note that the steps in the model are neither linear nor prescriptive. Lessons might begin with an independent task, followed by direct teacher modeling/demonstration, and ending with collaborative practice and application (see Figure 4.5).

Figure 4.5 GRoR in Practice

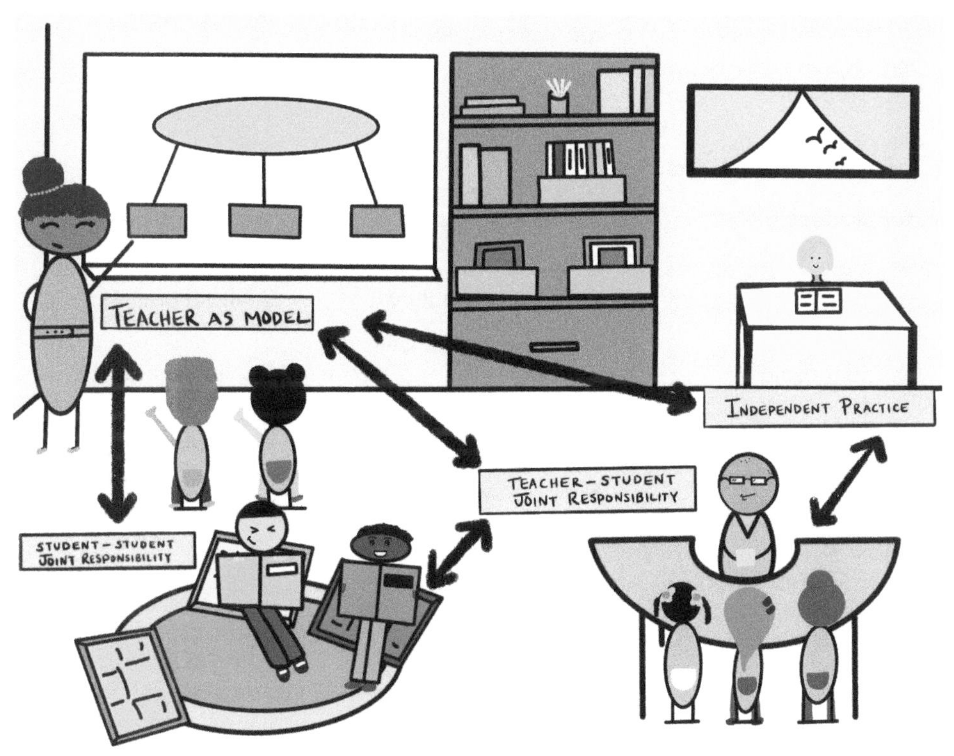

Universal Design for Learning (UDL)

UDL is a framework developed to "optimize teaching and learning for all people based on scientific insights into how humans learn" (CAST, 2018, para. 1). It was developed to ensure access to rigorous learning opportunities for all students, and its guidelines can provide a set of principles that can be adapted for lesson planning in support of the instruction of ELs/MLs. The overall structure of UDL provides choices for teachers to enhance student engagement in the learning process (WHY learn), student understanding of the content (WHAT to learn), and student responses to learning (HOW to learn). Figure 4.6 highlights these three principles with examples for enhancing instructional practices.

Figure 4.6 Universal Design for Learning: Instructional Practices for ELs/MLs

ENHANCE ELs/MLs ENGAGEMENT *WHY LEARN?*	ENHANCE ELs/MLs UNDERSTANDING *WHAT TO LEARN?*	ENHANCE ELs/MLs RESPONSES *HOW TO LEARN?*
Tap into students' interests	**Provide information in various ways**	**Vary student responses**
• Provide choices • Connect learning to students' interest and diverse cultural backgrounds • Develop relevant, authentic learning tasks	• Visual displays • Auditory representations • Multimedia representations	• Offer different ways for students to respond to their learning • Scaffold and support student responses through tools and technology
Foster student effort	**Build language use**	**Strengthen student communication**
• Provide clear goals and objectives • Consider using students' home languages for support • Devise opportunities for student-to-student collaboration • Offer detailed feedback	• Preview vocabulary • Review grammatical structures • Discuss language meaning in context • Support use of language-learning strategies	• Scaffold oral and written tasks • Provide sentence frames and stems • Use multimedia tools for students to communicate
Encourage self-monitoring	**Promote comprehension**	**Support use of general learning skills and strategies**
• Identify clear expectations • Assist students to set personal goals • Provide tools for self-guidance, reflection, and assessment • Teach organizational strategies	• Activate prior knowledge • Build ELs/MLs knowledge base • Support students to make text connections • Promote use of reading and writing strategies	• Offer checklists and other tools for goal setting • Provide time for students to reflect on their learning • Devise tools for students to remain organized and on target with their learning goals

Source: Adapted from CAST, (2018).

Sheltered Instruction Observation Protocol (SIOP) Model

The SIOP model is a research-based framework that combines content instruction and English language development for ELs/MLs (Echevarria et al., 2016). It consists of eight main components and thirty features that can enhance the detailed planning of co-planning teams. This model of instruction revolutionized the way ELs/MLs were being taught. It influenced the way ELs/MLs succeeded academically, including them in courses with rigorous grade-level learning targets coupled with instruction delivered in ways that made information comprehensible (Echevarria et al., 2016).

During the 2012–2013 academic year, we investigated the strategies an elementary school community used to implement co-teaching as a model of instruction for ELs/MLs (Dove & Honigsfeld, 2014). Although the main focus of the study was to investigate the implementation and instructional change of the co-teaching model, we also noted that the school's co-teaching initiative was coupled with the adoption of the SIOP model (Echevarria et al., 2010). The SIOP model was used to direct instruction and subsequently to co-plan. The framework, used as a checklist for planning, benefitted the novice co-teachers because it offered a detailed guide for instructional practices with ELs/MLs. Since that time, the use of SIOP for co-planning has become popular with many collaborative teams. In a February 2019 blog post, Carlota Holder et al. (2019) endorsed the use of the framework as follows:

> Lesson preparation is a foundational component of any successful lesson, but the combination of the features of the SIOP Lesson Preparation Component with the thorough, collaborative approach of co-planning, takes lesson planning to a whole new level . . . the content teacher brings in depth knowledge of the content standards and what students should know or be able to do as a result of the instruction. Meanwhile, the language teacher brings the expertise regarding which language domains (including forms and functions) would be most appropriate to practice with the content. (para. 2–3)

There are many resources available, both published and online, to support co-planning teams to incorporate the use of the SIOP model into their collaborative lesson planning. Figure 4.7 outlines the main components of the model.

Figure 4.7 The SIOP Model

1. Preparation—including written *content* and *language* objectives
2. Building background—emphasizing students' experiences and key vocabulary
3. Comprehensible input—using techniques to make content and language clear
4. Strategies—incorporating scaffolding techniques and higher-order questions
5. Interactions—frequent opportunities for students to use language productively
6. Practice/applications—hands-on activities that use all four language domains
7. Lesson delivery—monitoring lesson pace and increased student engagement
8. Review and assessment—providing comprehensive review and feedback

Shafali, EAL lead and Grade 5 EAL teacher at the American Embassy School, New Delhi, created a collaboration menu (see Figure 4.8) to support the alignment among the eight components of the SIOP model and collaborative practices her team engages in.

Figure 4.8 Collaboration Menu Using the SIOP Framework

Lesson Preparation	• Collaborate on defining and integrating content and language objectives • Engaging in task analysis
Building Background	• Previewing materials to anticipate language challenges and possibly creating a Tier 2 and 3 word list
Comprehensible Input	• Finding materials that are engaging and accessible • Adding visuals and creating graphic organizers
Strategies	• Thinking of differentiated question prompts • Developing sentence frames • Creating anticipation guides (reading comprehension)
Interaction	• Collaborate on creating strategy groups • Using appropriate protocols to facilitate equitable participation
Practice and Application	• Co-planning multiple ways to demonstrate understanding
Lesson Delivery	• Identifying co-teaching models appropriate for the lesson
Review and Assessment	• Co-creating assessments • Co-creating rubrics • Collaborating on report cards

Figure created by Shafali. Used with permission.

We recognize that both individual teachers and collaborative planning teams successfully use a range of research-informed frameworks such as ExC-ELL, Teachers College Readers and Writers Workshop, Q-TEL, Daily 5, and so on, for lesson planning. No matter which framework a team chooses or inherits from initiatives already in place, they offer significant guidance, organization, and a common language for teachers to collaborate for the instructional continuity of ELs/MLs. According to Kristina Robinson, "[When] any of the chosen frameworks are implemented with fidelity, teachers will see improved outcomes. Teachers shouldn't worry too much about which framework is perfect, but pick one that is workable for them and do it well" (personal communication, March 6, 2021).

Pause for a moment and jot down which of frameworks are in place in your context. Which one is most workable or accepted by your school community? Reflect on how collaborative the implementation is and how it may be improved.

____

____

____

____

Using Multiple Lenses for Planning

The dichotomy of content and language objectives has been with us since the early days of SIOP (Echevarria et al., 2003, 2012, 2016) and continues to inform planning and instruction for ELs/MLs in a range of instructional contexts. Even before SIOP was established, Snow et al. (1989) made a strong case for a conceptual framework of content and language integration, identifying several underlying rationales including that "cognitive development and language development go hand-in-hand" (p. 201). They further denoted that "language is learned most effectively for communication in meaningful, purposeful social and academic contexts" (p. 202). Considering the cognitive, language, and social aspects of learning, we challenge you not only to fully embrace content and language integration but also to expand your collaborative planning framework to include multiple lenses when preparing instruction for the sake of ELs/MLs as follows:

- **The cognitive lens**—factual, conceptual, procedural, and metacognitive knowledge
- **The linguistic lens**—core academic and discipline-specific language skills, oracy, literacy, and metacognitive awareness
- **The social-emotional lens**—self-awareness, self-management, social awareness, relationship skills, responsible decision-making, character, and citizenship

Let's begin by examining our common understanding of ELs'/MLs' learning for content attainment, English language and literacy development, and content and language integration before focusing on the multiple lenses and their corresponding components listed previously.

Planning Content and Language/Literacy Integration

In order to achieve content and language development and integration in classes taught with ELs/MLs in mind, we must first have a strong foundational understanding of the meaning of academic language, which may be best defined at three dimensions to determine (a) the special words and phrases, (b) sentence structures, and (c) text features, text types, and discourse practices associated with each lesson or unit (Ernst-Slavit & Egbert, 2006; WIDA, 2020b; Zwiers, 2014). Academic language has traditionally been viewed as productive or receptive in nature. When students interact with each other, with their teachers, and with different instructional materials (as well as with others outside the safety of the classroom and school space), they develop capacity with speaking and writing (productive or expressive skills). Through a range of reading and listening opportunities, we also intentionally support and help advance students' receptive (also referred as interpretive) skills.

Focusing on content attainment, we recognize the need to offer scaffolded supports and multimodal, multisensory, and multilingual access to the core content so ELs/MLs would be able to have not just a basic understanding but a mastery of grade-appropriate content, even if they do not yet have full command of English. In addition, we propose the systematic examination of the core content curriculum for language features that are critical to understanding, developing, and ultimately mastering so *all* students may be able to actively engage in the lessons while also participating in intentional instruction of academic language. Such close examination of academic language is suggested by many others, such as Soto-Hinman and Hetzel (2009), Gottlieb and Ernst-Slavit (2014), and Ottow (2019), just to highlight a few.

When we approach the challenge (and opportunity) to achieve content and language integration from the angle of language and literacy development, our call to action is to ensure that ELs/MLs develop metalinguistic awareness—the control of linguistic processing and the analysis of linguistic knowledge (Bialystok & Ryan, 1985) and how ELs/MLs use language(s) across content areas based on what is unique to each core academic subject. According to the recently updated guiding principles of academic language development, we must also recognize that "multilingual learners draw on their metacognitive, metalinguistic, and metacultural awareness to develop effectiveness in language use" (WIDA, 2020b, p. 12). ELs/MLs use these strategies to become more effective linguistically in different content areas. See Figure 4.9 for a summary of content and language integration.

Figure 4.9 Content and Language and Literacy Integration

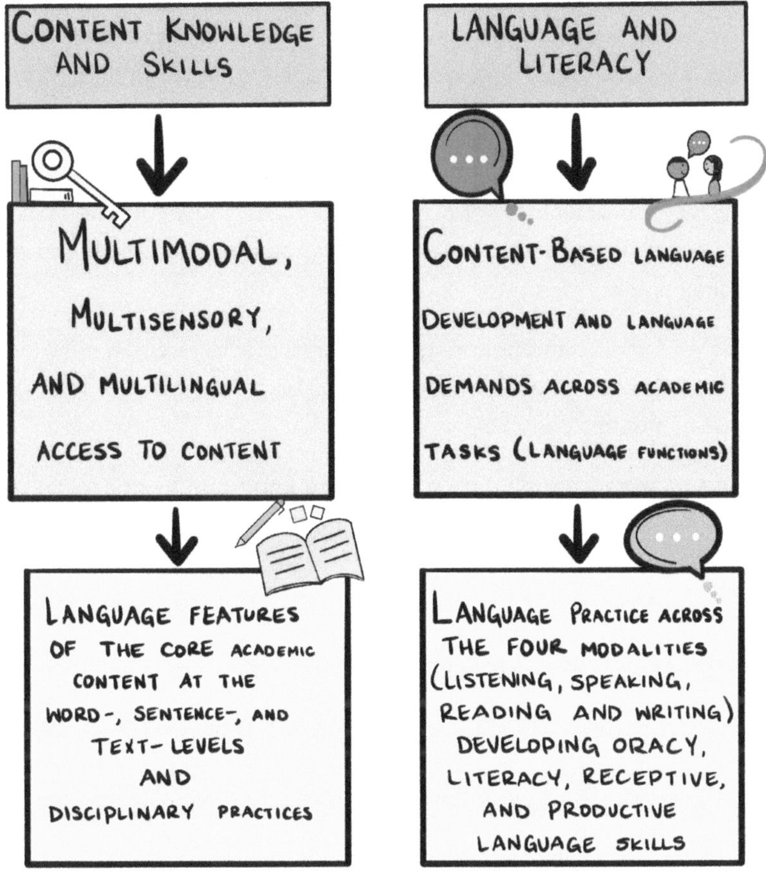

STOP AND PROCESS

iStock.com/bombuscreative

Based on your professional knowledge and teaching experience, which of these statements are best aligned with your beliefs about and experiences with academic language and literacy?

1. It is necessary and highly beneficial for ELs/MLs when teachers collaboratively plan integrated lessons to support simultaneous content and language development.
2. ELs/MLs who have a strong linguistic foundation and are literate in their home languages are likely to develop academic language and literacy skills in English faster.
3. ELs/MLs on all levels of language proficiency benefit from explicit instruction in academic language.
4. Academic content and skill development must be aligned to academic language development.

(Continued)

(Continued)

5. While academic vocabulary is often recognized as a key factor contributing to ELs'/MLs' success, a much broader set of academic language skills, including academic sentence and text levels and authentic discourse, are needed for them to develop academic language proficiency.
6. When ELs/MLs have ample opportunity to practice and learn academic language through oral activities, they are also getting prepared for reading and writing across the content areas.
7. ELs/MLs who understand how language is similar or different in new contexts (metalinguistic knowledge) are more likely to be comfortable using academic language in multiple contexts.
8. Routine and lesson planning frameworks are important to the co-teaching process.

Planning Instruction Through Multiple Lenses

Let's now shift our focus as we refine and further uncover the critical aspects of content and language development and integration for planning purposes by looking through the multiple dimensions of these three lenses—the cognitive lens, the linguistic lens, and the social-emotional lens.

1. The **cognitive lens** ensures that academic rigor and core content expectations are not compromised. Students' language proficiency levels may not be used as a predictor of whether or not they are capable of cognitively engaging with academic content and skills. We all must embrace this notion to provide equitable, engaging, and challenging yet well-supported content instruction to our ELs/MLs.
2. The **linguistic lens** allows for an explicit examination of the academic language and literacy opportunities and expectations embedded in the core content classes. Ottow (2019) notes that a language lens is used to "think about and operationalize the language of our content through which to plan, teach and assesses" (p. 5). She further argues that "not only does developing a language lens help us predict what challenges students may have, it can aid us in discovering opportunities to provide appropriate support and know how to plan explicit language goals" (p. 5). The linguistic lens we are suggesting here pushes our planning somewhat further by inviting all educators to consider academic language and literacy expectations for each lesson.
3. The **social-emotional lens** urges us not to overlook how our ELs/MLs (a) navigate their own emotions and aspirations, (b) build relationships

> with others, including learning about perspective-taking and collaborating, and (c) define their place in the world. Goleman and Senge (2014) refer to the three skill sets representing the *inner*, the *other*, and the *outer* spheres of our existence as the triple focus. In addition, using a social-emotional lens for planning will ensure ELs/MLs "connect emotionally to their learning" (Goodwin, 2018, p. 7). Further, as Ergas (2017) also reminds us, "schools need to teach us to live in this world, but we also need to learn to live with ourselves" (p. 247).

You might be wondering why planning needs to include these three lenses or how anyone might be able to consider so much for a single lesson. Our strongest argument is that by virtue of using multiple lenses during collaborative planning, we become more reflective about our students' needs, engage in deeper professional dialogue with each other, and show that we are committed to our students' growth and development in all these dimensions. Adding a social-emotional focus to planning takes us beyond the dichotomy of content and language goals or objectives and ensures students' affective connections to learning. Our goal with Figure 4.10 is to deconstruct the three major lenses into strands that more specifically address the complex endeavors ELs/MLs face when they participate in learning within the classroom and engage in academic tasks with their peers or on their own.

While considering all these dimensions for unit and lesson planning at the same time may be challenging, let's take a moment and reflect on the alternative. If teachers believe that the successful instruction of ELs/MLs is the same as good teaching, this notion "overlooks the nature of language development and its relationship to content learning, and obscures attention to ELs' sociocultural and socioemotional experiences" (Hopkins et al., 2019, p. 2301). ELs/MLs thrive in the general education classroom when the content is accessible cognitively, culturally, and linguistically, when they can develop academic language and literacy skills at the same time as their social-emotional developmental needs are also addressed. To achieve that, consider the following simple framework to initiate your planning conversation:

1. What content goals are all students supposed to meet?
2. What kind of language and literacy practices will be associated with mastering the content?
3. How will the students grow and develop socially and emotionally at the same time?

Designing multidimensional integrated units and lessons may require additional time and effort initially, especially if this may indicate a marked shift in your practice; yet when you work collaboratively with your colleagues and intentionally combine your expertise by looking at the same curriculum, unit, or lesson through multiple perspectives, the responsibility of using multiple lenses is also shared, and ultimately, students benefit.

Figure 4.10 Framework of the Three Lenses for Collaborative Planning

LENS	SPECIFIC FOCUS	HOW TO PLAN FOR THIS	UNIQUE CONSIDERATIONS FOR ELS/MLS	EXAMPLES OF WHAT IT LOOKS LIKE ACROSS THE CORE CONTENT AREAS
Cognitive (Based on Krathwol, 2002; Yilmaz, 2011)	Factual knowledge	Select essential information students need to retrieve and retain.	Rather than focusing on what facts ELs/MLs need to understand and remember, consider how they can apply, analyze, and evaluate information	In a social studies unit that utilizes interactive timelines with facts about key events, invite students to review how each contributed to the major event.
	Conceptual knowledge	Determine what prerequisite conceptual understanding is needed for the lesson/unit and how to sequence the new concepts to achieve understanding.	Consider what the big ideas are in a unit of study: What is the essential learning to be transferred to the next unit *and* to future learning, including real-life problems?	In ELA, when studying classic or contemporary literature, invite students to analyze the choices characters make and how they impact the story outcomes. Offer examples and literacy experiences that are relevant to students' lives and invite students to share their own examples.
	Procedural knowledge	Determine what skills and processes students need to engage in academic tasks.	Consider how ELs/MLs may participate in learning activities and interactions to have access to and develop mastery of the procedures.	In science, engage students in tasks that build on (a) previous skills and (b) multiple representations, such as diagrams, outlines, sketches, video-recorded responses. Offer multiple pathways to learning and demonstrating that learning has taken place.
	Metacognitive knowledge	Raise awareness about the thinking processes that students utilize. Introduce and consistently use Thinking Maps or other advance organizers.	Connect new learning to metacognitive, metalinguistic, and metacultural awareness. Help students identify their own learning strategies.	In math, engage students in math talk and draw special attention to (a) the way students explain their thinking and (b) the precision of language needed to fully engage in disciplinary practices. Invite students to reflect on and self-assess both their thinking processes and the outcomes of their math learning.

LENS	SPECIFIC FOCUS	HOW TO PLAN FOR THIS	UNIQUE CONSIDERATIONS FOR ELS/MLS	EXAMPLES OF WHAT IT LOOKS LIKE ACROSS THE CORE CONTENT AREAS
Linguistic (Based on Lesaux & Harris, 2015; WIDA, 2020; Zwiers, 2014)	Core academic-language skills Discipline-specific academic language skills	Focus on academic language skills and language uses across all content areas and genres. Identify what language features and what forms of language use are unique to each discipline.	Address all three dimensions of how language is used at the word-, sentence-, and discourse-levels for academic purposes and highlight what is unique about academic language use within each core discipline.	Across all content areas, ensure students have ample opportunities to engage in four key language uses to narrate, inform, explain, and argue (WIDA, 2020). Within each content area, help students approximate how experts of the field use language—they talk, read, and write like scientists, mathematicians, historians, and so on.
	Oracy	Focus on listening and speaking opportunities, especially academic conversations.	Offer verbal scaffolds. Allow for multilingual responses. Invite multiple modes of expression.	Engage in academic conversations—talk about a math problem, discuss an experiment in science, debate a point of view in social studies, and share original thoughts and reflections.
	Literacy	Focus on developmentally appropriate code-based and meaning-based competencies (Lesaux & Harris, 2015).	Offer structured minilessons that explicitly teach literacy skills while also engaging students in authentic, joyful opportunities to use their multiple literacies.	Engage in content-specific literacy experiences across the core academic subjects: deconstruct and reconstruct a word problem in math; capture scientific observations; analyze information originating in multiple sources in social studies; analyze text features of fiction and nonfiction selections.
	Metalinguistic awareness	Invite students to reflect on, recognize, assess, and utilize their multilingual skills.	Capitalize on ELs'/MLs' ability to access their full linguistic repertoires and activate awareness of how they use their languages across different contexts.	In all content areas, invite students to be language detectives and search for cognates; analyze words for word parts; compare and contrast how certain expressions are used in English vs. in other languages, and so on.

(Continued)

(Continued)

LENS	SPECIFIC FOCUS	HOW TO PLAN FOR THIS	UNIQUE CONSIDERATIONS FOR ELS/MLS	EXAMPLES OF WHAT IT LOOKS LIKE ACROSS THE CORE CONTENT AREAS
Social-Emotional (Based on CASEL, 2020)	Self-awareness	Invite students to reflect on, recognize, assess, and appropriately act upon their own emotions, needs, and beliefs.	Cultivate growth mindset (ensuring that students believe in themselves and their home language is recognized as strength). Help students develop self-confidence in a new learning environment and in a new language. Help students develop self-efficacy, competence, autonomy, and learner agency.	During the entire school day, see bilingual and bicultural identity as strength. Self-assess strength. Develop confidence. Celebrate successes. Cultivate optimism.
	Self-management	Help students to regulate their own emotions and behaviors while developing impulse control and organization skills.	Embrace self-advocacy. Learn stress management. Develop skills to overcome adverse circumstances. Develop self.	Invite students to reflect on what motivates them, what stresses them, and how they are able to manage the challenge of learning in two or more languages in each particular content area. Help students set, monitor, and make progress toward personal, linguistic, and academic goals within specific academic contexts.
	Social awareness	Invite students to reflect on how their behavior impacts others and how to better understand others' perspectives.	Develop empathy and respect for others. Understand others who come from a range of cultural backgrounds.	Read literature on a theme from multiple authors representing multiple cultural contexts and identities. Read about current events and content-specific nonfiction genres representing multiple perspectives.

LENS	SPECIFIC FOCUS	HOW TO PLAN FOR THIS	UNIQUE CONSIDERATIONS FOR ELS/MLS	EXAMPLES OF WHAT IT LOOKS LIKE ACROSS THE CORE CONTENT AREAS
	Relationship skills	Communicate with others representing different cultural and linguistic backgrounds, building meaningful relationships. Ask for and offer help to others.	Understand verbal and nonverbal social cues, develop conflict resolution and problem-solving skills. Develop trust in others. Experience a school and classroom climate where risk-taking is the norm without a fear of ridicule or embarrassment.	Design opportunities for collaborative work. Establish group norms and clear expectations for group participation. Have students work in station rotations. Introduce Kagan structures (Kagan et al., 2016) and use them across content areas for consistency.
	Responsible decision-making, character, and citizenship	Guide students to make choices, help them pay attention, and support them with developing short-term and long-term plans.	Develop cognitive and social-emotional flexibility and tolerance for ambiguity. Cultivate creative problem solving.	Create a climate of high expectations with high support—for example, in social studies and science classes, evaluate dilemmas and ethical decisions related to a current problem.

A SNAPSHOT FROM THE FIELD

Let's hear from a sixth-grade team consisting of an English language (EL) teacher, Jennifer Pomagier, an English language arts (ELA) teacher, Kristin Cochrane, and a special educator, Miriam Schuman, who use the three lenses—cognitive (content), linguistic (language), and social-emotional—to plan lessons for their students.

One of our ELA standards for 6th grade is for students to grapple with, annotate, and analyze a complex text. We align these content standards to success criteria to identify what the students can do as a result of this four-day lesson. The content objectives are also aligned to language objectives and social-emotional objectives using the Illinois Priority Learning Standards (2020). In addition, we review the WIDA Can-Do descriptors for the appropriate levels and domains that are applicable to our lesson (see Figure 4.11).

Figure 4.11 Alignments of Standards to Success Criteria

LESSON PLANNING	
CONTENT STANDARDS	**SUCCESS CRITERIA**
RI.6.2. Determine a central idea of a text and how it is conveyed through particular details; provide a summary of the text distinct from personal opinions or judgments.	• *To determine (figure out) the central idea of a text and its key details* • *To create an objective (no opinion) summary of the text*
RL.6.4. Determine the meaning of words and phrases as they are used in a text, including figurative and connotative meanings; analyze the impact of a specific word choice on meaning and tone.	• *To determine (figure out) the meaning of words and phrases as they are used in the text*

CONTENT STANDARDS	SUCCESS CRITERIA
RL.6.10. Read and comprehend complex literary and informational texts independently and proficiently.	• *To read and comprehend a complex informational text well*
LANGUAGE STANDARDS	**SUCCESS CRITERIA**
L.4A. Use context (e.g., the overall meaning of a sentence or paragraph; a word's position or function in a sentence) as a clue to the meaning of a word or phrase.	• *To use context clues to determine the meaning of unfamiliar words or phrases*
L.6. Acquire and use accurately grade-appropriate general academic and domain-specific words and phrases; gather vocabulary knowledge when considering a word or phrase important to comprehension or expression.	• *To better understand and use the meanings of grade-appropriate academic vocabulary*
SOCIAL-EMOTIONAL STANDARDS	**SUCCESS CRITERIA**
1A.3b. Apply strategies to manage stress and to motivate successful performance.	• *To apply (use) strategies to manage stress and perform well*
21.B.3a. Work cooperatively with others to accomplish a set goal in both competitive and non-competitive situations.	• *To work cooperatively with others to accomplish (meet) a common goal*

In addition, we review the WIDA Can-Do descriptors for the appropriate levels and domains that are applicable to our lesson as follows:

WIDA Can-Do Descriptors 6–8

- *Level 4 Reading*
  - *Students can process recounts by comparing content-related concepts*
  - *Students can process recounts by connecting ideas with supporting details to show relationships (e.g., characters' actions to their feelings)*
- *Level 5 Speaking*
  - *Students can discuss by building on the ideas of others*
- *Level 6 Listening*
  - *Students can process recounts by identifying key ideas expressed orally*
  - *Students can process recounts by identifying new information expressed by others*

This lesson (which lasts approximately four class periods) provides students with a preview of key concepts, format, and vocabulary presented in the complex text so that students can best comprehend and think critically about the content. The prereading supports EL students with visuals but also increases comprehension for students with

(Continued)

(Continued)

special needs and truly all learners in the class. The second part of the lesson is the reading itself. We want students to learn how to have some productive struggle and then to persevere through this lesson.

To start, we complete our first reading as a whole class read aloud, demonstrating how to carefully annotate and analyze a complex text together. This step allows for all students to access the text and practice the necessary annotation skills with teacher modeling and support. Each step of the process is broken down and displayed visually so that students are able to follow along. The lesson also focuses on specific skills to make sense of new vocabulary and complex language (i.e., using context clues and roots), particularly helpful for ELs.

Once students have completed a close reading of the text one time, they are tasked with reading the text a second time within small groups, persevering through a complex task with others. Students are each assigned something different to annotate for when listening to the text read aloud (vocabulary, essential question, connections and purpose and central idea) and then use reciprocal teaching to share their findings with their group members. The groups are heterogeneous to ensure all students are learning from each other.

To assess student understanding, all three teachers monitor the different groups and provide scaffolding with sentence frames as needed. Students are expected to take a picture or screenshot of their individual annotations and upload them to our student management system. We do have a formative comprehension check designed to assess understanding that will be completed individually as well. Finally, students will complete a similar assignment independently to help us as teachers gauge their ability to annotate and analyze a complex text after completing the lesson.

* * *

Jennifer Pomagier is a middle school EL teacher who co-teaches four sixth-grade English language arts block classes each school day. Her background is in secondary education and English, endorsed in English as a second language.

Kristin Cochrane is a middle school English language arts teacher who co-teaches four sixth-grade English language arts block classes each school day. Her background is in secondary education and English, endorsed in English as a second language.

Miriam Schuman is a middle school special education teacher who co-teaches four sixth-grade English language arts block classes each school day. Her background is in English literature and primary and secondary education, and she is an LBS1 and National Board certified teacher.

What Research Says

"Within the co-planning framework, conversations need to be streamlined and focused on the end goal. Asking questions such as 'What is the target for the course, for the month, or for the class session?' has proven to be effective. While this sounds very simple in print, it is much more difficult in practice because creative thinking in the context of collaboration can cause co-teachers to veer off target and be unproductive with their use of time. Having a structured time allotment supports the flow of co-planning. Establishing a goal and setting a time frame ensure co-teachers can stay on task and achieve necessary jobs." (Pratt et al., 2016, p. 3)

Co-Planning Routines

Not many of us become enthusiastic when we hear the word *routine*; its very mention may conjure up thoughts of everything that is unremarkable and mundane. However, we would like to invite you to view routines, for both co-planning and lesson delivery, as a part of a set of dynamic and powerful tools for effective collaborative teacher teams. In this section of the chapter, we will outline how teachers optimize their time and attention by establishing routines and protocols for their co-planning sessions. We will also showcase how teachers develop daily and weekly instructional routines in their classes that can be used to support the co-planning process.

A Co-Planning Routine Example

Time is a precious commodity for teachers, and to make the most of the available time for collaborative planning, we have found the most accomplished teacher teams develop and stick to a routine for their planning sessions. Therefore, to support the creation of action steps for planning, we offer a description of the following team-planning routine that consists of four parts—organization, preplanning, co-planning, and post-planning—as follows:

- **Organization.** Before embarking on a joint co-planning venture, teachers need to establish a system in which their team can effectively work. First and foremost, the team must agree on who will be a part of the planning process, what the team plans to accomplish, when and where the team will meet either face-to-face or virtually, what are each team member's expectations, time commitment, roles, and responsibilities, and how the team will communicate. Other considerations in organizing the team are as follows:
    - The selection of a mode for team member communication—email, text messaging, and so on
    - The choice of a platform to co-plan and share documents—for example, Google Drive, Dropbox, and One-Drive
    - The distribution or sharing of course materials for each team member—curriculum guide/map, scope and sequence, pacing guide, modules, texts, standards, and so on

  - Access to essential technology so that all teachers can connect with online course resources
  - The creation and/or selection of tools and templates for the planning process

- **Preplanning.** Having organized the team and with each member having the necessary tools at hand, this phase of the co-planning routine involves team members working apart from one another before a joint planning session. Each team member is generally responsible for reviewing the content curriculum, the standards to be addressed as indicated in a scope and sequence, the texts and materials to be used, and so on, in order to prepare for the co-planning session. The ELD teacher looks at what is to be taught through the lens of working with ELs/MLs, selecting the necessary background knowledge, vocabulary, reading strategies, modifications, and scaffolds required for ELs/MLs to be successful. Meanwhile, the content/grade-level teacher focuses on how to deliver the content to all students by shaping learning goals; developing knowledge of the discipline through critical thinking, inquiry, and authentic and collaborative experiences; and creating appropriate assessments to gauge the learning of content knowledge and skills. Tasks in the preplanning phase with ELs/MLs in mind additionally include the following:
  - Analyzing texts for assigned readings to determine the need for modifications and/or scaffolding
  - Identifying the basic and academic vocabulary needed to develop skills and concepts
  - Determining the language functions—describe, compare, predict, infer, persuade, and so on—necessary for students to be full participants in the learning experience
  - Selecting the language forms (simple and complex sentence structures) required to express ideas through speaking and writing
  - Considering whole-class/small-group activities and instructional strategies to support the acquisition of new vocabulary and language forms/functions
- **Co-planning.** Any teacher team will tell you that collaborative face-to-face time—virtual or in person—with other team members is invaluable when it comes to planning instruction with special student populations in mind. In this phase of the routine, teachers share the standards to be addressed, negotiate possible content and language-learning targets, identify collaborative and independent class activities, confirm the challenges students will confront, consider formative and summative assessments, divide roles and responsibilities, and determine needed materials. Other

considerations for effective co-planning include what we call ESCROW (Honigsfeld & Dove, 2019) to maximize the effectiveness of co-planning sessions as follows:

  - **E**stablish and stick to set meeting times
  - **S**tart by discussing big ideas and setting essential learning goals
  - **C**oncentrate on areas of special difficulty for ELs; scaffold learning, adapt content, modify assignments, and differentiate tasks
  - **R**eview previous lessons based on student performance data
  - **O**vercome the need to always be in control
  - **W**ork toward common understanding of ELs' needs (p. 73)

- **Post-planning.** After the team has met, each teacher will need to accomplish various planning assignments independently, such as creating materials for learning activities, scaffolding the different dimensions of each task (see Chapter 6 for scaffolding ideas), differentiating assessments, searching for multimedia resources, creating learning centers/stations for collaborative student work, and so on. Some tips for post-planning include the following:
  - Make sure you have access to the resources and materials needed for the post-planning process
  - Pace the completion of your post-planning tasks to prevent overwhelming or overextending yourself
  - Agree to develop differentiated activities and materials for yourself and others that can be accomplished in the amount of time you have
  - Divide and conquer—ask team members for assistance when needed

Additional Co-Planning Routines

One of the most important insights we have gained from observing teachers who work collaboratively is that they successfully do so by developing their own guidelines and parameters for working with one another. The following is a series of ideas from collaborative teacher teams that have maximized their time through their own co-planning routines. We offer them here as an inspiration for accomplishing collaborative work.

30-Minute Planning. Teachers divide their allotted co-planning time to remain focused and accomplish tasks within a short period as follows:

1. Initial 2 to 3 minutes (WHEN): Calendar review. Teachers identify when certain aspects of the course curriculum will take place including the length of the unit of study and when summative assessments need to take place. They also note any upcoming holidays, special events that

might take place, and reports that are due, as well as check for upcoming co-planning meetings.

2. 15 to 20 minutes (WHAT & HOW): Five-day plan. The team determines instruction for one full week specifying the content and language targets and the means of instructional delivery, including suggested resources and materials.

3. 6 to 8 minutes (WHO): Students' needs. Here, individual students are discussed and possible instructional supports are suggested.

4 + 1 Content Planning. This planning routine, developed by a secondary co-teaching team, was created to address the specific challenges ELs/MLs were having with acquiring and applying content knowledge. The team noticed that delivering new content material on a daily basis was overwhelming for some students, who inevitably fell behind as the class progressed through each unit of study. To improve student academic performance and linguistic development, this co-teaching team shifted their instruction and ultimately their planning to include 4 days of new content instruction with language support followed by 1 day of review and enrichment. In this way, students who needed a review of the content material were able to do so as well as have increased opportunities to apply new language skills through speaking and writing while those students who mastered the content had the opportunity to dig deeper into the subject through additional readings, multimedia presentations, small-group projects, and creative writing assignments.

Full-Day Planning. An ELD teacher who co-taught in several classes with various grade-level teachers prompted this planning scheme. The co-taught schedule was arranged so that for 4 days, Monday through Thursday, the ELD teacher spent all of her time in assigned classes for co-taught instruction; she had no preparation periods set for those 4 days. In turn, Fridays were set aside as a day for teacher collaboration and co-planning, in which the ELD teacher used her deferred preparation periods to co-plan the whole day with her fellow teaching partners. This scheme required that all of the ELD teacher's instructional partners had an aligned preparation period with one of her preparation periods every Friday.

Planning With Instructional Routines in Mind

Instructional routines generally go hand-in-hand with co-planning routines. Both daily and weekly instructional routines can not only be a guide for co-planning sessions but also create a foundation for collaborative conversations that need not be renegotiated week after week. For example, daily routines may consist of a specific set of instructional strategies that are rotated to open a lesson, facilitate a lesson, and close a lesson. When all team members have a clear understanding of each set of strategies, it is much easier to plan instruction by selecting from a list of possible tasks students complete as well as differentiate those tasks. See Figure 4.12 for a sample planning chart using daily instructional routines.

Figure 4.12 Instructional Routines Planning Chart

CLASS:	TOPIC:	
DAY OF THE WEEK	STRATEGIES: SELECT ONE FOR LESSON SECTION	DESCRIPTION AND DIFFERENTIATION
Monday	**Opening** ❑ A–Z Charts ❑ Anticipation Guide ❑ Stand Up, Hand Up, Pair Up ❑ Four Corners ❑ KWL Charts	
	Facilitating ❑ Student Groupings—Multiple Groups ❑ Sentence Frames/Starters ❑ Word Walls ❑ One Pagers ❑ Graphic Organizers ❑ Alternative Materials	
	Closing ❑ Exit Ticket ❑ 3-2-1 Reflection ❑ Two-Dollar Summary ❑ Gallery Walk ❑ Google Form Quiz	

online resources Available for download at **resources.corwin.com/CoPlanningforELs**

Daily instructional routines may follow a set of published lesson components, such as the GRoR (Fisher & Frey, 2014), the Daily Five (Boushey & Moser, 2014), or SIOP (Echevarria et al., 2010, 2016), a more generalized framework, such as speak-write-interact-read-listen or SWIRL (Dove & Honigsfeld, 2018), or a teacher-created or team-developed daily routine.

In addition to daily routines, common weekly routines might be established that can enhance teachers' conversations during planning time and shift discussions to specific content and students' needs instead of the context of instruction—how the lesson will proceed—because it can already be assumed by having routine structures already in place. Figure 4.13 is an example of a weekly routine for an elementary literacy class, and Figure 4.14 showcases a routine for middle school English language arts.

Figure 4.13 Weekly English Language Arts Routine: Elementary

	MONDAY	TUESDAY	WEDNESDAY	THURSDAY	FRIDAY
Class Activity I	Introduce New Word Wall Words	Reader's Workshop	Word Wall Activity	Writer's Workshop	Word Wall Activity
Timeframe	40 minutes	40 minutes	30 minutes	40 minutes	30 minutes
Co-teaching Model	One Group: One Lead Teacher and One Teacher *Teaching on Purpose*	Multiple Groups: Two Teachers Monitor/Teach	One Group: One Lead Teacher and One Teacher *Teaching on Purpose*	Multiple Groups: Two Teachers Monitor/Teach	Two Groups: One Teacher Re-teaches, One Teaches Alternative Information
Class Activity II	Shared Reading	Guided Reading	Writer's Workshop	Guided Reading	Reader's Workshop
Timeframe	30 minutes	30 minutes	40 minutes	30 minutes	40 minutes
Co-teaching Model	Two Groups: Two Teachers Teach the same content	Multiple Groups: Two Teachers Monitor/Teach	Multiple Groups: Two Teachers Monitor/Teach	Multiple Groups: Two Teachers Monitor/Teach	Multiple Groups: Two Teachers Monitor/Teach

Source: Reprinted from *Collaborating for English Learners: A Foundational Guide to Integrated Practices* (Second Edition) by Andrea Honigsfeld and Maria G. Dove. Thousand Oaks, CA: Corwin, www.corwin.com.

Figure 4.14 Weekly Middle School English Language Arts Routine

MONDAY	TUESDAY	WEDNESDAY	THURSDAY	FRIDAY
Motivational activity or Do now	Motivational activity or Do now	Motivational activity or Do now	Motivational activity or Do now	Motivational activity or Do now
Introduce new vocabulary	Vocabulary review: definitions	Vocabulary analysis	Vocabulary journal	Vocabulary expansion
Preview text	Small-group reading	Writing lesson	Small-group reading	Writing lesson
Read aloud introduction	Questions/prompts for discussion	Writing application	Questions/prompts for discussion	Writing application
Write text predictions individually	Recap text selection—whole class	3-2-1 reflection individually	Recap text selection—whole class	Exit ticket individually

Increasing the Effectiveness of Collaborative Routines

We advocate for teacher collaboration to be a priority and for regular and consistent time during the school day for co-planning teams to meet. We also recognize that many teachers continue to work in isolation, not always by choice but due to lack of time. Fullan (2016) observes that the "teaching profession, with some notable exceptions, is typically not a place where teachers collectively learn." He goes on to say that "this is not just an individual problem. It is a system problem" (p. 122). Although some teachers may be reluctant participants, we find most teachers are not to blame for their lack of participation in collaborative planning. In order to embrace collaborative planning, there truly needs to be a schoolwide initiative for it to take place. Teacher collaboration and collective professional learning need to be a part of the general school culture, and for these to occur, school leaders play crucial roles in creating a school culture and norms that help make it happen routinely.

Tools of the Trade

The following are a collection of co-planning templates (Figures 4.15 through 4.18) for your consideration to enhance the effectiveness of your collaborative planning sessions whether you co-teach or not. We invite you to consider the potential of each of them as well as combine, adapt, or rearrange them to meet the needs of your particular program.

Figure 4.15 Daily Planning Template

DAY/DATE	CONTENT OBJECTIVE (INCLUDING TARGET STANDARD)	LANGUAGE OBJECTIVE (INCLUDING TARGET STANDARD)	CO-TEACHING MODEL(S)

(Continued)

(Continued)

LEARNER ACTIVITIES (INCLUDING ACCOMMODATIONS—ADAPTATIONS OR MODIFICATIONS)	CONTENT TEACHER'S ROLE	ELD/ELL TEACHER'S ROLE

FORMATIVE ASSESSMENTS (INCLUDE ACCOMMODATIONS FOR LANGUAGE PROFICIENCIES)	NOTES ON INDIVIDUAL STUDENTS

Source: Adaped from Honigsfeld and Dove (2008) and Long Island RBERN (2015). Reprinted from *Co-Teaching for English Learners: A Guide to Collaborative Planning, Instruction, Assessment, and Reflection* by Andrea Honigsfeld and Maria G. Dove. Thousand Oaks, CA: Corwin. www.corwin.com.

Figure 4.16 A Week-at-a-Glance Co-Planning Template

ELD/ELL Teacher: ___________ Classroom Teacher: ___________ Grade: ___________

For the Week of: ____

WEEKLY OVERVIEW WHAT IS THE FOCUS FOR THE WEEK? WHAT CONTENT-AREA TOPICS WILL WE ADDRESS?			
	CONTENT AND LANGUAGE OBJECTIVES WHAT ARE WE GOING TO TEACH?	*KEY INSTRUCTIONAL STRATEGIES* HOW ARE WE GOING TO REACH ALL STUDENTS?	*RESOURCES/ MATERIALS* WHAT MATERIALS DO WE NEED? WHO IS PREPARING WHAT?
Monday			
Tuesday			
Wednesday			
Thursday			
Friday			
Formative and Summative Assessment Plan:			

Source: Adaped from Honigsfeld and Dove (2010). Reprinted from *Co-Teaching for English Learners: A Guide to Collaborative Planning, Instruction, Assessment, and Reflection* by Andrea Honigsfeld and Maria G. Dove. Thousand Oaks, CA: Corwin. www.corwin.com.

Figure 4.17 Co-Teaching Weekly Planning Template

DAY/ DATE	CONTENT OBJECTIVE (INCLUDING TARGET STANDARD)	CO-TEACHING MODEL(S) (IDENTIFY SPECIFIC TEACHER ROLES)	MATERIALS AND LEARNING AIDS NEEDED	ACCOMMODATIONS (ADAPTATIONS AND MODIFICATIONS)	FORMATIVE AND SUMMATIVE ASSESSMENTS	POST-LESSON REFLECTIONS
Mon.	Content Objective (Including Target Standard)					
	Language Objective (Including Target Standard)					
Tue.	Content Objective (Including Target Standard)					
	Language Objective (Including Target Standard)					
Wed.	Content Objective (Including Target Standard)					
	Language Objective (Including Target Standard)					
Thur.	Content Objective (Including Target Standard)					
	Language Objective (Including Target Standard)					
Fri.	Content Objective (Including Target Standard					
	Language Objective (Including Target Standard)					

Adapted from Martinsen Holt (2004) and Long Island RBERN (2015), funded by the New York State Education Department. Reprinted from *Co-Teaching for English Learners: A Guide to Collaborative Planning, Instruction, Assessment, and Reflection* by Andrea Honigsfeld and Maria G. Dove. Thousand Oaks, CA: Corwin. www.corwin.com.

Figure 4.18 Unit Planning Example

UNIT CO-PLANNING TEMPLATE FOR THE DIGITAL CLASSROOM

Unit Title: Guided by a Cause: A Long Walk to Water **Anticipated Duration:** 3–4 Weeks

Teacher A: Mrs. Cordeiro

Teacher B: Ms. Flores

Digital Platform: Google Classroom

Essential Question: How can resilience lead to empowerment?

Unit Objectives Aligned to Standards:

CONTENT	LANGUAGE
I can analyze how dialogue or specific incidents reveal information about characters or move the plot forward. *I can analyze how an author develops and contrasts the points of view of characters and narrators in a literary text.* *I can analyze the interactions between individuals, events, and ideas in a text.* *I can write an informative essay focusing on a specific topic and including relevant and interesting ideas and details.*	*I can make and orally describe inferences from the text.* *I can explain how the author develops different points of view.* *I can summarize the events and interaction of the text by using Somebody-Wanted-But-So-Then strategy.* *I can utilize transition words and sentence frames.*

Activating/Providing Background Knowledge: Question Formulation Technique—students will work in small groups to generate questions, each around a different assigned image that relates to the text ALWTW (Google Slides).

Digital Instructional Strategies/Tools:

Teacher Modeling (When & How)	**Guided Practice** (When & How)
Zoom: Video modeling (QFT) Screencastify (how to use digital tools)	Google Slides Synchronous meetings (Zoom)
Group Work (When & How) Google Slides Google Hangouts	**Independent Work** (When & How) Google Slides, Google Docs, Google Classroom, Google Drawings FlipGrid (Point of view discussion) EdPuzzle (Video on water for Sudan project)

(Continued)

(Continued)

SCAFFOLDS				
Sensory	Graphic	Interactive	Digital resources	Social-emotional
Screencasts to give verbal directions YouTube for read aloud Voice over in Google Slides	Graphic organizers	Video conferences	YouTube videos NewsELA	Mindful journaling Small group video conferences Access to Google Voice

Unit Assessment Plan: Informative Essay

Figure created by Kelley Cordeiro and Erica Flores. Used with permission.

Celebrations

A Learning Lab Approach to Collaborative Planning

Mary Pettit—fifth-grade teacher, NBCT, shared with us how she initiated a learning lab approach to co-planning at her grade level and beyond that with Alyce Smith.

In an effort to foster a more inclusive environment, our district implemented a version of co-teaching—a learning lab model—that allowed for a more flexible heterogeneous grouping of English language learners in the general education or inclusion setting. When English language learners were grouped in prior years, an ENL (English as a new language) teacher would remove them from the class and take them to a separate room where they worked on skills that supplemented the work we were doing in our classroom. This was typically called a pull-out model. As the negative impact of homogeneous grouping was noted in the field, student achievement remained stagnant, and students' social/emotional learning suffered from feeling separated from their classmates. Therefore, efforts to change our mindset and practice were clearly necessary.

In an attempt to implement a peer mentor/coach approach to planning, my co-teacher, Alyce Smith, a special education teacher, and I, along with other colleagues in our district, organized a lesson that I volunteered to videotape so we could reflect on it together (see the lesson plan in Figure 4.19). I identified some teaching strategies I would be working on to improve, and my colleagues were invited to note observations during the lesson.

Establishing this trust through the above activity was the first step in forming a co-planning partnership that we hoped to continue developing. After conferring with each other before the lesson about its goals and objectives, the videotaping began. As expected, this experience was extremely enlightening. Even as a veteran teacher of 23 years, observing yourself on video and being critiqued through the eyes of your colleagues was a humbling reminder that we all have something to learn from each other every day. Collaboration post-lesson gave us the opportunity to reflect on teaching so that we could maximize opportunities for future planning. In fact, Mrs. Smith and I used the video several more times to reflect on during collaborative lesson planning for weeks after.

This kind of peer mentoring/coaching can invoke a feeling of vulnerability at first. Volunteering to videotape a lesson can feel nerve-wracking and intimidating, but as educators who know the value of learning from colleagues and the importance of adapting our planning and practices to best meet the needs of our students, we realized the invaluable opportunities this kind of collaboration can provide.

Goals for Future Conversations

Our co-planning partnership began with conversations about what our students' strengths are and how we could celebrate and build upon them. Our goals for co-planning efforts were driven by asset-based attributes using an anecdotal system of informal observations of reading and writing as well as our formal assessments and benchmarks. It is important to note that in a true inclusive setting, we each strive to keep notes on all of our students. We agreed that co-teachers should not separate and group students based on their general education, special education, or language proficiency status. Getting to know all the students in our class helps us to collaborate more effectively. After establishing "what our students already know," we use the grade-appropriate reading and writing workshop model to guide us toward planning the goals and objectives of each lesson. Strategies for co-teaching, key concepts, vocabulary, literary language, listening comprehension, and writing skills are designed to be purposeful, embedded in everything that we do and say, and differentiated based on our constant observations of student performance.

Collaborative planning is evidenced in every corner of the classroom down to the purposeful placement of furniture. Our goal is to establish a classroom environment that appears like it "runs itself." Results of effective collaborative planning shine as evidenced by our attitudes toward learning, our pride and confidence in our growth, and our willingness to continue an open dialogue with each other. Establishing this learning lab co-planning model has energized our efforts, helped to form professional partnerships in and out of the classroom, and provided opportunities for community engagement and connections. In addition, our learning lab video lessons could be utilized in larger group professional development settings and could potentially unite colleagues to move to the next level in their planning. Figure 4.19 is not only an example of a learning lab collaboration with first-grade colleagues; it also reveals our intentional planning around cognitive, social-emotional, and language development goals.

Figure 4.19 A Collaborative Planning Session

Grade 1 English Language Arts

Read Aloud: "Spaghetti in a Hot Dog Bun" by Maria Cisni Desmondi

HOW TO PLAN LENS: COGNITIVE FOCUS: CONCEPTUAL KNOWLEDGE	EL/ML CONSIDERATIONS	WHAT DOES IT LOOK LIKE?
Prerequisite conceptual understanding needed: • In this unit of study, students will learn and practice strategies for noticing character feelings, traits, problems, lessons learned, setting, and the role dialogue plays in helping readers understand story elements. • Sentences are framed for visual cues and consistent use of literary language. Example: The lesson the character learned in the story is_____. • Transitioning from using concept unit vocabulary during whole group and pair-share read alouds to using the same strategies during independent reading will be modeled using a journaling method.	**Connections to real life:** **Prereading:** • Teachers will use real-life storytelling strategies to model how unit vocabulary is used and applied. Providing sentence frames during storytelling allows students to visualize how concepts can be applied in real-life situations. • Opportunities for pair sharing using the same sentence frames gives ELs/MLs time to practice using unit vocabulary and concepts in the context of their own storytelling. • ENL teacher anticipates challenges students with varying levels of English proficiency may have and creates a mini anchor chart using the same story elements with one of the students' own stories.	• Students sit next to their *pair-share* partner on the rug and listen to the teacher offering a personal storytelling. • The preplanned and purposeful stopping points give students opportunities to apply elements from the teacher's story to their own life experience. • Co-teachers participated in sharing and adding words to the anchor chart. • The story continues as the storyteller adds pieces of the story to the appropriate part of the chart. When the story is finished, the co-teachers model through thinking aloud how the chart helps to tell the story (see Figure 4.20) for the collaboratively developed anchor chart.
Focus: Procedural knowledge ***Preplanned, purposeful stopping points to model a strategy or think aloud:** 1. Stop after the first two pages to notice the two characters talking. Ask children to identify the Post-it on the anchor chart that says, "Dialogue" by identifying the number of the Post-it using raised fingers. Co-teachers scan the room for understanding.	**EL/ML considerations:** • Each preplanned stopping point gave student pairs an opportunity to use varying levels of language skills. • Providing sentence frames as context for pairs to share their thinking supported the learning that ELs/MLs needed to feel successful.	**Pathways to learning:** • Using personal book journals with anchor charts for reference, students choose an element off the chart to journal about. • Several journal samples are displayed as models for students. Allowing students to choose an element to journal about allows them to take ownership over their learning.

HOW TO PLAN LENS: COGNITIVE FOCUS: CONCEPTUAL KNOWLEDGE	EL/ML CONSIDERATIONS	WHAT DOES IT LOOK LIKE?
2. Page 5 think aloud: "When characters roll their eyes, it doesn't usually mean a good thing . . . let's read to find out the 'KIND' of character Ralph is" (setting up for trait work). 3. Page 6 ask kids to turn and talk about the setting (place Post-its with the words *classroom* and *school* on the anchor chart). 4. Page 7 turn and talk about a feeling the character is having. Place feeling words such as *worried* and *embarrassed* on the anchor chart next to "FEELINGS." 5. Page 9 pause to think aloud about why Ralph may be sitting alone at lunch. 6. Page 10 use a Post-it shaped like a speech bubble to ask students to turn and talk about what the speech/thought bubble might say above the character's head. (Note additional understandings about character feelings based on responses from students.) 7. Page 12 model think aloud: *This makes me think that Papa Gina is trying to teach Lucy a lesson about how to solve her problem . . . Let's read to find out.* 8. Lesson continues repeating strategies such as think alouds, Post-its, turn and talks, and so on.	• ELs/MLs who have a more proficient command of language are able to use more implicit strategies requiring them to put themselves in the character's place and discuss what the character might be thinking in a particular scene. *ELs/MLs who need a higher level of support will be able to use their personal anchor chart illustrating their own story. This support will help them put story element vocabulary in a context that makes sense to them. *Another consideration resulting from our co-planning was assigning "Partner A" and "Partner B" titles. It is anticipated that some student pairs will have students who do more sharing than others. In anticipation of this, when a teacher says, "turn and talk," we could switch up who shares first each time. • Additional considerations for ELs/MLs include co-planning content-area lessons to include opportunities to journal.	• Book journaling also allows students to express their understanding and interpretation of the reading in their own way. • Students use their journals during one-on-one conferences to guide discussion and retelling of the story. • Journaling also leads to more authentic discussions, opportunities for various expressions of comprehension, and a transfer of knowledge to future assignments in writing about reading. • Journaling allows *all* students to express their understanding and meet with success at their own level. For example: emergent readers and writers are able to journal using sketches and pictures to guide their discussion while proficient readers and writers are able to use more complex journaling strategies to guide discussion at their level.

(Continued)

(Continued)

HOW TO PLAN LENS: SOCIAL-EMOTIONAL FOCUS: SELF-AWARENESS	EL/ML CONSIDERATIONS	WHAT DOES IT LOOK LIKE?
Opportunities for students to reflect on, recognize, assess, and appropriately act upon their own emotions, needs, and beliefs. • Journals are an extension of each child's learning. • Students design their own journal cover. It is laminated and filled with blank paper. • The only "rule" about using their journals is whatever writing goes in it must be writing about the reading or learning in class. • Journal writing helps them take ownership of their success.	EL/ML need: • Opportunities to engage in conversations to share their understandings • Sentence frames to guide discussion • To experience language through storytelling and journaling • Read alouds, audiobooks, and leveled books with diverse characters they can relate to • Connections to real life and opportunities to celebrate success	• Purposeful planning includes using time for a "walking museum" of journals. • Students showcase their journal work and other students are able to make notes of journal entry ideas for their future journaling and practice conversational skills • Students are able to leave Post-it notes with questions or comments on student desks next to journals using sentence frames as a guide if needed. • Establishing a personal journal technique and using entries as a guide to facilitate conversation builds student confidence. • Participation in a walking museum gives students a sense of pride and belief that they are capable, part of a learning community, and successful.

HOW TO PLAN LENS: LINGUISTIC FOCUS: DISCIPLINE-SPECIFIC ACADEMIC LANGUAGE SKILLS AND ORACY	EL/ML CONSIDERATIONS	WHAT DOES IT LOOK LIKE?
• Anticipate sentence frames needed for a read aloud; post them next to the anchor chart on sentence strips as a visual cue. • Develop sentence frames that can be used in the future for consistency and practice. • Examples: 1. The character in the story is feeling ___________ in this part. 2. The character is showing that they are a ___________ kind of person. 3. This part of the story makes me think ___________. 4. This part of the story is happening ___________.	EL/ML students need: • Opportunities to effectively communicate using models for academic language and oracy • Models for situations in context that they can replicate independently • Sentence frames for display around the room to scaffold understanding of language skills • To be able to transfer oracy practice into writing practice using sentence frames while journaling	• Purposeful placement of sentence frames around the classroom provides ELs/MLs and others the opportunity to apply language and oracy skills in specific situations. • For this specific lesson, preplanned stopping points throughout the read aloud gave students several chances to use sentence frames in context. • Using a think-aloud method, co-teachers can physically point to the appropriate sentence frame while speaking. Students can then pair share using appropriate academic language, inflection, and context.

Figure created by Mary Pettit and Alyce Smith. Used with permission.

Figure 4.20 Collaboratively Planned Anchor Chart*

When I read, I notice...

*This anchor chart was designed to use as a visual guide for "turn and talk" opportunities during read aloud or a shared reading experience. In addition, the chart was replicated and placed in journals for students to use as a guide for writing about reading.

Figure created by Mary Pettit and Alyce Smith. Used with permission.

COLLABORATIVE REFLECTION QUESTIONS

1. The opening sentence of this chapter suggests that teachers need to change not only what they do but also how they think in order to co-plan for the sake of ELs/MLs. After reading this chapter, how has your thinking been influenced? What might change as a result of working as a team to plan instruction for ELs/MLs?

2. The general tenets for language instruction—language progressions, language opportunities (demands), language scaffolds, and language supports—should be a critical focus when planning instruction for ELs/MLs. Which aspects of this framework do you think are more easily incorporated into lesson plans that focus on integrated content and language teaching? Which might be more challenging to do?

3. Consider the multiple lenses that support planning for ELs/MLs—the cognitive lens, the linguistic lens, and the social-emotional lens. How might attention be paid to each lens that would lead to more effective instruction for ELs/MLs?

4. Examine the various frameworks and routines presented in this chapter. Review the templates for unit and lesson planning. Which of these structures or routines might enhance your team collaboration? How might they be adjusted to meet the needs of your student population or program requirements?

5. What are the greatest obstacles your team might face with consistent co-planning? How might you plan to overcome these challenges?

Watch Andrea and Maria discussing some highlights of Chapter 4. How might you negotiate the use of frameworks or instructional and co-planning routines with your fellow collaborators?

COLLABORATIVE ACTION STEPS

Consider what you have uncovered while reading this chapter and identify how this chapter has shaped your thinking about the use of frameworks and routines for co-planning.

1. Assess how your co-planning is organized. Consider what you are presently using to guide your collaborative conversations. If you have yet to formally collaboratively plan, where might you begin?
2. Review the various frameworks and instructional and co-planning routines. Investigate additional frameworks or map out your own instructional or co-planning routines.
3. Determine what is working and what might need improvement.
4. Consider how you might incorporate some of the chapter's ideas into your already established practices or how you might begin routine collaborative conversations with fellow teachers.
5. Draft a plan for implementing a collaborative planning routine.

Planning for Integrated Language and Literacy Development

5

> *"I see content as the soil that nurtures the seed of language and literacy development. Learning content can never be at the expense of learning a language."*
>
> —Tan Huynh, IB middle year program educator
> KIS International School, Thailand

> *"In order to meet the diverse needs of our English learners, intentional planning with high quality scaffolds are key to bridging language and content learning. Intentional planning involves being proactive in anticipating potential barriers to learning and providing access for all learners."*
>
> —Shadia Salem, director of English learning
> North Palos School District 117, Illinois

In this chapter, we present the power of collaborative work teachers engage in to create integrated language- and literacy-rich learning opportunities and environments to make instruction across all grade-level and core content areas accessible as well as develop facility and fluency in English for English learners/multilingual learners (ELs/MLs). Genesee and Lindholm-Leary (2013) remind us that when content and language instruction are integrated, there is "authentic communication in the classroom about matters of academic importance" (p. 6). If ELs/MLs have limited access to the core content and do not engage in authentic, meaningful exchanges with their English-speaking peers, their language development falls short of engagement with grade-appropriate, content-based explorations.

Zoom In

In a suburban middle school with a large population of ELs/MLs, Angela and Yessenia are beginning their school day in their eight-grade math class. They take out their iPads and begin the opening activity posted on the board, even before the bell rings. Their task is to recall commonly used vocabulary that signifies addition, subtraction, multiplication, and division in word problems. They are directed to a link that displays a four-page Jamboard, one page set for each math function, and using an electronic sticky note, they begin to post the words they recall. They are directed not to duplicate any words that are already posted. Both Angela and Yessenia are beginning-level English learners, so they rely on their personal math vocabulary notebooks to support them. These notebooks contain various foursquare graphic organizers, which provide word definitions, synonyms, word problems, and number sentences to illustrate each targeted vocabulary word. Home language support is also included. Additionally, they work in a team with two other students to complete the opening activity with the support of the English language development (ELD) teacher, who co-teaches the class alongside the math teacher.

The activation of prior knowledge and the attention paid to vocabulary in the beginning of the class support Angela and Yessenia to comprehend the math content as the lesson progresses. In addition to vocabulary associated with math functions, other key terms, such as *variable, systems*, and *equations*, are addressed during direct instruction at the onset of the lesson. Next, the students are divided into two groups, which are determined by a quick review of their homework; each group works with one of the teachers to analyze word problems, determine how to write the appropriate equations, and ultimately solve them. At this time, Angela and Yessenia and their group work with the ELD teacher, who guides them step-by-step to analyze each problem and carefully consider how the words are strung together to make meaning. Afterwards, Angela and Yessenia are given the choice—in teams or in a small group supported by the ELD teacher—to practice problem solving. They choose to complete their work alongside the ELD teacher, who provides them with further encouragement and assistance.

Zoom Out

During this math class, academic language instruction was intentionally woven into the lesson at multiple key points—at the beginning of the lesson, during the lesson, and at the end of the lesson. At the start, key vocabulary for math functions was the main focus of the opening task, helping students to recall and rediscover the common language signified in word problems (see Figure 5.1).

Figure 5.1 Keywords for the Four Mathematical Operations

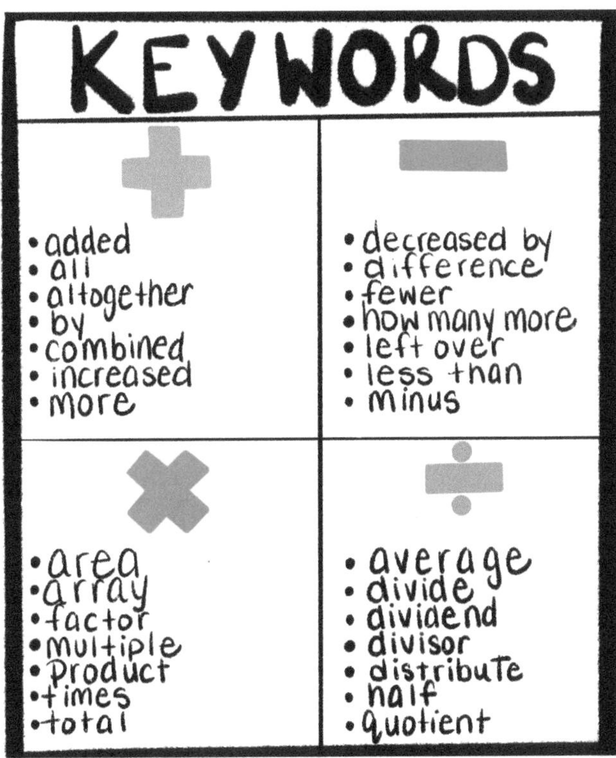

Next, as part of direct instruction on the nature of systems, key terms were highlighted during the class discussion and the meaning of these terms were consistently reviewed throughout the lesson. During the guided practice, when the class was divided into two groups, there was a targeted focus on understanding and making sense of each word problem, with careful attention being paid to how key words are strung together to create meaning. Finally, all students worked collaboratively to discuss the meaning of and solve math problems involving systems; this activity provided students with the opportunity to practice not only their new math skills but also the language of math. This lesson exemplifies how academic language can be addressed in the content class on multiple levels—at the word level (vocabulary), at the sentence level (dissecting sentences in word problems), and at the discourse level (verbally explaining problem solving).

Content and Language: What Is the Relationship?

Content instruction may not take place without considering the language that we need to teach the content. When we zoom out, we look at the literacy practices that we as educators need to include in teaching core subject matter and invite our students to engage in these same practices within the unique context of each core content area. When we zoom in, we may ponder more specific questions such as the following:

- What words are needed for conceptual understanding?
- What typical sentence structures are used within the context of the course content to formulate a thought, to express an opinion, to support a claim, to offer an explanation, and so on?
- How are sentences woven together within the context of the lesson to explain one's learning, to elaborate on one's thinking, or to argue for or against a particular perspective?
- How does capacity with academic words and more complex sentences and text lead to academic discourse in an authentic way?

Let's also keep in mind that student discourse—spoken or written—in any context will only happen if it is meaningful, functional, and authentic. Therefore, it is essential to focus on meaning-making before concentrating on the accuracy of grammatical forms. Students of all ages across all grade levels and content areas need multiple authentic opportunities to engage in oral and written discourse for meaning-making to develop their conceptual understanding simultaneously with their oracy and multiliteracies.

We have adapted Bacon's (2017) framework on critical literacy in English language teaching (ELT) to our current purposes by recognizing that ELs/MLs experience language and literacy development across three potentially overlapping processes:

1. **Incidental language and literacy learning:** ELs/MLs are exposed to English language and literacy through everyday social and school experiences.

2. **Explicit language and literacy learning:** Teachers select and focus on specific English language and literacy skills aligned to the lesson.

3. **Integrated language and literacy learning:** Teacher-directed and authentic learning opportunities are infused; teachers understand and plan for the type of academic language and literacy needed to access content and to demonstrate mastery, so they embed the instruction intentionally and provide authentic learning tasks for students to use it.

In our work with educators, we have found that collaboratively and intentionally planning for content and language integration is well worth the effort. When planning for such integrated instruction, we have previously advised teams to consider the following key tenets (Dove & Honigsfeld, 2018):

- Language is recognized as dialogical—it is developed through meaningful interaction with others.
- Students must participate in social and academic learning activities that allow for sustained authentic language use.
- Content and language are recognized for being interconnected; language is the vehicle that helps ELs/MLs make reasonable progress toward meeting grade-level content goals.
- Activating and building background knowledge for student understanding and successful task completion must be supported.
- Learning tasks should contain all four language domains (speaking, writing, reading, and listening) as well as allow for viewing and visual representations (Rubin et al., in press) with particular emphasis on the productive skills of speaking and writing.
- Lessons should be scaffolded to break down language and literacy practices and engagement with core content without oversimplification (see Chapter 6 for more on scaffolding).
- Lessons must systemically build on the individual and cultural assets students bring to the learning—learning must be relevant and connect to ELs'/MLs' lived experiences.

If you agree to plan with these premises in mind, your ELs/MLs are more likely to experience instruction characterized by the following:

- Instructional consistency that systemically supports content and language development along with social-emotional growth

- Curriculum continuity with clear goals and objectives
- Reduction in fragmented, disjointed learning experiences or isolated, skill-based language-learning tasks
- A recognition that there are multiple pathways to content and language learning and mastery
- More integration and less student isolation in the classroom and in the community

Integrated Planning for Instruction

An integrated approach to content, academic language and literacy development, and social-emotional learning goes beyond addressing the four language domains (reading, writing, and speaking/listening) merely when there is time for it, when it fits in the lesson, or when it is convenient. Planning for language development must be purposeful and intentional, and it requires systemic collaboration to have a measurable impact on student learning (Dove & Honigsfeld, 2020b; WIDA, 2020b). It is too important and too complex to do it alone!

While incidental language acquisition does happen for some learners, our responsibility as educators is to ensure that students have the skills needed to be successful, literate citizens, so we can't leave it to chance. When we create complex and comprehensive learning experiences for ELs/MLs, we must also devise targeted opportunities for them to develop the facility needed to engage in oral and written academic discourse. For this reason, building ELs'/MLs' language skills incrementally—meeting students at their level of proficiency (making content comprehensible) and adding to their linguistic and metalinguistic knowledge through focused instruction—is key. Language learning can be nurtured alongside content by carefully selecting appropriate vocabulary and phrases, sentence forms, and mentor texts for students to consider in order for them to develop comprehension and the ability to produce more complex texts.

Use the following checklist to self-assess and reflect on what kind of language-learning experiences ELs/MLs have access to.

ELS/MLS HAVE ACCESS TO

- Academic language practices that are both rigorous and authentic
- A text-rich environment with a variety of text formats available, including audio books, daily newspaper stands or websites, reference materials, resources for take-home reading, journals, and podcasts

- Primary documents of all types (including multilingual resources and multicultural perspectives) so that students can easily access and develop comfort levels for reading in different time periods and language styles, particularly in social studies and science
- Secondary sources that highlight the art of opinion, debate, and the comparison and contrast of essential ideas reflective of mainstream and nonmainstream writers as well as varying perspectives
- "Power" words or domain-specific vocabulary needed for content understanding in specific disciplines
- Multiple opportunities for close reading, annotating, and multimodal access to text as well as multimodal expressions
- Various authentic texts with stories, dramas, and poetry highlighted using feedback from other students as "reviews"
- Places and spaces for reading, writing, and sharing ideas (Book talks and literature circle areas should be designed and designated to maximize student interaction and mirror the way adults interface in successful book groups.)

What Research Says

When we think of integration, we also consider meaningfully connecting language domains, modes of communication, and oracy and literacy practices for ELs/MLs. Seminal literature has well supported the connection between listening/speaking and literacy as well as academic proficiency.

1. Applebee et al. (2003) carefully reviewed the literature on discussion-based learning and nonmainstream students—defined by them as low achievers, children of the poor, and second-language learners. They concluded that rather than learning in a traditional classroom environment,

    > [these diverse learners] do much better when instruction builds on previous knowledge and current ideas and experiences, permits students to voice their understandings and refine them through substantive discussion with others, and explicitly provides the new knowledge and strategies that students need to participate successfully in the continuing discussion. (p. 689)

2. Specifically, Saunders and O'Brien (2006) confirmed that "there is no controversy about the fundamental importance of English oral language development as part of the larger enterprise of educating ELLs" (p. 14).

3. August and Shanahan (2006) (National Literacy Panel) found that strong oral language skills enhance the development of literacy in second-language learners.

4. Additionally, Fred Genesee and his colleagues (Genesee et al., 2006) reported that oral language proficiency in the native language and second language both contribute to literacy development.

Research has shown this strong connection between oracy and literacy for decades; yet ELs/MLs may not have enough opportunity to talk and engage in authentic academic discourse regularly. How can we ensure more opportunities for integrating oracy and literacy?

Planning for Academic Language on Three Dimensions

As suggested by Figure 4.10 in Chapter 4, a multiple-lens approach is beneficial for ELs'/MLs' academic, linguistic, and social-emotional development. Here, our goal is to narrow our focus on how to plan for academic language using a three-dimensional framework: **Word level—Sentence level—Discourse level.**

Academic language has been defined differently by individual researchers and practitioners. Gottlieb and Ernst-Slavit (2013) suggest that "*academic language* refers to the language used in school to acquire new or deeper understanding of the content and to communicate that understanding to others" (p. 2). O'Hara and Pritchard (2016), members of the Complex Language Development Network team, originally worked with Jeff Zwiers to develop a framework for academic language and literacy development that consists of three dimensions of academic language depicted in Figure 5.2. In this adapted version of the framework, several challenges (also perceived as opportunities) that are faced by multilingual learners and essential instructional practices are added based on WIDA (2020b) and our own work in the field. The ultimate goal for collaborative planning is for successful academic language integration in the target core content class on the word, sentence, and discourse levels.

ELs/MLs need both authentic opportunities to use all dimensions of language across academic practices as well as explicit guidance in examining language as it works on each of these three levels and across the various content areas. Let's further examine language to see how the micro- and macro-level pieces fit together, while keeping in mind that students will only develop competence with language and literacy if they have the opportunity to participate in social and academic practices in appropriate, authentic contexts.

Figure 5.2 Academic Language Dimensions, Features, Challenges, and Essential Instructional Practices

DIMENSION	ACADEMIC LANGUAGE FEATURES	CHALLENGES (AND OPPORTUNITIES) FOR ELS/MLS	ESSENTIAL INSTRUCTIONAL PRACTICES TO PLAN FOR
Word level (vocabulary or phrases)	• Generic and discipline-specific academic terms • Figurative and idiomatic expressions • Words with multiple meanings • Roots and affixes	• Volume of vocabulary needed • Nuances of word meanings • Phrases and collocations • Precise use of words and phrases • Pronunciation	• Exposure to vast vocabulary through interactions with language-rich texts and experiences • An interactive environment in which verbal exchanges are encouraged and not silenced • Word-learning strategies
Sentence level	• Sentence structure • Sentence length • Sentence complexity • Grammatical structures • Pronouns • Context clues • Proverbs	• Complex sentences with low-frequency words • Advanced grammatical features (passive voice, participles, nominalization)	• Sentence frames, sentence starters • Sentence dissection (sentence chunking with discussion on the form and meaning of each segment) • Mentor text • Sentence varieties
Text level	• Text organization and cohesion • Text craft and structure • Text density • Clarity and coherence • Text types and genres	• Reading and Lexile levels • Complexity of ideas • Background knowledge students need to comprehend • Styles and structures unique to each genre or text type	• Strategy instruction across the content areas • Genre study • Read alouds and shared reading • Scaffolded and independent reading • Inquiry groups • Text analysis • Text annotation • Text deconstruction and reconstruction

Source: Adapted from Pritchard and O'Hara (2016); WIDA (2020b).

Suggestions for Planning Word-Level Academic Language Integration

Research and practical strategies regarding vocabulary instruction can fill libraries. Here we will focus on four essential practices to guide your planning of vocabulary integration: (1) vocabulary self-assessment, (2) tiered vocabulary instruction, (3) intentional choice for targeted vocabulary work (*frontload, embed, blend, and send off*) and (4) multi-approach, targeted, and sustained academic vocabulary instruction.

Vocabulary self-assessment. When students examine their own learning, it can reveal authentic evidence of their understanding and comprehension. For this reason, let's begin with developing student agency. By inviting students to assess their own level of vocabulary usage, we not only raise awareness about word knowledge but help develop independence, metalinguistic and metacognitive awareness, and goal-setting. Ritchhart (2015) reminds us that "the chief goal of instruction, right alongside the development of content understanding, is the advancement of thinking" (p. 33). On the other hand, Taboada Barber (2016) notes that morphological awareness helps students recognize prefixes, roots, and suffixes and how to manipulate them to form words.

To advance independent thinking about students' own learning, introduce the Vocabulary Self-Assessment Tool in Figure 5.3, which is an adapted version of a classic by Beck and colleagues (2002).

Figure 5.3 Vocabulary Self-Assessment Tool

VOCABULARY	MY KNOWLEDGE OF KEY WORDS			
	I HAVE NEVER HEARD OF IT	I HAVE HEARD OF IT, I THINK I KNOW WHAT IT MEANS	I KNOW IT VERY WELL	I CAN TELL OR WRITE A SENTENCE WITH IT

online resources Available for download at **resources.corwin.com/CoPlanningforELs**

Tiered vocabulary instruction. Selecting words for vocabulary instruction is generally determined by what students need most to comprehend text and engage in discourse. Yet ELs/MLs most often need support in understanding basic and general academic words in addition to content-specific vocabulary. Based on Beck and colleagues' (2002, 2008) ground-breaking work, we suggest planning vocabulary instruction using this three-tier model:

- **Tier 1:** Basic words that are often recognized and used with ease by speakers of English (e.g., book, girl, happy, he, etc.) may continue to be challenging for some ELs/MLs at the early stages of language development. They may need vocabulary instruction also targeting these words and may face a special challenge if these words are polysemous—having multiple meanings (table, work, place, arms, bank, and so on).

- **Tier 2:** General academic words tend to be more complex. Some of them travel across content areas (e.g., origin, system, primary, volume, and so on) and have different meanings; whereas others perform similar textual or discourse-level functions regardless of the content (e.g., therefore; for instance; nevertheless).

- **Tier 3:** Domain-specific words and less commonly used words that are critical for understanding the subject matter of the instruction (e.g., photosynthesis, circumference, expedition) as well as developing more complex academic language skills. Precise word usage supports conceptual learning, so Tier 3 words are essential for content attainment.

The ultimate purpose of the three-tiered categorization goes beyond merely identifying the level of complexity words represent. Instead, we are calling all teachers to make important instructional decisions based on this categorization and commit to intentionally building students' vocabulary, including Tier 2 vocabulary across the content areas, to offer the most access to critical words that afford students participation in a range of academic tasks, and clarify Tier 1 words when needed.

Targeted vocabulary: Frontload, embed, blend, and send off. We adapted an approach for vocabulary development from Carr et al. (2006), who suggest a different way of grouping target vocabulary words. We, too, recommend that you frontload key vocabulary to engage the students, to build background, or to anchor the lesson. Words that may be successfully taught without the context of the lesson should be chosen. Lesson-embedded words are those that are introduced during the lesson while students are engaged in a range of authentic learning tasks, thus these words are fully contextualized and meaningfully presented. You can blend vocabulary instruction by introducing new words "during front-loading, when common definitions and examples from students' prior knowledge are addressed; then during content instruction, they are revisited and refined with scientific definitions" (pp. 47–48).

Finally, at the end of the lesson, review vocabulary related to the big ideas and enduring understanding based on the lesson objectives and send the students off with them.

Multi-approach, targeted, and sustained academic vocabulary instruction. This approach centers on maintaining consistent vocabulary instruction throughout the course of several lessons. Based on the *What Works Clearing House's* (Baker et al., 2014) recommendation, start by choosing a small set of words and then offer in-depth, varied learning opportunities focused on the same words for several days. Words that meet some or most of the following criteria should be prioritized for selection:

1. Essential for understanding the text/lesson
2. Frequently appear in the text/lesson
3. May also be used in other content areas
4. Have multiple meanings
5. Ideal for word analysis (prefixes and suffixes)
6. Cross-language connections (cognates)

Taking this approach to vocabulary instruction is also aligned to what Blachowicz et al. (2006) suggest as good vocabulary instruction:

- It takes place in a language- and word-rich environment that fosters [. . .] "word consciousness."
- It includes intentional teaching of selected words, providing multiple types of information about each new word as well as opportunities for repeated exposure, use, and practice.
- It includes teaching generative elements of words and word-learning strategies in ways that give students the ability to learn new words independently. (p. 527)

Additionally, most effective vocabulary instruction in a school or district must be based on a common philosophy and shared practices among teachers to ensure greater continuity and instructional intensity (Calderón, 2016). At the same time, we must recognize that students come to school with a vast range of prior knowledge, background experiences, active and passive vocabulary, and language skills; thus differentiated instruction and targeted language development must also be considered.

A SNAPSHOT FROM THE FIELD

Nikki McDougal, English learning team leader at North Palos, District 117, shared with us how building on students' home languages can support academic development and validate students' home cultures and prior knowledge:

At H. H. Conrady Junior High School, we have a significant number of English learners who are in the beginning stages of their English language development. In order to support them in content classes, our teachers work diligently to provide opportunities for students to bridge their knowledge in their home language to what they are learning in English. I put together this document (see Figure 5.4) with them, and it allows teachers (and students) to directly and immediately translate any vocabulary terms or phrases using Google Translate formulas. I learned about using codes for translating with Google Sheets from Sara Knigge, consultant and author with Read en Espanol Inc. After she showed me how the codes worked, I created this tool for our teachers and students to utilize. The codes used for the translation can be found on the Library of Congress site (https://www.loc.gov/standards/iso639-2/php/code_list.php).

Although Google Translate is not perfect, it allows students to see that their home languages are important and valued while also supporting them in being able to bridge and translanguage in their classes regardless of whether there is a bilingual teacher present.

Figure 5.4 Multilingual Vocabulary Support

Language codes	Spanish	Polish	Arabic	Chinese	Bengali	Vietnamese
convey	transmitir	przenieść	يقنع	传达	বহন করা	chuyên chở
elaborate	elaborar	opracować	يشرح	精心制作的	সম্প্রসারিত	kỹ lưỡng
cycle	ciclo	cykl	دورة	循环	সাইকেল	đi xe đạp
revolution	revolución	rewolucja	ثورة	革命	বিপ্লব	Cuộc cách mạng
measurement	medición	pomiary	قياس	测量	মাপা	đo đạc
fraction	fracción	frakcja	جزء	分数	ভগ্নাংশ	phần

Figure created by Nikki McDougal. Used with permission.

Suggestions for Planning Sentence-Level Academic Language Integration

The three approaches to planning sentence-level academic language integration we suggest include (a) sentence dissection—similar strategies are also known as juicy sentences, language dives, and sentence cross-examination; (b) language functions with language frames; and (c) sentence patterns as mentor texts.

Sentence dissection. This strategy provides students with a format for closely analyzing sentence structures. Sentence dissection can be performed on all text types on all grade levels. It is especially important to apply this strategy to content-based academic texts, so students can gradually become independent readers of textbooks and other high-density, more complex informational texts. Introducing ELs/MLs to one "juicy sentence" a day based on a shared text is a similar strategy also promoted by Lilly Wong Fillmore (2009). Other closely related strategies are language dives (EL Education, n.d.) or sentence cross-examination (Honigsfeld & Dodge, 2015). These are significantly overlapping approaches to explicit sentence-level work, with some nuanced differences in how each engages students in rich conversations about language found in sentences. We suggest you start with the one that most appeals to your planning team.

Though sentences are no longer diagrammed and grammar is no longer taught (or should not be taught in isolation and out of context), sentence dissection—a close sentence-level language analysis—can be helpful for ELs/MLs. During a structured session of no longer than 8 to 10 minutes, offer students exposure to and guided exploration of a carefully selected, sufficiently complex sentence (or two). It is best if the excerpt comes from a text you are using for literacy or content-based instruction and is rich in information as well as opportunities for discussing grammar and usage.

Below is an example of how to plan for sentence dissection. Follow these steps with any variations needed based on students' needs:

1. Choose a sentence from the target textbook or other assigned reading that has an important message in the text while also lending itself to rich conversations about meaning and grammatical structure.
2. Present the sentence on chart paper, traditional blackboard, or Smartboard.
3. Facilitate an in-depth discussion of what the sentence meant, how the author expressed his/her idea, and so forth, inviting student input into meaning-making first.
4. Ask probing questions—about the *who, what, when,* and *where* of the sentence.
5. Pinpoint one or more unique linguistic features of the sentence (passive voice, relative clauses, heavy noun phrases) to call students' attention to select language complexities.
6. Use color-coding or other visually engaging methods to chunk the sentence into clauses or phrases.

7. Utilize think alouds as they pinpointed grammatical or stylistic choices in some (*but not all of the*) language chunks to keep the activity brief and engaging.
8. Invite students to use the sentence as mentor text and to create similar sentences of their own to be able to internalize the language complexity.

See an example below: The first sentence dissected in Figure 5.5 is excerpted from a science journal article written for teens (Boutle et al., 2020).

Figure 5.5 A Dissected Sentence From a Science Journal

Sentence: "So we might think a planet is uninhabitable because it lacks these gases when in fact they are just hidden by dust" (Boutle et al., 2020, p. 3).

SENTENCE CHUNK	POSSIBLE DISCUSSION POINTS	LINGUISTIC FEATURES
So we might think	What does "might" mean in this sentence? Why does the author choose to say "we might think" instead of "we think"?	Auxiliary or helping verbs (may, might)
a planet is uninhabitable	Uninhabitable is a long word, but you might recognize some word parts. What are those parts and how do they help you make sense of the word?	Roots, prefixes, suffixes
because it lacks these gases	What lacks gases? What does "it" refer to? Why does this clause begin with the word "because"? The sentence refers to "these gases." Where do we find in the text what "these gases" actually are?	Causal relationship between clauses Context clues and identifying the antecedent to demonstrative pronouns
when in fact	Why is the phrase "in fact" used here? (Hint: What do we the readers expect based on the first half of the sentence? What is another way to say the same [in reality . . . ; the truth is . . .]?)	Phrases to add emphasis: Actually . . . In reality . . . The truth is . . .
they are just hidden by dust.	What are hidden by dust? What does the pronoun "they" refer to? How can we change this sentence structure to start with the word "Dust . . ."	Passive voice Referential pronoun (they)

The sentence-level academic language work utilizing language dives (EL Education, n.d.) or sentence cross-examination consists of three predictable steps. With guidance and support, ELs/MLs engage in a three-part process that consists of the following:

1. Deconstruct the sentence by discussing what the sentence means, how each segment contributes to its meaning, and what essential phrases and chunks are included in the sentence.
2. Reconstruct the sentence by inviting students to put the sentence back together chunk by chunk and consider sentence variations as well. For example, another sentence from the science article previously cited reads, "*The more water is lost over time, the more land is exposed*" (Boutle et al., 2020, p. 3). Here, students work with language chunks as if they were puzzle pieces (see Figure 5.6).

Figure 5.6 Sentence Deconstruction

3. Practice chunks of the sentence. Create your own sentences based on the language model extrapolated from the target sentence.

As explained by a recent curriculum guide published online by EL Education,

> As part of this inquiry-based process, students acquire academic language through analysis, conversation, and usage, appreciating the time provided to focus on just one sentence. They commonly become filled with curiosity about language and delight in unlocking its mysteries. This is more effective than having language explained through lectures, rules, and memorization. (EL Education, n.d., p. 2)

Language functions with language frames. Among others, Dutro and Kinsella (2010) suggest a different structured approach to sentence-level work by examining language functions and language frames (see Figure 5.7). Both of these tools scaffold ELs'/MLs' classroom participation and contribution to academic conversations. Language functions refer to how language is used to accomplish communication tasks in school settings. For example, a student might be asked to compare two characters in a story, explain how to solve a math problem, question the outcomes of a science experiment, or draw a conclusion. Language frames refer to phrases, structures, and prompts that guide ELs/MLs in forming meaningful sentences and, thus, help ELs/MLs accomplish various language functions. Language frames can include what are known as sentence starters, sentence frames, or signal words.

Let's look at an example from an elementary science lesson on butterflies and moths. If students are asked to *compare* and *contrast* two things, an entering-emerging-level student might be given a sentence starter that includes a lot more information than a more advanced student may use:

> "Moths and butterflies are both ________." Or "Both are ________."

A sentence frame not only offers the beginning of the sentence but some additional wording as well:

> "Moths and butterflies are different because moths are ________, but butterflies are ________."
>
> Signal phrases such as "—er than" will also help perform the language function of compare and contrast. An intermediate or developing-level student, on the other hand, may be introduced to sentence starters and sentence frames that may include more complex structures or less information, such as "________ and ________ are similar because they both (are/have) ________" as well as signal phrases including "similarly" or "in contrast." Finally, ELs/MLs at higher language proficiency levels may be challenged to further elaborate on how they compare two items by using sentence frames or sentence starters, such as "Neither ________ nor ________ have ________" or "Their shared/common attributes are ________." Further, advanced learners can be given signal words such as "whereas" or "as opposed to" to use in a sentence discussing differences.

Sentence patterns. Examining sentence patterns contained in various types of text supports ELs/MLs to better understand how words are strung together to make meaning. Among others, Oczkus (2007) recognizes the importance of borrowing from authors: "When students study the textual patterns in fiction and nonfiction, first analyzing and then borrowing another author's organizational pattern or word choice, their writing improves" (p. xiv). At the elementary level, using patterned writing and patterned speech are more commonly accepted practices; at the secondary level, sentence patterns can also be recognized in both fiction and nonfiction with the intention of helping diverse learners become familiar with the way

- words are strung together to make meaning,
- verb tense is used appropriately,
- parts of speech fit together, and
- simple, compound, and complex sentences are formed.

Figure 5.7 Aligning Language Functions and Language Frames

MATCHING LANGUAGE FUNCTIONS TO LANGUAGE FRAMES		
COMMON FUNCTIONS (IN ALPHABETICAL ORDER)	KEY WORDS AND PHRASES	POSSIBLE SENTENCE STARTERS AND SENTENCE FRAMES
Analyze	Examine Investigate Determine	Given the information/facts/evidence, we can interpret/conclude that . . . . Based on . . . , we can claim that . . . After examining . . . , we can draw the conclusion that . . . .
Cause and Effect	If . . . , then . . . As a result Therefore/thus Consequently	. . . was caused by . . . . . . was a result of . . . . . . led to . . .
Classify	Belongs to . . . Sort and label Traits/features/categories	. . . is an example of . . . . . . consists of several categories, such as . . . . . . is a type of . . .
Compare and Contrast	(ADJ)-er than . . . ; (ADJ)-est On the other hand Similarly Despite	. . . and . . . are similar because they both . . . One similarity between . . . and . . . is . . . . . . and . . . are different because . . . . . . is, whereas . . . is
Describe	ADJECTIVES and ADVERBS	The diagram/map/graph illustrates how . . . The illustration/photo/image depicts . . .
Evaluate	Assess/assessment Agree vs. disagree Value	Based on . . . , we determine that . . . After examining . . . , we conclude that . . .
Infer	Due to . . . Since In light of . . .	We can infer that . . . Based on . . . , we can make the inference that . . .
Inform	Fact Details Draw a conclusion . . .	My understanding about . . . is . . . . The information in this article suggests that . . . The authors claim that . . . The facts indicate that . . .
Inquire/Seek Information	Who; What; When; Where; How; Why According to . . .	Could you explain . . . , please? I don't understand what you mean by . . . I wonder . . . May I ask you about . . . ?

MATCHING LANGUAGE FUNCTIONS TO LANGUAGE FRAMES		
COMMON FUNCTIONS (IN ALPHABETICAL ORDER)	KEY WORDS AND PHRASES	POSSIBLE SENTENCE STARTERS AND SENTENCE FRAMES
Justify	Because of For this reason Due to Claim and evidence	My main reason to believe this is . . . My primary reason to claim . . . is . . . . Based on the evidence I found in . . . , I conclude . . . .
Predict	Guess Estimate Believe	Based on . . . , I predict that . . . Considering . . . , I anticipate that . . . .
Sequence	Previously Finally Before . . . After . . .	First, ... Next, ... Then, ... Finally, ... First, ... Second, ... Third, ... Finally, ... Initially, ... Later, ...
Summarize	In sum In summary Overall In conclusion	Overall, the text is about . . . . The author indicated . . . . The basic message is . . . .
Synthesize	Together Combine A synthesis of . . . and	The main point of . . . is . . . . The significance of . . . is . . . .

Invite your students to be *sentence pattern detectives* and introduce the strategy *Read it, Speak it, Write it* into your teaching (Honigsfeld & Dove, 2013). Plan on highlighting a sentence or two in each lesson (or lesson sequence) that lends itself well to becoming a mentor sentence that the students can both analyze and then emulate. Anderson and La Rocca (2017) recognize that students are naturally curious about language, and when teachers "step in and share the patterns of power in bite-sized, digestible chunks" (p. 7), they help their "learners to experiment and play with these patterns with loads of talk, support, and modeling" (p. 7).

Let's return to the previously cited science article for teens and examine the following sentence, which may be well suited for sentence pattern work at the secondary level.

> *The only chance for a planet orbiting a red dwarf to be warm and suitable for life (or habitable) is for it to be very close to the star.* (Boutle et al., 2020, p. 1)

After students discuss the meaning of the sentence, they use the sentence frame extrapolated from the mentor text and create sentences reflective of their own experiences to develop ownership of the structure.

> The only chance for ________ is for it to be ________.

Sentence-level analysis is an important activity for ELs/MLs as well as all students to better understand how words truly combine to form complex text. By examining and emulating the patterns presented in model sentences, students are better able to expand their capability to express their ideas, make sense of the order of words and word combinations in sentences, and subsequently improve their reading comprehension and ability to write for academic purposes.

Suggestions for Planning Discourse-Level Academic Language Integration

Discourse or text-level features of academic language that ELs/MLs may find most challenging include organization and cohesion. For example, consider what students need to know to understand and fully appreciate the following excerpt from Abraham Lincoln's June 26, 1858, speech upon accepting the Republican nomination for Senate. Notice how Lincoln begins with a (now famous) topic sentence, how the next sentence explains what he referred to in the first place, and the final two sentences further elaborate on his original claim. The repetition of certain phrases and the parallel sentence structure within the text are all examples of text organization and rhetorical devices:

> *A house divided against itself cannot stand. I believe this government cannot endure, permanently half slave and half free. I do not expect the Union to be dissolved—I do not expect the house to fall—but I do expect it will cease to be divided. It will become all one thing or all the other.*
>
> (Excerpted from http://www.abrahamlincolnonline.org/lincoln/speeches/house.htm)

What do ELs/MLs need to be successful with complex texts such as the speech above?

Pause for a moment and jot down what you think ELs/MLs need to be successful with complex texts such as Lincoln's 1858 speech.

____

____

____

____

Have you considered any or all of the following: background knowledge; key vocabulary and sentence structures; text density; organization and cohesion; context and register; and more? When planning for the discourse dimension of academic language, we must remember to take into account the variety of speech/written texts that are available for students to explore and engage in across the curriculum and how critical it is for ELs/MLs to have opportunities for extended discourse in all language domains. Brisk (2015) reminds us, "the text achieves its cohesion through paragraphs that flow through well-connected themes and new information" (p. 8). For this reason, we would like to offer two approaches for planning for discourse-level work:

- Engaging with and creating **multilingual, multimodal, and multilevel** texts
- Implementing **genre studies with mentor texts**

Multilingual, multimodal, and multilevel texts. ELs/MLs need both access to and opportunities to comprehend and produce oral and written discourse that is multilingual, multimodal, and available at multiple reading levels. Using these various dimensions for introducing and creating text will allow ELs/MLs to have multiple entry points into the content they are learning as well as provide supports to build competency in language use.

Multilingual discourse practices and multilingual texts allow ELs/MLs to draw on their multiple linguistic resources and help develop multiliteracies. Relying on students' home languages and tapping into their cultural histories affirms their personal identities and further supports learning additional languages. With the technology available today, we no longer need to depend on the language knowledge of the classroom teacher to support multilingual discourse. Therefore, we must strongly consider how to best make the shift from deficit-based thinking about students who speak languages other than English and English-only instruction and discourse to regarding students' home languages as assets and not as obstacles to learning.

Multimodal approaches to serving ELs/MLs are getting increasing attention, whether they are recognized as scaffolding tools or more. We agree with Grapin (2019), who advocates for a strong version of multimodality according to which language should be viewed as a meaning-making tool across all the content areas and all modalities. One compelling argument for this approach is that "it turns a deficit view of ELs as lacking the linguistic resources needed to participate meaningfully in the content areas into an asset view that capitalizes on the diverse meaning-making resources they bring to the classroom" (p. 35). Multimodal discourse includes a wide range of possibilities, such as listening to a podcast, watching a video recording or screencast, or presenting information through a combination of visual and textual resources. Multimodal expression honors ELs/MLs across all grade levels, all proficiency levels, and all content areas.

Multilevel discourse recognizes that students progress through their language and literacy development in stages over time. When students have access to content, more specifically to text on multiple reading levels, they may be able to access key concepts and information and engage in learning activities with their peers. When text is provided on two or more levels, students may work on the independent level alone, on a higher-level text with peers, and at the grade-level (instructional level) text with their teachers.

A SOUND BITE

According to WIDA (2020),

> Multimodality, the use of multiple means of communication, is an essential way for all students to access and engage in the content areas. In addition to the use of spoken and written language, students also communicate through gestures, facial expressions, images, equations, maps, symbols, diagrams, charts, videos, graphs, computer-mediated content, and other means. (p. 12)

Do you agree? What are your experiences with multimodality? In what ways do you see multimodality as a method to increase ELs'/MLs' participation, learning, and demonstration of knowledge?

Icon: iStock.com/Vectorig

Genre study. Genres are commonly defined as "categories or kinds of writing, with distinctive features or rhetorical elements that speak to their purpose" (Fearn & Farrnan, 2001, p. 227). We recognize that different genres place different demands and expectations on ELs/MLs in their various literacy roles as readers and writers or as consumers and producers of multimodal texts. Explicit knowledge of and experience with a range of genres help make academic language more visible and accessible. Genre knowledge enhances ELs'/MLs' capacity with (a) understanding the purpose of the text; (b) recognizing the recurrent linguistic features of each genre; (c) being able to deconstruct and reconstruct text; and (d) constructing original text in the target genre first jointly, then independently.

We appreciate the way Duke et al. (2011) organize the reading and writing genres for a focused study into five major categories. See Figure 5.8 for a summary of these categories aligned to their purpose of the genre.

To support ELs/MLs in their thinking, talking, reading, and producing (writing) texts across grade-appropriate genres, we suggest an inquiry-based approach. When students are actively engaged in developing new understandings about each genre or text type, they develop deeper understanding, read with more comprehension and anticipation of what the genre is expected to represent, and write more effectively within each genre.

The mentor text approach to support genre studies. Just as teachers in the classroom act as language models, readings selected from appropriate texts can act as mentor texts and be used as models. Mentor texts help ELs/MLs anchor their understanding about how each genre works. With guidance and support, ELs/MLs need opportunities to deconstruct and reconstruct simple and increasingly more complex texts across genres. Memorable, outstanding examples of well-written texts also serve as models and may inspire or ground students in their own writing (Brisk, 2015; Gallagher, 2011). Mentor texts not only provide students with models for how words are strung together to express facts, opinions, thoughts, ideas, emotions, and so on, but also can support students to better understand

Figure 5.8 Categories of Genres, Their Purpose and Planning Tips

GENRE GROUPS	PURPOSE	GENRE TYPES	EXAMPLES FROM THE CLASSROOM (READING AND WRITING IN THE GENRES ARE COMBINED)	TIPS TO PLAN TO MEET ELS'/MLS' NEEDS
Narrative Genres	Sharing and making meaning of experiences	Fictional narratives, personal narratives, memoirs, family narratives, community narratives	Students read and write about real and imaginary events (such as create a family narrative about a celebration)	Include stories that reflect students' lived experiences; invite students to share their own stories
Procedural Genres	Learning how to do something and teaching others	How-to texts, manuals for classroom or school procedures, directions for games/activities	Students read how-to texts. They may produce similar texts (such as one to explain the steps needed to play a game they developed as a culminating project for a unit of study)	Allow students to share how-to texts representative of their own funds of knowledge
Informational Genres	Developing and communicating expertise	Reports, research projects, guides, informational booklets, informational websites	Students read informational texts and online sources as well as create a guidebook or website about a topic they research (for example, the community where they live)	Explicitly teach research skills, offer mentor texts
Dramatic Genres	Exploring meaning through performance	Plays, skits, readers theater scripts, poetry	Students read plays and scripts as well as write and perform short skits for an assembly on a topical issue	Invite students to express themselves via dramatic expressions
Persuasive Genres	Affecting change	Persuasive essays, magazine articles, formal letters and persuasive speeches, advocacy projects, pamphlets and posters	Students read articles and write a letter to the principal or school board requesting a change of a school rule or policy	Build on student in-school and out-of-school expertise

Source: Adapted from Dodge and Honigsfeld (2014) and Duke et al. (2011).

writing for different purposes—description, explanation, narrative, and so on, the importance of point of view, how to develop a story plot or characters, the use of figurative language, and so on. Mentor texts can also inspire students by making connections to their lived experiences and thereby serve as a motivation for students to express themselves.

Keep these questions in mind as you plan for the three levels of academic language:

1. What words or phrases are necessary for communication or content understanding?
2. What sentence types are necessary for communication and fluency of expression?
3. What varieties of oral and written text are necessary for expressing ideas?
4. What supports are used to represent meanings of important words and concepts?
5. How will the learning experience engage students in practicing and using language with a classmate or family member?
6. What are different ways in which students can be speaking, writing, interacting, reading, and listening (SWIRL-ing) about the content and their learning?

Source: Adapted from WIDA (2020b).

A SNAPSHOT FROM THE FIELD

Sara Knigge, consultant and author, applied the three dimensions of academic language—word level, sentence level, and discourse level—to the Picture Word Inductive Model (PWIM) and created a planning template as a guide for collaborating with fellow teachers on strategies for developing academic language (see Figure 5.9).

Figure 5.9 PWIM Planning Template

Level		Step
Word Level	**List**	1. Teacher chooses image dealing with upcoming content area/text/novel.
		2. Elicit words/phrases, "What do you see?"
		3. Label image, repeating words.
		4. Direct students to spell and say words aloud.
	Sort	5. Categorize words on separate chart. "Can we put any of these words in like groups?"
		6. Review chart over a series of days (pointing out phonics, syllables, cognates).
		7. Elicit more words under chart categories. Teacher leads students to key words/phrases in upcoming unit.
Sentence Level	**List**	8. Reference image and chart to brainstorm titles for image. Choose a title.
		9. Students (in small groups or whole group) create sentences using chart and image. Teacher can lead to sentence patterns for content area.
	Sort	10. Categorize sentences according to topic.
Discourse Level		11. Whole group can rearrange sentences into paragraph form while teacher "thinks aloud."
		12. Revisit paragraph over a series of days.

English Language Proficiency (ELP) Leveled Extension Activities:

ELP 1-2	ELP 2-3	ELP 4-5
• Label picture again. • Label a similar image. • Word study activities. • Illustrate sentences.	• Illustrate sentences. • Pick a sentence and expand it (add noun phrases, verbal phrases prepositional phrases, adjectives, adverbs, etc.). • Write alternative introductory or closing statements for the paragraph.	• Pick a sentence and expand it. • Search for and write a paragraph about a similar image. • Conduct research on the topic. • Convert the statements into questions.

Role of Teacher A:	**Role of Teacher B:**

Possible roles:

List key vocabulary prior to lesson.

Write example sentences or paragraphs students might provide.

Decide on and set examples of sentence patterns students can follow.

List cognates within image/topic.

Plan extension activities.

Assess students listening, speaking, reading, and writing.

Figure created by Sara Knigge. Used with permission.

Multidimensional Intentional Planning

Planning for Oracy and Literacy

Walqui (2019b) cautions us to move away from merely aiming at oral skills to focusing on oracy—having the facility to express one's thoughts and ideas and understand and respond to others using appropriate language and communication skills. She supports her claim by suggesting that "talk that develops knowledge and the ability to use it in action has to be purposefully and deliberately constructed, and it must invite all students in a class to become engaged" (p. 185). It is a well-recognized necessity to integrate reading and writing in all subject matter and use a wide variety of materials as well as class configurations and collaborative-learning groups for students to use language authentically and purposefully (Learned, 2018). It is also increasingly acknowledged that literacy may not develop as successfully as possible without students engaging in oral discourse (Motley, 2016; Robb, 2016; Zwiers, 2019). How can we expect our ELs/MLs or anyone to write about something they have not yet had the opportunity to discuss, ponder, read, and then discuss a bit more? We, too, agree that when planning integrated content and language instruction for ELs/MLs, we must include structured conversations and scaffolded, intentional academic exchanges as well as student-led discussions so all students get opportunities to engage in high-quality academic conversations. Based on research recognizing the connection and interdependence between oral language development and literacy, we are proposing talk-rich versions of the reader's and writer's workshop.

Talk-rich reader's workshops. When this approach is adapted for ELs/MLs, the reader's workshop begins with a mini-lesson in which a concept or particular reading strategy is introduced to students through conversation. The teacher models and demonstrates the skill and gives students a brief period of time for guided practice and real-life application. After the mini-lesson, students apply what has been taught by discussing the application of the strategy and reading books at their independent reading level in small groups, in pairs, or when ready, alone. Other reader's workshop activities enhanced with a focus on oracy may include students talking, dictating, or writing about what they have read in a journal, sharing the journal writing with a partner, reading aloud to or conferencing with the teacher, and participating in guided reading and academic discussion groups. Teachers generally end the reader's workshop by meeting with the whole class once again to review the mini-lesson concept and gather feedback from students about their various reading activities.

Talk-rich writer's workshops. A valuable activity for students to practice and demonstrate their knowledge of the basic features of print, the writer's workshop provides students with opportunities to practice writing in genres independently. One way to introduce a talk-rich writer's workshop is with an interactive read aloud with lots of discussions, using a reading selection that might also serve as a mentor text for student writing. Teachers may choose to continue with a mini-lesson to teach a particular writing concept. With young learners or diverse students of any age, lessons might focus on some print convention, such as beginning sentences with capital letters, indenting when starting a new paragraph, or ending sentences with the correct punctuation marks. Most of the time spent during writer's workshop should be on student writing.

Planning Across Levels of Literacy

How do you plan for levels of literacy when considering ELs'/MLs' needs? Fang and Robertson (2020) have recently recognized that "an emerging shift is taking place from teaching basic language skills (e.g., fluency, vocabulary) and generic cognitive strategies (e.g., inferencing, summarizing) to teaching discipline-specific language and literacy practices" (p. 240). This shift to disciplinary language and literacy instruction—the idea that all teachers are teachers of the English language and literacy unique to their disciplines—may be perceived as additional responsibilities on the shoulders of grade-level and content-area teachers. Yet the development of language and literacy skills for all students is integral to all content-area teaching and is necessary for student success in higher education and employment.

Among many others, Shanahan and Shanahan (2008) redefined literacy instruction by distinguishing among levels of literacy. *Basic literacy* refers to literacy skills that are crucial for understanding letter–sound correspondence, decoding, and accessing high-frequency words that are necessary for all reading tasks. The next level, *intermediate literacy*, indicates skills that are common to many reading tasks and include developing basic fluency when reading, understanding generic academic words and phrases, and applying general comprehension strategies to everyday and academic readings. Finally, there is *disciplinary literacy*, which specifies literacy skills that are essential to understanding and producing text that is unique to the various content areas, such as literature, history, science, mathematics, music, or any other subject matter (Shanahan & Shanahan, 2020). According to one of the most frequently cited definitions, disciplinary literacy is "grounded in the beliefs that reading and writing are integral to disciplinary practices and that disciplines differ not only in content but also in the ways this content is produced, communicated, and critiqued" (Fang, 2012, pp. 19–20).

To better visualize the complexity of literacy development and the connections between and among the levels, consider a simple drawing of a house, such as the one in Figure 5.10.

The foundations that hold up this complex structure represent the basic literacy skills that are essential—they must be solid and well developed to hold up the entire house. The first floor of the building represents the intermediate literacy skills: This level

Figure 5.10 The Architecture of Literacy

is where most of the interactions with literacy take place, essential comprehension skills are developed, and cross-disciplinary practices of reading and writing are experienced. Finally, the second floor and any other extensions to the house stand for the disciplinary literacy skills that scholars use in specialized content-area contexts. Digital or media literacy may represent the special "wiring" needed throughout the house. The top floor of the house and the embellishments of the roof also symbolize that one can develop disciplinary literacy in various spaces—one may acquire more advanced literacy skills for reading poetry and other fictional literary works; whereas others may immerse themselves in the literacy associated with hobbies and extracurricular activities and so on.

Let's also recognize that the same student might have acceptable skills for accessing complex historical documents yet show emerging skills with the technical language of computer science. Based on ELs'/MLs' proficiency levels and the objectives of the lesson, we must consider one or more levels within the context of the same lesson or unit. The most important recommendation is not to wait for ELs/MLs to develop fluency in English before planning for all three levels of literacy. For example, consider the use of a tool such as Figure 5.11 as a planning template to map out the literacy needs of ELs/MLs across proficiency levels and literacy levels.

Figure 5.11 Planning Template for Language and Literacy Levels

LEVELS OF PROFICIENCY	LEVELS OF LITERACY		
	BASIC	INTERMEDIATE	DISCIPLINARY
Entering-Emerging	• Decode words and interpret sound-symbol relationships • Recognize common words and phrases	• Understand common academic words in simple text • Find information in simple text	• Develop vocabulary for essential content concepts • Write simple phrases or sentences to express content concepts
Developing	• Understand most common (Tier 1) words • Read and comprehend two- to three-paragraph text with predictable content	• Comprehend main idea and details in short, factual academic texts • Convey ideas and opinions in simple paragraphs	• Develop strategies to understand texts that are increasingly complex or contain unfamiliar topics • Develop ability to write organized and cohesive text
Expanding–Bridging	• Find main idea and details consistently and understand key words in full-length academic readings • Work alone or in pairs to comprehend texts that are increasingly complex	• Generally make appropriate inferences, understand authors' purpose and point of view • Write about a variety of topics, display clear organization and topic development	• Read and comprehend grade-level texts that are conceptually and/or linguistically complex • Write about various topics and use a variety of sentence structures for stylistic purposes

Planning Across Literacy Roles

Fang (2012) further cautioned of the multiple literacy roles students participate in and must develop competence with to be successful with complex literacy tasks. When applied to ELs/MLs, the challenge of developing these four roles may become even more complex (see Figure 5.12), and thus intentional planning for literacy roles should be part of collaborative planning.

1. **As code-breakers**, diverse learners must have access to a range of skills and resources to process print and nonprint input (signs, symbols, and visual and graphic representations of information).

2. **As meaning-makers**, they must have the opportunity to interact with the target text and with each other to understand the overall meaning of the text.
3. **As text users,** they must have regular and meaningful access to a range of texts written in different genres for different audiences and purposes. These target texts must also serve an authentic purpose in the students' academic and literacy development to ensure high levels of motivation and engagement.
4. **As text analysts and critics,** they must be equipped with the necessary scaffolds to critically interpret, analyze, synthesize, and evaluate multiple texts.

Figure 5.12 Multiple Literacy Roles

Planning for Language and Literacy Development Across Disciplines

Students need experience with how language is used in a variety of ways and in a variety of contexts—formally and informally, in written and spoken formats, and in varied genres and situations. If students internalize the knowledge they have about how language functions in different contexts, they are likely to comprehend more fully when reading and listening or make more effective choices when speaking and writing. Interdisciplinary collaborative planning can help teachers align the language and literacy expectations across core courses, and the teachers, in turn, can guide their students on how to use language in a new context. Lee and Spratley (2010) identified a list of cross-discipline reading strategies for students to become competent readers in their content-specific classes. These strategies focus on the ability to do the following:

- Build prior knowledge
- Develop specialized vocabulary
- Learn to deconstruct complex sentences
- Use knowledge of text structures and genres to predict main and subordinate ideas
- Map graphic (and mathematical) representations against explanations in the text
- Pose discipline-relevant questions
- Compare claims and propositions across texts
- Use norms for reasoning within the discipline (i.e., what counts as evidence) to evaluate claims (p. 16)

Based on research presented in *The Handbook of TESOL in K–12* (de Oliveira, 2019) and other recent resources, here are some practical suggestions for planning across the content areas.

What to keep in mind when you plan lessons and units for ELs/MLs in science. In authentic contexts, scientists do their work in a multimodal fashion. Moje (2015) argued, "Multimodal representations are de rigueur in laboratories, archives, and field work. Opportunities to read and write (or compose) multimodal forms are critical for fostering disciplinary literacy skills because they are part and parcel of actual disciplinary practices" (p. 264). Additional strategies include the following:

- Plan for hands-on inquiry-based and discovery-oriented lessons.
- "Use multiple modes of communication (gestures, oral, graphic, textual)" (de Oliveira et al., 2019, p. 281).
- Design differentiated instructional materials that include verbal and visual adaptations and modifications.

- Include literacy practices through word walls, sentence stems, and sentence frames.
- Incorporate carefully designed graphics in your lesson and invite students to design their own graphic or multimodal representations of their learning (using a combination of drawing and writing).
- Have ELs/MLs work with lab partners as well as in groups of varied sizes and configurations.
- Accept language and register-mixing.
- Employ traditional (paper-and-pencil-based) and digital platforms for capturing students' conceptual development through concept maps and data visualization.

What to keep in mind when you plan lessons and units for ELs/MLs in math. A recent publication co-sponsored by the National Council for Teachers of Mathematics (NCTM) (Chval et al., 2021) perhaps put it best to address the cultural and linguistic needs of ELs/MLs within the context of mathematics education.

> Multilingual learners deserve the same social and academic opportunities to learn and be successful as their English-speaking peers. All students should learn how to interpret the meaning of problems, make conjectures, analyze mathematical thinking and solutions, monitor and evaluate their progress, and understand the approaches of others in comparison with their own. These expectations emphasize the vital role of language and communication in solving mathematical problems, including the different domains of language (i.e., reading, writing, speaking, and listening) in developing mathematical thinking, and demonstrating knowledge in classroom interactions. (xv)

See Figure 5.13 for how the NCTM Principles may be aligned with ELs'/MLs' academic and linguistic needs and instructional strategies.

What to keep in mind when you plan lessons and units for ELs/MLs in social studies. Parker (2015) describes social studies as a unique discipline as follows:

> It is a concept, a social construct. It is human-made like a pyramid, not natural like a tree; its meanings change with time and place, and with political context. Social studies is contingent, buffeted by social forces, and it reflects the anxieties, power dynamics, and "culture war" of the day. (p. 5)

While it is important to keep these differences in mind when teaching social studies to ELs/MLs, Honigsfeld et al. (2018) argue that taking a language-based approach and focusing on conceptual understanding for ELs/MLs is a viable entry point. They have adapted the Language-Based Approach to Content Instruction (LACI) model (de Oliveira, 2016) to social studies instruction and added guiding questions to support collaborative planning.

Figure 5.13 NCTM Principles and ELs'/MLs' Academic and Linguistic Needs and Instructional Strategies

PRINCIPLE	DEFINITION	INSTRUCTIONAL STRATEGIES FOR ELS/MLS
Equity	Excellence in mathematics education requires equity—high expectations and strong support for all students.	Even if ELs/MLs are still developing their English language skills, they are capable of high levels of math work: Offer them the right type and amount of support (see Chapter 6). Make sure ELs/MLs are not automatically excluded from advanced math classes: They must have opportunities to participate in high-level math classes.
Curriculum	A curriculum is more than a collection of activities; it must be coherent, focused on important mathematics, and well-articulated across the grades.	Remember that some ELs/MLs might have limited or interrupted formal education: They will need support with concepts and skills they have not yet mastered prior to starting school in the United States. Consider backmapping the curriculum to build foundational skills.
Teaching	Effective mathematics teaching requires understanding what students know and need to learn and then challenging and supporting them to learn it well.	When you teach mathematical concepts and skills, remember to teach the language of mathematics as well: Key technical words, common words used in unique ways in math, sentence frames that appear a lot in word problems, and so on.
Learning	Students must learn mathematics with understanding, actively building new knowledge from experience and prior knowledge.	Incorporate ELs'/MLs' lived experiences and prior learning of mathematics into your lessons. Find out how they have already used the math concepts you are teaching or how those concepts can be used outside the classroom.
Assessment	Assessment should support the learning of important mathematics and furnish useful information to both teachers and students.	Many ELs/MLs need accommodations on math assessments. Make dictionaries or translated versions of the test or quiz available.
Technology	Technology is essential in teaching and learning mathematics; it influences the mathematics that is taught and enhances students' learning.	Support ELs'/MLs' academic language skills by using hand-held devices, tablets, laptops. and computers along with a diversity of web-based tools strategically.

Source: Adapted from Kersaint et al. (2009, p. 43).

THE SIX CS OF LACI

CONNECTION: Pedagogy and curriculum are connected to students' backgrounds and experiences, making content explicit.

- **How do you as collaborating teachers make connections to students' backgrounds and experiences, making content explicit?**

CULTURE: Cultural and linguistic resources, or "funds of knowledge," that ELs/MLs already possess are used to support academic learning as ELs/MLs develop new resources to be able to participate in new situations, bridging home and school.

- **In what ways are students' cultural and linguistic backgrounds used as resources?**
- **How do your ELs/MLs develop new linguistic resources to actively participate in learning?**

CODE-BREAKING: Code-breaking integrates language and content as instructional components and involves explicitly teaching ways of doing school; academic literacy; and disciplinary, linguistic, and cultural codes of content learning.

- **How do you integrate content and language?**
- **How do you explicitly teach students ways of doing school, focusing on academic literacy, and disciplinary, linguistic, and cultural codes of content learning?**

CHALLENGE: Classroom goals and activities explore disciplinary literacy and higher-order thinking and reasoning. High challenge and high academic standards and content are maintained for ELs/MLs.

- **In what ways do the classroom goals and activities explore literacy and language skills needed for social studies as well as higher-order thinking and reasoning?**

COMMUNITY and COLLABORATION: Collaboration is a key component of practice, as communities of learners socially co-construct knowledge.

- **What are the key components of practice you use to develop communities of learners that are co-constructing knowledge?**

CLASSROOM INTERACTIONS: Classroom interactions focus on "interactional scaffolding," use of oral discourse to prompt elaboration, build academic literacy, and move learning forward through linking prior and new experiences; appropriating and recasting students' contributions; and using the initiation, response, feedback (IRF) sequence.

- **How do you implement classroom interactions (teacher to student and student to student) to focus on oral language development?**

In addition, Learned (2018) also claims, "Disciplinary literacy teaching can not only leverage youths' interests and identities in the service of historical learning but also create opportunities for young people to socially construct and shape historical interpretations" (p. 209). To do so, ELs/MLs must engage in literacy practices that emulate what historians do, such as (a) sourcing (evaluating where information comes from); (b) contextualizing (understanding the larger social and historical context where historical documents come from); and (c) comparing and contrasting (considering how various historical documents offer different accounts of the same person or event) (Shanahan & Shanahan, 2008, 2014).

What to keep in mind when you plan lessons and units for ELs/MLs in English language arts (ELA). One common approach to addressing ELs'/MLs' needs in the context of ELA instruction is differentiating between the language students need in everyday situations and for general literacy (reading and writing) development and the language needed to develop competency in the subject of ELA. Pearson and colleagues (2020) remind us "that the job of comprehension is not complete until one uses the resulting understanding to do something—tell a story, explain a situation, argue with an author or a classmate, or maybe even plan to change the world" (p. 286).

Support for ELs/MLs differs according to their grade level and their stage of literacy development—are the students learning to read and write or are they reading and writing to learn? We suspect with ELs/MLs, it might be a little of both. For this reason, consider conducting close and critical reading of texts based on the advice of Fisher et al. (2016) as follows:

- **Text selection.** No matter what grade level, the chosen text should be above students' independent reading level. Close and critical reading with rich text will provide multiple opportunities for deeper comprehension (Fisher et al., 2017).
- **Initial reading.** For younger students, share the text by reading aloud. For older students, allow them to read independently or give them a choice to hear the text being read.
- **Annotation.** Model for students how to annotate text; use think alouds to demonstrate how to summarize key points, ask questions, make inferences, and identify concepts and key vocabulary while reading pieces of text to encourage critical thinking.
- **Repeated readings.** Depending on age and reading ability, students may reread alone, in pairs, with teacher's support, or through additional read alouds. Use of audio or video presentations of the reading might also be used.
- **Text-based discussions.** Text-based questions are the focus of these targeted discussions giving students teachable moments to analyze the overall

meaning and structure of the text and provide them with opportunities for inferencing.

- **Responding to texts.** Students work alone, in pairs, or directly with the teacher to write collaboratively or form individual responses to texts. Students are often given prompts to guide their writing. They also work together to investigate and debate probing questions.

What to keep in mind when you plan lessons and units for ELs/MLs in all other content areas. As you plan to collaborate and collaborate to plan instruction for ELs/MLs across all content areas, keep in mind that ELs'/MLs' language and literacy experiences are dynamic and multilayered. In response, planning should also be multidimensional. As an easy way to remember that multiple approaches to supporting ELs/MLs will be needed, we designed a mnemonic. Think of the word *multiple* or the prefix *multi* and connect it to as many pedagogical concepts from this chapter (and beyond) as you can. See Figure 5.14 for some examples of how the prefix *multi* or the word *multiple* may help unpack the complex processes and many different approaches to plan for when you consider ELs'/MLs' assets and needs.

Figure 5.14 Multidimensional Response to ELs'/MLs' Needs

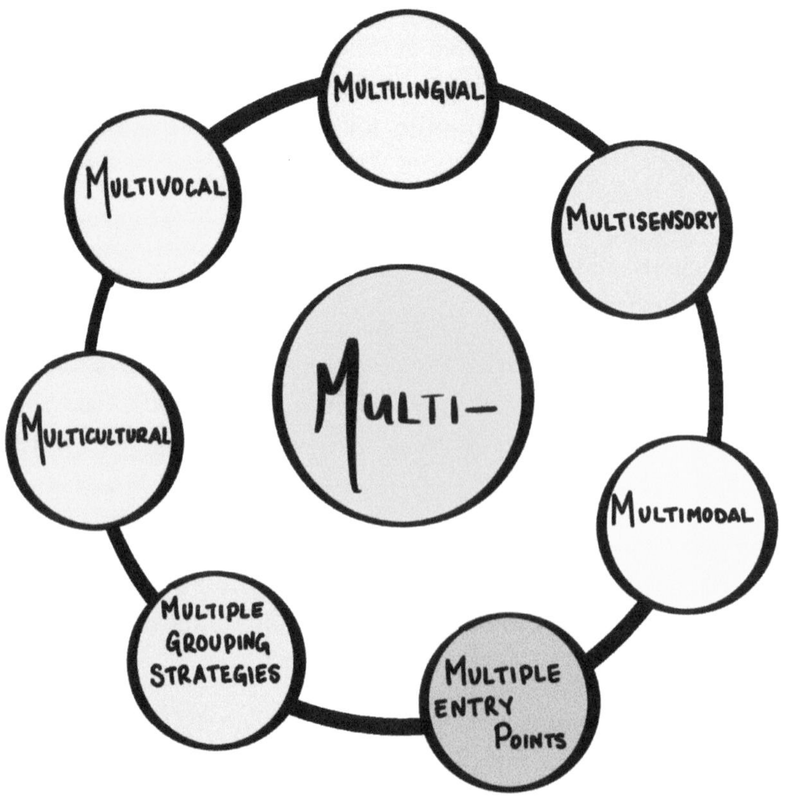

Tools of the Trade

Teaching Channel has served educators as a platform rich with videos and blog posts addressing issues of education across grade levels and content areas. See this link for suggestions on language-rich content-based instruction: https://learn.teachingchannel.com/ells/ell-instruction.

Sam Daunt, a UK-based educator, developed a passion project to support language and literacy development through a rich collection of images, illustrations, digital art, and animation.

https://www.onceuponapicture.co.uk

The Understanding Language: Stanford University initiative is designed "to increase recognition that learning the language of each academic discipline is essential to learning content. Obtaining, evaluating, and communicating information; articulating and building on ideas; constructing explanations; engaging in argument from evidence—such language-rich performance expectations permeate the new standards." (Stanford University, n.d., para. 1.)

https://ell.stanford.edu

A bilingual website for educators and families, Colorin Colorado! offers a robust collection of videos, research briefs, practical strategies, and other resources on https://www.colorincolorado.org/content-instruction-ells.

Celebrations

Change Is All Around Me: A Unit Integrating Social-Emotional Learning, Language Development, and Content

This four-day unit, *Change Is All Around Me*, in the Brockton Public Schools, highlights the integration of social-emotional learning, language development, and academic success for ELs/MLs. The series of lessons is taught as a dedicated ELD unit within either the Sheltered English Immersion or Dual-Language program models offered at various schools. The unit can be flexibly adapted and implemented across different instructional delivery approaches (e.g., push-in/co-taught, pull out/self-contained, or embedded) within the different program models.

Brockton has been engaged in a collaborative initiative whereby teachers have been supported in curriculum development and sharing curricular resources in an online portal. Further supported with systematic common planning time in grade-level teams, teachers can share data from teaching units, and from making formative adjustments and new resources, continuously and collaboratively improve curricular materials over time.

Social-Emotional Learning (SEL)

Through the social-emotional learning goals embedded in the unit, lessons aim to support students' self-awareness, integrating personal, cultural, and linguistic identities of each student and making instruction relevant and engaging. These social-emotional goals are the starting points for building students' agency, identity, and critical stance, even at the earliest grade levels. Grade 2 teachers Barbara Lora, Melissa Vergne, and Maria Pina selected the text *Fall Is Not Easy*, by Marty Kelley, to design a carefully planned progression of learning tasks related to the theme of managing change connected to their students' language and literacy development. Students make personal connections with their teachers and peers and identify their emotions in order to process their feelings, values, and thoughts throughout the unit.

Maria Pina

Melissa Vergne

Barbara Lora

This integration of social-emotional learning with language and literacy development serves to provide many opportunities for teachers to learn about their students as they consider their needs and different ways to engage them and connect with their lives in meaningful ways. The social-emotional learning focus also supports building community in the classroom, expectations for interactions, and common values for supporting each other in school.

Language and Content Integration

In connection with social-emotional learning, students are also developing language in rich, meaningful, and culturally sustaining contexts within grade-level, standards-referenced content themes. This focus on standards ensures that all students are working toward meeting grade-level expectations as they develop their English language proficiency (or dual language proficiency). High expectations are maintained as students engage as critical thinkers, readers, and writers in the unit. Content learning is integrated and aligned in planning for English language development.

Focus Language Goals (FLGs) in the unit frame (see Figure 5.15) show how teachers integrate key language uses and language expectations in the curriculum, based on the 2020 WIDA English Language Development Standards Framework and Massachusetts Next-Generation ESL Curriculum initiative (Massachusetts Department of Elementary and Secondary Education, n.d.). The FLGs also incorporate analytic practices embedded in our Massachusetts Frameworks (state content standards for academic achievement) and content themes and contexts that support

ELs/MLs in preparation for grade-level content instructional expectations. Lessons then are unpacked from the FLGs into academic language skills and knowledge, including forms and features that are appropriate for students' English language proficiency growth. These skills and knowledge are represented through lesson-level language objectives that are carefully planned in a teaching and learning cycle and contextualized in grade-appropriate content.

Figure 5.15 Change Is All Around Me ELD Unit: Grade 2

Unit Focus Language Goals (FLGs)	1. Explain using English structures to communicate context-specific messages. (Student-friendly: We will explain by describing how the tree feels some seasons are easy and others are not easy using the key words from the story.) 2. Discuss by comparing and contrasting to participate in grade-appropriate exchanges of information.	
Content Connections	Analytic content practices of using evidence from text, participation in grade-appropriate exchanges, comparing and contrasting.	
Social-Emotional Goals	Students will practice self-awareness through the activities in the lessons to specifically focus on • integrating personal, cultural and linguistic identities; • identifying one's emotions; • linking feelings, values, and thoughts of others; and • having a growth mindset.	
Unit Length	4–5 days including final assessment	
Daily Lesson Objectives	Lesson 1: Explain by describing how the tree feels some seasons are easy and others are not easy using the key words from the story. Lesson 2: Discuss by contrasting things we can do now with things we could not do as babies. Lesson 3: Explain by identifying six steps to becoming resilient.	
Text and Description	Fall Is Not Easy by Martin Kelley Fall is a tough time of year for a lot of us. Kids have to go back to school, teachers and football players have to go back to work, and parents have to look for new places to hide holiday presents. But perhaps fall is hardest of all on trees. After all, they have to change their entire appearance every year! This book is the rhyming story of a tree's humorous struggles to change its colors for fall. It is a perfect introduction to the seasons for young children and to a discussion of change, feelings, and resilience.	
ACADEMIC LANGUAGE AND LITERACY KNOWLEDGE AND SKILLS		
Academic Language Knowledge	**Academic Language Skills**	**Analysis of Text**
Word level: fall, spring, winter, summer, easy, grow, bare, patience, change, resilience and resilient, affirmation	Use the simple present tense in a full sentence. (affirmations) Introduce past tense (can/could, grow/grew) with sentence frames.	Structure: poem Concept: change, patience, dealing with change Sentence level: all simple present

(Continued)

(Continued)

<table>
<tr><th colspan="3">ACADEMIC LANGUAGE AND LITERACY KNOWLEDGE AND SKILLS</th></tr>
<tr><td>Sentence level: simple present tense; simple sentence structure.
Discourse level: Explanation about self and others with evidence and examples.
Compare and contrast language: (similar/same/alike) (different from, different)</td><td>Describe what people do to deal with a change.
Identify specific things that resilient people do when there is a change by watching a video.
Compare and contrast ideas as a group. Write an explanation of what is hard and solutions.</td><td>Vocabulary: autumn, fall, winter, spring, springtime, summer, bare, melt, "in the air," rain, glow, breeze, strange, right, wrong, belong, should.
Rhyming words.</td></tr>
<tr><td>Cultural Connections/ Relevance:</td><td colspan="2">Do you have any special things you do in different seasons? How do you deal with change? (Consider sociocultural circumstances in approaching content.)</td></tr>
<tr><td>Differentiation and Supports for Individualized Instruction</td><td colspan="2">Whole class discussion of pictures in book, processing in bilingual grouped pairs, read aloud, video, word bank, sentence frames/paragraph frames, teacher-student assistance with writing through instructional conversation</td></tr>
<tr><td>Prereading Instruction</td><td colspan="2">1. Daily check-in (repeats): How are you feeling?
2. Text features/look at and talk about the pictures
3. Introduce the words
4. Use the words in sentences</td></tr>
<tr><td>During Reading Instruction</td><td colspan="2">1. Ask questions.
• Wh- questions for comprehension check
• Text-to-self connections/questions (If you were the tree . . . ?)
• Inference questions (Why is the tree upset?)
2. In context of read aloud, discuss vocabulary.
3. Ask students to think about the tree's feelings as you read about each season.</td></tr>
<tr><td>Post-Reading Instruction</td><td colspan="2">1. Review the four seasons and tree's feelings in each.
• Ask: "How does the tree feel in the fall?" (angry, unhappy, confused, etc.)
• Ask students to explain why the tree feels that way.
2. Have students practice using full sentences, using the word because.
3. Model how to change present tense verbs grow and feel to past tense grew and felt.
4. "Flowers grow each year." "They grew a lot in the spring." "The tree feels happy in the winter, but it felt sad in the fall."
5. Infuse comprehensible input with pictures, realia, or videos each time as possible.
6. Formative check-in with fingers.</td></tr>
<tr><td>Performance Assessment Activity and Wrap-Up</td><td colspan="2">Refer back to mini-lesson skills and review targeted vocabulary through a group activity and questions.
Final assessment options:
1. Tell something that is not easy to learn but would be worth it. Why do you think this?
2. Explain what it takes to be resilient. Use resilient in your answer.
3. Can you draw a picture of a job that you think takes a lot of resilience?</td></tr>
<tr><td>Real-World Application and Extension</td><td colspan="2">Brainstorm professions that you think would be hard. Write why they are hard. Then write affirmations in bubbles that workers may tell themselves to keep going.</td></tr>
</table>

Figure created by Maria Pina, Melissa Vergne, and Barbara Lora. Used with permission.

It is important to point out a dual process for instructional design that is assumed behind this unit frame, which consists of integrated language and content goals as follows:

1. First, backward design and unpacking of linguistic expectations necessary in planning for language development informed this and other unit-level FLGs for Grade 2 students in Brockton. Coherent and aligned academic language skills and knowledge were then unpacked from the FLGs for each of the unit lessons addressing the English language proficiency ranges of students.
2. This unit and approach provides necessary flexibility in adjusting instruction that happens in tandem with the skillful, dynamic assessment the teachers make. These adjustments provide diverse pathways to achieving unit goals in different ways and for heterogeneous student needs.

This two-process approach addresses common challenges in curricular planning for ELs/MLs based on standards. First, language learning must be connected to the sociocultural context. Language development is not a neatly packaged sequential scope and sequence of language forms and features to be taught in isolation. Therefore, two sets of standards must be skillfully integrated. The development process for ELs/MLs is also individual and requires constant monitoring and adjustment during instruction. Individual students' proficiencies in reading, writing, listening, and speaking are not static either and differ in development. These considerations must all be integrated into a standards-based curriculum.

Collaborative Practices in Design and Implementation of Integrated Standards

As the very first school district in the United States to offer bilingual education back in 1970, Brockton knows the benefits and challenges of collaborative practice and works hard to create structures that are sustainable and that impact student success. In this unit, Barbara, Melissa, and Maria planned for instruction in ways that are similar to how they expect their students to engage in learning in the classroom—collaboratively. Their collaboration now benefits the other grade-level team members through their work, and vice versa.

Continuous improvement happens each time the unit is implemented for a particular group of Brockton students. Teachers are able to provide immediate feedback and new resources into the unit portal, including instructional notes addressing different students' needs. Through common planning time, the teacher team is supported in working together in their grade-level teams, in sharing responsibility for their students across classrooms, unpacking language and content standards, supporting new teachers with coaching, and sharing high-quality practical materials to support new teachers. These teams also incorporate the specialized expertise different teachers hold across Brockton's multilingual programs (special populations of students, special education, gifted and talented, newcomers, etc.). All the teachers are supported by the director of bilingual and ESL, the citywide language assessment specialist, and coaches in continuous improvement and planning through common planning times. The new interactive portal and technologies support all with immediate access and supports, while curriculum, instruction, and assessment priorities for common planning time ensure sustained job-embedded professional learning for the long term.

COLLABORATIVE REFLECTION QUESTIONS

1. Over a decade ago, Zwiers (2008) noted that "teachers sometimes do two things: (1) they do not use enough academic language when they model and scaffold content-area thinking and doing, and (2) they too often accept oral and written responses that are not sufficiently academic in nature" (p. 50), thus students are not exposed to or expected to use rigorous academic language consistently. Do you think it is important and why? How does this chapter support all teachers with embracing that for language to develop and flourish, it must be recognized as a powerful tool and it needs purposeful attention in all content areas by all teachers?
2. Akhavan (2009) insightfully remarks that

   writing is a gatekeeping skill. Those students who write well do well in the upper-elementary grades, in high school, and beyond. Those who are never given the opportunity to learn to write never get the chance to think, connect, and excel in classes that demand of them the ability to show what they know. (p. xii)

   What ideas from this chapter support teachers in planning for enhanced literacy development, and how can we ensure that ELs/MLs thrive as writers?
3. Hammond et al. (2018) aptly state that "students [must] have opportunities **to talk to learn and to learn to talk** (and read and write) academic English" (p. 65). How do you plan to accomplish this with ELs/MLs on multiple language proficiency levels?
4. Many evidence-based, important concepts were introduced in this chapter. What is one concept that resonated with you, and what action will you take to apply new learning in that area?

Watch Andrea and Maria discussing some highlights of Chapter 5. Reflect on their positions in favor of integrated language and content instruction. In what ways did they affirm or challenge your thinking about this topic?

COLLABORATIVE ACTION STEPS

Consider the collaborative planning process of integrating language, content, and social-emotional learning.

1. Determine the key collaborators with whom you will coordinate your efforts to affirm and support the practice of the integration of language, content, and social-emotional learning.
2. Decide which key components of the integration of language, content, and social-emotional learning can be immediately incorporated into your instructional and collaborative planning routines.
3. Identify instructional procedures and practices that will support your actions to meaningfully integrate language and content instruction with social-emotional learning for ELs/MLs.
4. Examine how language and content instructional goals, objectives, or learning intentions along with social-emotional learning can be achievable and accurately assessed to continue to inform your instruction.
5. Determine how you will share success stories and the challenges related to the integration of language, content, and social-emotional learning with fellow collaborators.

Multidimensional Scaffolding: Rigor, Relevance, Relationships, and Research Informed (4 Rs)

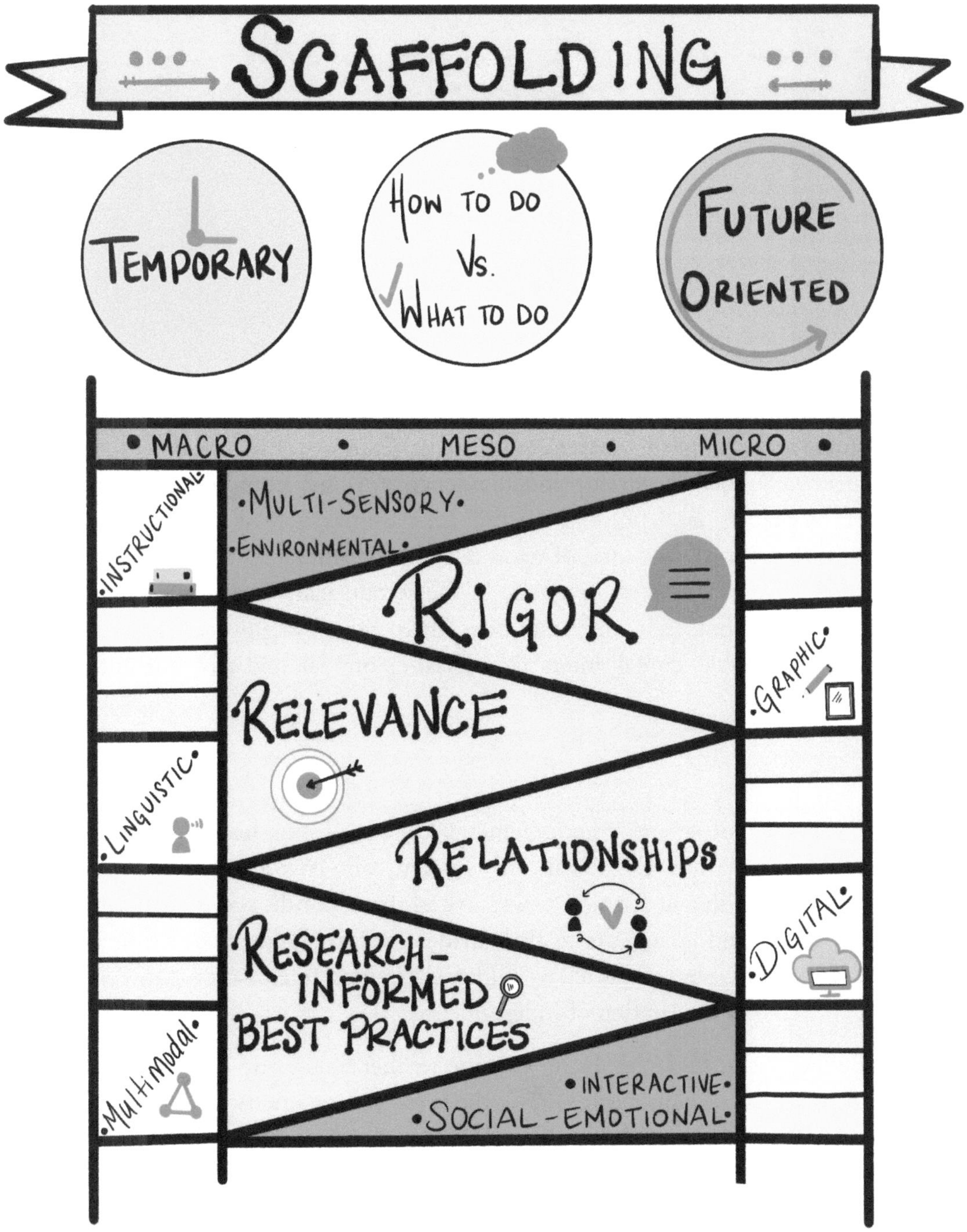

"Scaffolding for learning is not as clear as scaffolding for a building project. Teachers can't see finished walls and know the scaffolding must come down. Appropriate scaffolding for multilingual learners requires teachers to know their students well, stay committed to rigor, and understand that scaffolding is unique to every student. Ultimately, all scaffolding is removed so the building can stand on its own, and so must our students."

—Kristina Robertson, English learner (EL) program administrator
Roseville, Minnesota

"Understanding the big picture before a unit starts helps me with knowing where we are going, what we need to know, how we will know it, and why we need to know it. First, we focus on macro-scaffolding content and language integration, then we look at our students and ask ourselves: How are ALL of THEM going to get it? Here is where we micro-scaffold the lesson—we decide on activities and resources, graphic organizers, visuals, sentence starters, strategic student groupings, and co-teaching models with our respective roles."

—Alis D. Gorcea, EAL 7 specialist/co-teacher
Saigon South International School, HCMC, Vietnam

In this final chapter, our goal is to offer several additional angles for collaborative planning, with a focus on scaffolding, commonly recognized as temporary learning support for English learners/multilingual learners (ELs/MLs) and others who ultimately need to develop independence with task completion. In the first half of the chapter, we define and redefine the classic strategy of scaffolding to include a 4 Rs framework consisting of rigor, relevance, relationships, and research-informed and evidence-based best practices. In the second half, we make a case for considering scaffolding techniques that offer instructional, linguistic, multimodal, multisensory, graphic, digital, interactive, social-emotional, and environmental supports to ELs/MLs.

Zoom In

Oscar, one of several entering/emerging ELs/MLs in his fifth-grade class in a Midwestern city, is seated near other students who have a wide range of proficiency in both English and Spanish. Oscar arrived three months ago from Guatemala with his family, and he appears to have made a positive adjustment to his new school environment. He and his fellow students are about to embark on an analysis of the United States Declaration of Independence.

Before Oscar views the document, the teacher focuses on what she calls "the big ideas" of the text and begins to ask the class probing questions such as *What does it mean when a country declares (declara) independence (independencia)? What are some reasons (razones) why a group of people or a nation (nación) would want independence? What might be some reasons why the Declaration of Independence was written? Have any other countries declared their independence? If so, which ones?* The teacher opts to clarify essential words during the discussion instead of preteaching a long list of terms with associated translations. She notes on an idea web that is projected on the board—key vocabulary and information students share in response to her questions. The teacher also provides sentence frames that support Oscar and others to join in the discussion and encourages responses partly or fully in English and Spanish. Students volunteer to translate Spanish responses into English and English responses into Spanish.

The teacher activates students' prior knowledge, builds background knowledge, and further explains key vocabulary through the use of an anticipation guide that includes broad-based and specific statements such as *Most colonists supported independence from Britain* and *The Stamp Act was responsible for colonists desiring independence.* This unit of study is explored over a three-week period in which the teacher guides students to unpack the meaning of the Declaration of Independence a few sentences at a time.

Some students, like Oscar, are given a bulleted, illustrated, one-page summary in English containing pieces of the document along with the full document written in both English and Spanish as references. Other students receive simplified versions of the Declaration of Independence in English along with the original version. As each section of the document is explored, students have opportunities to work in heterogeneous groups to complete tasks and engage in discussion. Oscar participates in small-group tasks, including the analysis of the famous painting of the signing of the Declaration of Independence by John Trumball, interpreting the meaning of the specific language used in the document, and debating what the document meant by "all men are created equal." The teacher circulates the room and checks for student understanding during group work. During this time, she is able to support Oscar's attempts to use English through on-the-spot mini conferences and one-to-one conversations to clarify content, vocabulary, sentence forms, and language functions. In this way, Oscar is assisted throughout the unit of study by the use of various strategies that scaffold instruction and nurture Oscar's understanding and use of English.

Zoom Out

This unit of study requires the teacher not only to balance her instructional delivery so that the rigor and authenticity of the Declaration of Independence is maintained but also to unfold the meaning of the document the way her students, like Oscar, can best understand its content and concepts while making connections to their lived experiences. The document is highly abstract and lexically dense, which makes it even more challenging for ELs/MLs. To make the meaning of the document accessible and memorable, the teacher incorporates multiple scaffolding strategies designed to support various student needs throughout the unit.

Scaffolding must be implemented with intention and clarity and may be designed for at least three levels of support, according to Bunch et al. (2015):

1. **Macro-scaffolding** is planned for longer-term implementation across a unit or multiple lessons and gives students the opportunity to gradually build understanding, skills, and competence in their academic practices that include language, literacy, and content development. In the preceding lesson, the teacher uses a broad-brush approach when opening a discussion about the reasons for desired independence, a theme that carries throughout the unit. The significance of key vocabulary unfolds throughout each lesson, one lesson building on the other, with a heavy emphasis on the use of English and Spanish cognates and the promotion of translanguaging—using multiple languages together. Students are given ample opportunities to use new words in spoken and written discourse. This discourse is consistently supported by the sentence frames and starters devised by the teacher. The instructional routines set for learning this social studies unit are carried through each subsequent unit of study. In essence, "at the macro level, the overall design of the unit supports students by linking lesson to lesson in articulated ways, deepening and enriching understandings of central ideas, processes, and the language required to express those ideas" (Bunch et al., p. 12). Therefore, the curriculum is collaboratively planned to be spiral in nature so that concepts and skills are revisited and there are ample opportunities to engage in the use of academic language.
2. **Meso-scaffolding** refers to design features that offer structures to support ELs/MLs through the flow of each lesson. Think of it as the arc of teaching. For example, the learning engagement of Oscar and his fellow students is reinforced by the use of graph organizers, such as the idea web that captures essential information during a whole-class discussion. Additionally, the teacher activates students' prior knowledge using an anticipation guide, which sparks further discussion of information and concepts. During small-group conversations, students are asked to examine a famous drawing using an artifact analysis template, which prompts them to consider various aspects of the drawing. All of these techniques provide students with additional time and attention to consider, process, comprehend, or uncover new information.
3. **Micro-scaffolding** is the small-group or individual support teachers offer as needed. This approach allows teachers to focus on specific academic, language, and literacy skills that are embedded in the lesson. Bunch and his colleagues (2013) captured the essence of this practice as follows:

   While the teacher carefully plans tasks which will develop her students' potential over time, the most important part of scaffolding occurs

> in the moment, as the teacher observes how students work, what skills are maturing, which ones need further support to ripen, and what may be misunderstood. Then, teachers contingently offer the appropriate support to redirect, deepen, or accelerate specific students' development. (p. 16)

For example, when Oscar is completing tasks collaboratively or alone, his teacher checks in with him to determine if he requires additional support to understand the lesson content, comprehend how to reach task completion, or express his ideas using written or spoken English. This targeted individual attention provides Oscar with added opportunities to acquire immediate interventions.

When attention is paid to the three levels of scaffolding, macro-, meso-, and micro-, it can provide the supportive learning environment that all students need to become actively engaged learners and to increase their academic and language proficiency.

Scaffolding Defined

Scaffolding is most commonly known as a temporary support needed until students can participate in or complete a task independently. As a practice to support learning, it has been around in a range of contexts since Vygotsky (1978) first described the zone of proximal development (ZPD) within his socio-cultural theory. It was characterized as "the distance between the actual developmental level as determined by independent problem solving and the level of potential development as determined through problem solving under adult guidance or in collaboration with more capable peers" (p. 86). Bridging the distance between what learners can do by themselves and what the next level of learning is that they can achieve with the help of a more knowledgeable other heavily depends upon social interaction for learning to take place.

Bruner (1960/2009) is among the first to define instructional scaffolding as a teaching strategy that offers support based on each learner's ZPD primarily because he considered what children can do with assistance may be even more indicative of their development than what they could do alone. His frequently quoted message still holds: "We begin with the hypothesis that any subject can be taught in some intellectually honest form to any child at any stage of development" (p. 33). Later, Bruner (1983) also suggested that scaffolding is "a process of 'setting up' the situation to make the child's entry easy and successful and then gradually pulling back and handing the role to the child as he becomes skilled enough to manage it" (p. 60). As such, the ultimate goal of scaffolding is to help students achieve independence; so we must be intentional and strategic with our scaffolding practices as well as avoid turning scaffolding into rescuing our students and doing most of the work for them (Thompson, 2021).

Scaffolding in support of academic success for ELs/MLs was aptly dubbed a *pedagogy of success* by Walqui and van Lier in their seminal 2010 publication. They recommend that pedagogical scaffolds "should be constantly changed, dismantled, extended, and adapted in accordance with the needs" of the students (Walqui & van Lier, 2010, p. 24). Many researchers and practitioners agree that scaffolds and instructional supports better serve ELs/MLs in the general education context than oversimplified texts, leveled materials, and isolated skills-based lessons. It is widely recognized that scaffolding is one critical way to offer the necessary support to all students but especially to those who might benefit from linguistic, academic, or socio-cultural guidance. Gibbons (2015) highlights the three major characteristics of scaffolding as follows:

> It is *temporary* help that assists a learner to move toward new concepts, new levels of understanding, and new language.
>
> It enables a learner to know *how to do something* (not just what to do), so that they will be better able to complete similar tasks alone.
>
> It is *future oriented:* in Vygotsky's words, what a learner can do with support today, he or she will be able to do alone tomorrow. (p. 15)

There is a growing body of research exploring the ways ELs/MLs may be supported; among them is scaffolding. Many of them build on the work of Walqui (2006), who emphatically claims that instead of simplifying the tasks we provide ELs/MLs or the language we use in class,

> Teaching subject matter content to English learners requires amplifying and enriching the linguistic and extralinguistic context, so that students do not get just one opportunity to come to terms with the concepts involved, but in fact may construct their understanding on the basis of multiple clues and perspectives encountered in a variety of class activities. (p. 169)

Among many others, Bunch et al. (2015) suggest that scaffolding works by creating multiple pathways for ELs/MLs and envisioning what students will be able to do in the future on their own and responding with the right amount of support offered at the right time. Scaffolding is designed to build independence and autonomy over time (Walqui & Heritage, 2012).

Research on scaffolding continues to expand. One common takeaway from current research is that scaffolding is not to simplify and reduce content. Its purpose is to offer the amount and type of support when needed and if needed and eventually to remove the support from the teaching and learning experience. The rest of the chapter will guide you through how to do just that!

Based on your professional knowledge and teaching experience, which of these statements are best aligned with your beliefs about scaffolds?

STOP AND PROCESS

iStock.com/bombuscreative

1. The use of scaffolds must be strategic; types of scaffolds, lengths of use, and availability of supports will impact student learning.
2. Scaffolds are always temporary; they go up and come down dictated by student needs.
3. Scaffolds enable students to have access to complex content.
4. Offering too much scaffolding can be detrimental to student growth and development.
5. Scaffolds encourage students to begin to use their emerging language skills with more confidence.
6. Scaffolds ensure that ELs/MLs successfully participate in social and academic tasks before they develop full proficiency in English.
7. Scaffolding is a tool for equity.
8. If a student relies on scaffolding to complete a task, they may not be assessed the same way as others who do not use scaffolds.
9. Scaffolding may not be the sole responsibility of teachers; students may offer peer support to each other in support of language and literacy development.

Scaffolding Redefined for the 4 Rs

We have found that researchers and practitioners may slightly differ in their ways of defining or advocating for scaffolding for ELs/MLs. Our approach is built on decades of research and practitioner knowledge (Calderón et al., 2019; de Oliveira, 2019; Gibbons, 2015). We have redefined scaffolding around the 4 Rs of *Rigor, Relevance, Relationships, and Research-Informed best practices*. In the forthcoming section, we will unpack scaffolding from each of these perspectives.

Scaffolding for Rigor

High expectations based on standards and rigorous academic core curricula require all teachers to consider ways to make content accessible to all students. The combined goal of content area learning and English language and literacy development also presents a unique challenge and opportunity at the same time for examining what rigor means for ELs/MLs. It would not go amiss to acknowledge that more concrete ideas make way for increasingly complex concepts and more abstract language as students move up grade levels. For ELs/MLs to be successful within the context of rigorous learning opportunities and to "undertake this complex process of comprehending and producing academic text, deep and flexible knowledge of the

A SOUND BITE

All teachers need to "create the instructional conditions in which ELs can productively engage in the key [standards-informed academic] practices" (Bunch, 2013, p. 329). Hopkins et al. (2019) suggest that "when teachers view ELs as bringing valuable knowledge and experiences and see them as eager and capable learners, they are more likely to foster learning environments that engage and challenge ELs" (p. 2298).

Do you agree? What is your experience with ELs/MLs being viewed as knowledgeable, capable, and eager learners? In your experiences, what instructional conditions and learning environments are most essential to address? What conditions and what aspects of the learning environment do you have most control over, and how do you mitigate them to better respond to all students' needs?

Icon: iStock.com/Vectorig

often abstract and complex" (Lesaux et al., 2014, p. 1161) academic language used in each core content area and the particular target registers are needed. In our consideration of scaffolding for rigor, we have divided our discussion of the topic into four categories—content, process, product, and language (see Figure 6.1).

Rigor With Content

What it is: Developing conceptual understanding through increasingly complex tasks that build upon each other. Honoring students' ways of knowing and their funds of knowledge.

What it is not: Giving ELs/MLs difficult, inaccessible, incomprehensible texts, lectures, tasks, and assignments.

Rigor With Process

What it is: Breaking down, chunking, modeling, allowing multiple meaningful opportunities to interact with new content, and practicing new skills while building endurance, resilience, and tolerance for ambiguity.

What it is not: Giving multistep directions to new learning processes that lead to frustration and fear of failure or simply assigning rigorous tasks.

Figure 6.1 The 4 Rs of Scaffolding

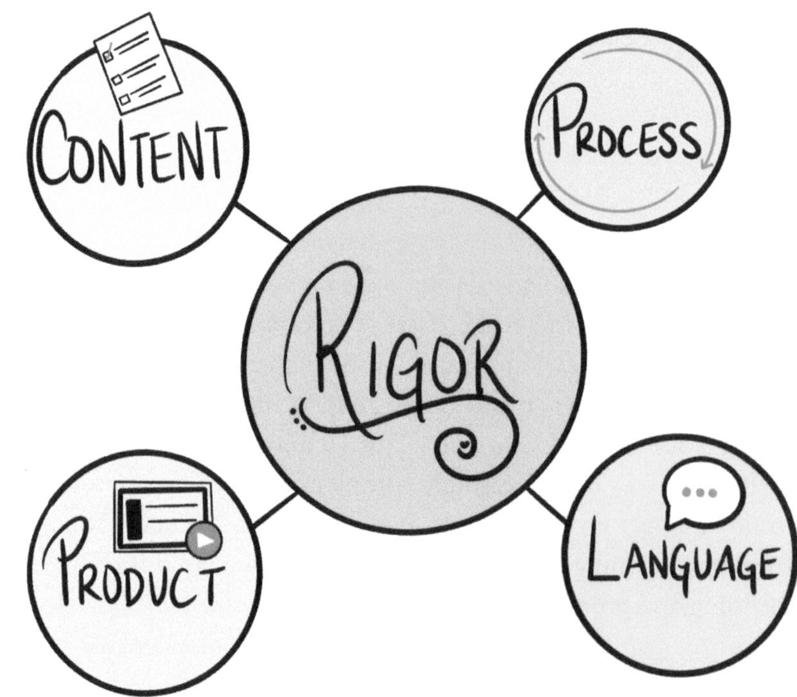

Rigor With Product

What it is: Allowing for multimodal, multilingual, multidimensional expressions of student learning. Offering authentic learning opportunities that ensure both collaborative and self-directed learning. Providing models for students but expecting creativity and individuality.

What it is not: Creating situations in which students simply copy your example and provide cookie-cutter answers and identical final products.

Rigor With Language

What it is: Leveraging ELs'/MLs' full linguistic repertoires, including translanguaging. Focusing on students' evolving levels of understanding of the intricacies of how the English language works and guiding them to see patterns and emulate features of oral and written communication that are essential for the task at hand. Recognizing commonly used language features within and across different content areas.

Tonya Ward Singer (2018) cautions,

> If your linguistic supports lead students to mimic without thinking or to disengage, your supports are too limiting. Drop the scaffold and work to generate original thought and authentic participation—no matter how incorrect the grammar. Then use more complex, varied, and open-ended supports to help students stretch their thinking and language use in new ways. (p. 141)

What it is not: Overcorrecting every grammatical error, hyperfocusing on vocabulary, insisting on speaking in complete sentences only and using standard English or insisting on an "English-only" learning environment. Setting low expectations for ELs/MLs.

Key Ideas for Scaffolding for Rigor

When you use *rigor* as your guiding principle for scaffolding, you choose to

- Examine your personal and professional beliefs and attitudes about what students can do
- Have high expectations for students to develop knowledge and skills even if their English expression is merely approximating
- Examine the academic (or cognitive) demand as well as the language or literacy demand of the lesson/task
- Scaffold up rather than water down as you provide extralinguistic support and a variety of multimodal processes
- Focus on clarity of instruction with multiple entry points and multiple pathways to mastery

- Adapt written materials (via study guides, outlines, summaries, visually or digitally enhanced or annotated versions of the target texts)
- Adapt oral language (via wait time, visually or digitally enhanced explanations, guided questioning, built-in repetitions or redundancy)

A SOUND BITE

In *Teaching Controversial Issues: The Case for Critical Thinking and Moral Commitment in the Classroom*, Noddings and Brooks (2017) argue that

> a prime purpose of critical thinking in the public domain is to consider and evaluate the arguments made on controversial issues. This requires a continual search for meaning and understanding. The object is not necessarily to win a debate [. . .] The idea is to use critical thinking in contributing to healthy human relations and the maintenance of a strong participatory democracy. (p. 1)

Do you agree? What are your experiences with infusing critical thinking into your planning to ensure rigorous instruction? Which aspect(s) of this statement might need specific attention to better support ELs/MLs in your context? How do you teach ELs/MLs to engage in conversations courageously and critically? How do they learn to self-advocate?

Icon: iStock.com/Vectorig

Scaffolding for Relevance

The word *relevance* comes from the French *relevant* "helpful" and originally from the Latin *relevare,* "to lessen, to lighten" (https://www.etymonline.com/word/relevant). Today, and especially in our context, what relevance stands for is something that is important and helpful for ELs/MLs, for their immediate and long-term needs, and is connected to their lives, families, and communities.

What it is: Knowledge, skills, and competencies that have recognized importance to ELs/MLs.

What it is not: Everything that is in the curriculum that we want to cover and that will be on the test.

When you use relevance as your guiding principle for scaffolding, you choose to recognize that ELs/MLs need relevance in the scaffolds and supports afforded them (instead of remedial reading courses or academic intervention services that focus on a limited set of predetermined skill sets). Solórzano and Yosso (2002) ask a critical question, "Whose stories are privileged in educational contexts and whose stories are distorted and silenced?" (p. 36), echoing the line from the musical *Hamilton* (Miranda, 2015), "Who tells your story?" A thoughtful, sincere response to this question may significantly impact how you select your instructional resources and supplementary materials. What is being taught must be made meaningful and culturally relevant for the student to comprehend and engage with actively and meaningfully. When we scaffold for relevance, we make intentional connections between what students do and experience in school and what is happening in their lives out of school.

It has been widely recognized that "progress among ELs/MLs is not uniform. Some students make good progress, whereas others do not, an observation that argues for the importance of attending to the individual needs of students as part of whatever instructional approach is implemented" (National Academies of Sciences, Engineering, and Medicine, 2017, p. 306). As a result, an intentional approach to scaffolding will help avoid over-support and ensure that scaffolds will fade with time and there is a transfer of responsibility to students.

Key Ideas for Scaffolding for Relevance

How to scaffold for what is relevant to the students' lived experiences:

- Consider ELs'/MLs' funds of knowledge and funds of identity (what cultural knowledge and identity they bring to school)
- Build on their cultural and linguistic assets (home language and literacy/oracy skills)
- Create peer-supported learning opportunities to enhance social and academic interactions as well as opportunities for ELs/MLs to learn ways of collaboration and other soft skills
- Tap into their personal interests outside of school
- Connect their learning to what they have previously read, learned, or experienced

How to scaffold for what is relevant to the grade-appropriate core content curricula:

- Employ back mapping to identify essential building blocks and specific content knowledge
- Design language and literacy development opportunities that are closely aligned to the core curriculum
- Consider enduring learning and essential questions
- Apprentice ELs/MLs into language and literacy practices in the disciplines: How do scientists formulate questions? How do historians explain what led up to key events? How do readers analyze a piece of literature? How do economists explain the causes of unemployment?
- Connect what they are learning to what is happening in their personal world or the greater world around them

How to scaffold for what is relevant to the students' unique academic, linguistic, and social-emotional needs:

- Offer explicit instructional support

- Consider each student's unique background and learning goals to plan for personalized learning
- Ensure that translanguaging is accepted, valued, and embedded into daily pedagogy. As García and Wei (2014) note, translanguaging is a process in which "bilingual speakers select meaning-making features [from multiple languages] and freely combine them to potentialize meaning-making, cognitive engagement, creativity, and criticality" (p. 42).
- Design problem-based, *rich* educational tasks "that have substantial intellectual value and are designed to have a relevance beyond the classroom" (Hammond et al., 2018, p. 55)
- Celebrate their individual and unique ways in which they learn

Scaffolding for Relationships

Relationships—having a strong sense of belonging in and outside the classroom—matter. It is widely recognized that when teachers successfully "*reach*" their students and relate to them on multiple levels, they make connections that far outlast the 45-minute class period, the school day, or even the school year! Scaffolding for relationships is especially important for ELs/MLs who are new to the United States, a community, a school, or a classroom.

What it is: Creating a supportive, culturally and linguistically responsive and sustaining learning environment for all language learners across all program models.

What it is not: Expecting ELs/MLs to assimilate into the mainstream class and school culture.

Key Ideas for Scaffolding for Relationships

ELs/MLs need to form relationships for authentic language use, for staying motivated (language is not acquired in isolation), and for social-emotional and academic growth. Creating a learning environment that is exemplified by respect, care, and empathy must be a priority for all educators. For ELs/MLs to thrive, they need a variety of high-quality teacher-to-student and student-to-student interactions and relationships defined by cooperation, collaboration, and willingness to work together across racial, ethnic, and gender lines. Let's also recognize that students may make meaningful connections with an entire community of educators, staff, and students, from the principal to the custodian, from the nurse to the librarian, from the coach to members of sport teams and clubs outside the immediate circle of friends and classmates that ELs/MLs usually have. Our goal is to ensure ELs/MLs develop agency and autonomy and feelings of competence. To accomplish this, we must

- Create a system of support in each classroom and larger learning environment
- Get to know our students and frequently ask about their lives
- Avoid any unnecessary competitiveness or pressure
- Recognize that learning is a joint activity through collaborative, interactive "high touch" experiences
- Encourage communication that is appropriate for the task and social context over grammatical correctness
- Explicitly teach students how to build on each other's ideas
- Use humor and other coping skills
- Offer generic and specific praise as frequently as possible and reasonable
- Provide frequent affirmations and celebrate students' work, effort, progress, and positive contributions to the class

Scaffolding for Research-Informed and Evidence-Based Best Practices

Along with Bunch (2013) and others, we, too, caution against "curricularizing" language into linguistic units of study or considering language as a prerequisite for content learning; instead, we embrace the notion that "language is an essential mediator of teaching and learning" (p. 329), and **the goal is for ELs/MLs to develop a rich repertoire of linguistic competences to be able to develop English in a range of academic and nonacademic settings**. It has been widely recognized that language development and content attainment are not just closely connected but thoroughly intertwined, and as such, academic language and literacy practices will more stridently develop as a result of engagement with rigorous, relevant, and accessible curriculum and instruction.

What it is: Careful consideration of the current and seminal research findings and systemically reported practice-based evidences and an application thereof to the classroom context.

What it is not: Transferring theory to practice based on personal beliefs without adequate resources.

Research has been growing steadily to identify what leads to high-quality educational outcomes for students who are learning English. Figure 6.2 offers a summary of the research-based recommendations based on the key findings (August, 2018), a rationale for each, and a concise list of essential practices.

Figure 6.2 A Summary of Research-Based Recommendations With Scaffolding Practices

RECOMMENDATIONS BASED ON RESEARCH	WHY DOES IT MATTER?	ESSENTIAL PRACTICES TO SCAFFOLD FOR IT
1. *Provide Access to Grade-Level Course Content*	Academic achievement depends on it.	❑ Rely on standards and benchmarks to ensure grade-level standard instruction ❑ Use authentic multilevel, multimodal, multilingual instructional materials ❑ Apply the gradual release of responsibility model to ensure teacher and peer support throughout the learning process
2. *Build on Effective Practices Used With English-Proficient Students*	Vast body of research can inform evidence-based instructional practices for all students.	❑ Adapt practices designed for English-proficient students with necessary accommodations and modifications ❑ Consider instructional and linguistic support for ELs/MLs
3. *Provide Supports to Help ELs/MLs Master Core Content and Skills*	Supports and scaffolds ensure equitable learning opportunities for ELs/MLs.	❑ Focus on visual supports (pictures, illustrations, videos, graphic organizers, concept maps, diagrams, multimedia, etc.) and verbal supports (home language, glossaries, discussions via varied group configurations, etc.)
4. *Develop ELs'/MLs' Academic Language*	Competence with language across all four domains ensures participation in academic activities.	❑ Help students develop generic and academic vocabulary ❑ Have ELs/MLs engage in academic conversations ❑ Create opportunities for students to practice writing to extend their learning
5. *Encourage Peer-to-Peer Learning Opportunities*	Social and academic interactions ensure authentic language use and collaborative meaning-making.	❑ Enable students to interact in all four modalities along with interaction (SWIRL—speak, write, interact, read, and listen) with peer support ❑ Set up peer-assisted learning opportunities and collaborative and cooperative learning ❑ Have students engage in group learning of various sizes and configurations
6. *Capitalize on Students' Home Language, Knowledge, and Cultural Assets*	Students' identities, strengths, and assets are recognized, validated, and celebrated.	❑ Draw on what students already know ❑ Preview and/or review new learning in ELs'/MLs' preferred language ❑ Assess, activate, and build on prior knowledge ❑ Make multilingual and culturally relevant instructional materials available ❑ Ask students to share their cultural and linguistic insights related to the content ❑ Lift up students' voices
7. *Screen for Language and Literacy Challenges, Monitor Progress, and Support ELs/MLs Who Are Struggling*	Continuous assessment and appropriate interventions prevent school failure.	❑ Personalize and individualize instruction based on unique student needs ❑ Implement and collaboratively interpret progress monitoring data

Source: Author created, using data from August (2018).

What Research Says

While in Figure 6.2 we shared several recommendations and essential scaffolding strategies, here are some additional evidence-based suggestions based on recently emerging research:

- Offer students multiple meaningful opportunities to encounter new material and practice through interleaving or intermittently changing the skill area they are expected to practice (Goodwin, 2018).
- "Ensure students have access to *message abundancy* through opportunities to visit and revisit similar curriculum language and concepts via whole-class, group, and pair work" (Hammond et al., 2018, p. 65).
- Praise students enthusiastically to offer them generic and specific recognition of their growth and contributions (Banse et al., 2019).

Collaborative Planning With the 4 Rs in Mind

Some might make the case for instructional planning being the opposite of rocket science, but we would have to respectfully disagree. Planning collaboratively, like rocket science, requires multiple skill sets as well as years of experience to confidently execute all the moving parts of instruction and assessment. As in previous chapters, we have offered various tools for collaboratively planning instruction. Yet we also know that each collaborative team has different areas in which they need to direct their focus. Therefore, we developed this checklist for collaborative planning with the 4 Rs (see Figure 6.3) for those teams who would like to concentrate their efforts on providing scaffolded instruction for rigor, relevance, relationships, and research-informed instruction.

Figure 6.3 Collaborative Planning With the 4 Rs

	QUESTIONS TO CONSIDER	YES	NO
Rigor	*Have we identified the cognitive and linguistic demands of the lesson/unit?*		
	Have we set clear expectations for procedures and assessment measures?		
	Have we created multiple entry points for students with various needs to access information and complete tasks?		
	Have we adapted oral and written materials yet maintained rigor?		
Relevance	*Have we considered the relevance of our plans to students' cultural and personal identities?*		
	Have we planned how to capitalize on students' cultural and linguistic assets in our lesson/unit?		
	Have we provided an adequate amount of time for students to interact with one another?		
	Have we considered students' prior learning, experiences, or interests?		

(Continued)

(Continued)

	QUESTIONS TO CONSIDER	YES	NO
Relationships	*Have we created a system of support so students can thrive during this lesson/unit?*		
	Do the activities we have planned foster an environment for cooperation and collaboration?		
	Have we collaboratively developed and modeled guidelines for effective communication skills?		
	Have we set sufficient time to celebrate students' efforts, progress, and contributions to the class?		
Research-Informed Practices	*Have we provided students access to the general grade-level course curriculum?*		
	Have we devised appropriate multimodal supports for students to master core content?		
	Have we planned for the development and assessment of ELs'/MLs' English language skills?		
	Have we set sufficient time for students to interact in all four modalities—speak, write, read, and listen?		

Available for download at **resources.corwin.com/CoPlanningforELs**

Unpacking the Nine Dimensions of Scaffolding

In this section, our goal is to support collaborative planning efforts by introducing or reintroducing nine dimensions of scaffolding to recognize the multidimensional nature of the work (see Figure 6.4). In a stark summary, the team at the National Academies of Sciences, Engineering, and Medicine (2017) claim the following:

> Instruction that fails to address appropriately the linguistic, cultural, socioemotional, and academic needs of English learners (ELs) when they first enter elementary school leads to their lack of progress and to the growing number of long-term ELs in secondary schools, which in turn can lead to disengagement in these students. (p. 326)

We believe that supporting ELs/MLs is a complex, multilayered endeavor, without one right approach, technique, or strategy. What we cannot compromise on is the pedagogical stance that ELs/MLs are able to participate in grade-appropriate learning with the right amount and type of scaffolds and supports.

Much of what is coming might look familiar, perhaps in bits and pieces. We expanded upon previous scaffolding overviews that have presented three (WIDA, 2013) or five (Dove et al., 2015) ways to scaffold. The nine scaffolding approaches have emerged from practice-based (Gibbons, 2015; Levine et al., 2013), research-based (August, 2018), and standards-based publications (WIDA, 2020b) as well as from our own field-based research and observations. Under each heading, we will define the scaffolding practice first, support it with a *quotable* quote, offer some further evidence to

Figure 6.4 The Nine Dimensions of Scaffolding

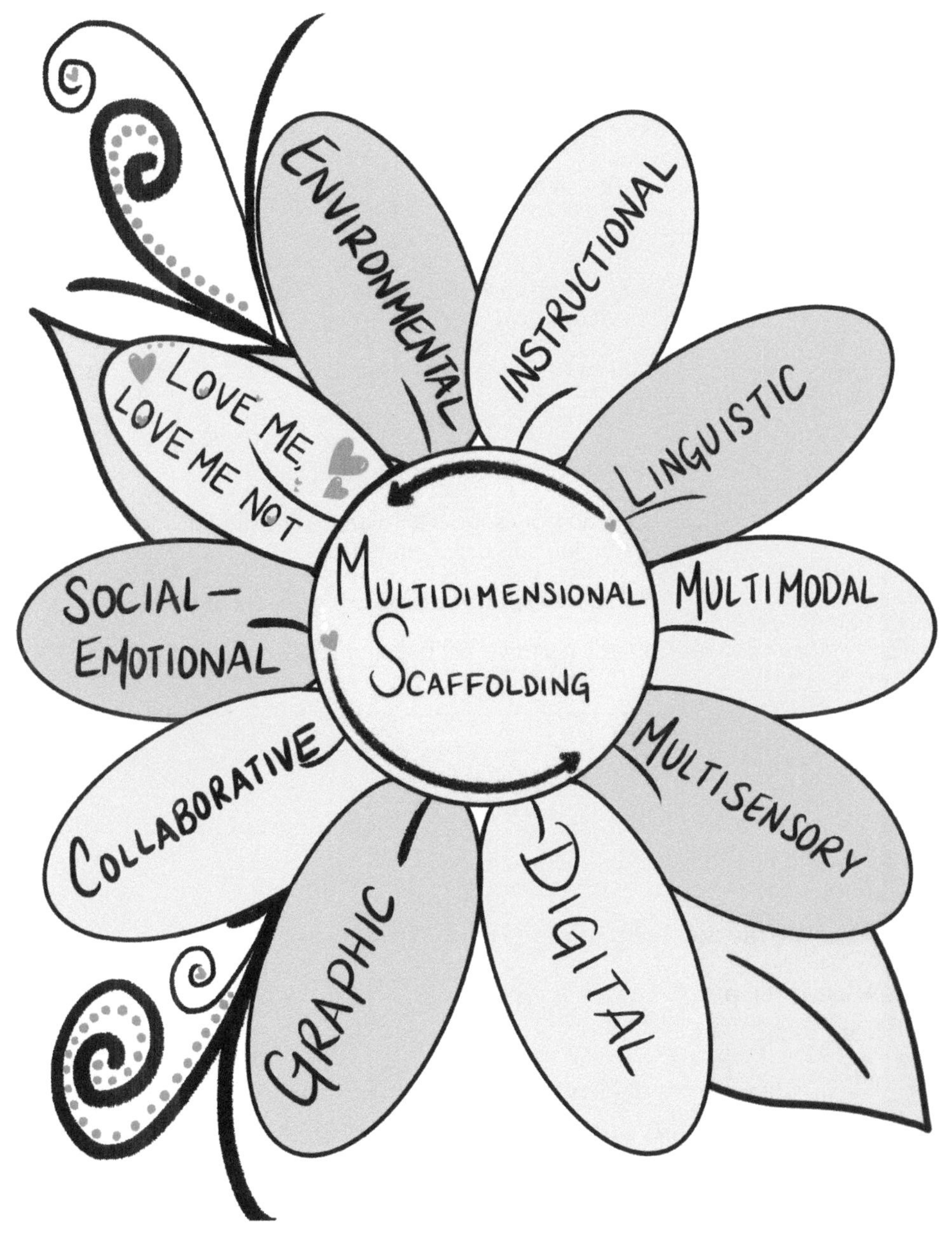

undergird its importance, present actionable ways to implement it, and share some authentic examples from the field. We invite you to consider this as a choice menu—not every scaffolding technique will fit every lesson; not every scaffolding approach will result in the desired outcomes for all students; and you can definitely not include nine types of scaffolds in every 42-minute or even 80-minute class period, so you will need to choose. We must also recognize that some of these scaffolding approaches overlap. See Figure 6.5 for a preview of all the scaffolding approaches that we are introducing here. You can also use this tool to determine the utility and applicability of each to your own context.

Figure 6.5 Summary of Scaffolding Approaches

SCAFFOLDING APPROACH	BRIEF DESCRIPTION OF EACH APPROACH
Instructional	Supporting ELs/MLs through the entire learning experience by strategic lesson delivery
Linguistic	Supporting language and literacy development at the word, sentence, and discourse levels
Multimodal	Expressive (speaking, writing, visually representing) and interpretive modes of language (listening, reading, viewing)
Multisensory	Auditory, visual, tactile, and kinesthetic experiences
Graphic	Schematic or visual representations
Digital	Technology-based tools and techniques
Interactive/Collaborative	Participatory supports to enable communication and role definition and task completion
Social-emotional	Affective supports and relationship building
Environmental	Physical and virtual learning context

Key questions to answer when you and your collaborating teachers make a choice about scaffolding include the following:

- What are the most urgent needs of our students?
- What is the purpose of each type of support, and who will benefit most from each?
- What subgroups of students will need differentiation, and how will scaffolds accomplish that?
- What types of scaffolds does the upcoming unit or lesson require for equitable access to the core curriculum and language and literacy development?
- What types of scaffolds does the upcoming unit or lesson require for meaningful student engagement in academic practice?
- How do we ensure that the scaffold will fade and make way for student independence?

Let's take a closer look at nine ways to infuse scaffolding intentionally into instruction. After defining what it is, each scaffolding approach will be supported by a powerful quote, a solid rationale, specific implications for ELs/MLs, implementation tips, and one or more authentic examples from K–12 practitioners.

1. Instructional Scaffolding

What Is It?

Through instructional scaffolding, you structure lessons in ways that are accessible to learners at all levels of academic and linguistic readiness, by offering modeling and incrementally increasing the complexity of the learning through guided and (eventually) independent practice.

Words of Wisdom

"Scaffolding provides a gentler entry, but the destination remains the same" (Coe et al., 2020, p. 32).

Why Is It Important for All Students?

Instructional scaffolding supports the natural learning progression, so students can develop confidence in their academic and linguistic abilities and fluency with academic skills and language and literacy practices across all content areas. Learning becomes independent in the following classic format of the gradual release of responsibility (GRoR) model (de Oliveira & Smith, 2019; Fisher & Frey, 2014). Teacher modeling is followed by joint construction of meaning or guided practice leading to collaborative construction or shared practice, ending the teaching-learning cycle with independent construction or practice. (Return to Chapter 4 for more discussion of GRoR.)

How Does It Specifically Relate to ELs'/MLs' Needs?

Grade-level instruction might present itself as both complex and difficult for ELs/MLs. Complexity refers to the type of knowledge, thinking process, and action needed for students to successfully participate in a learning experience. Difficulty is a more subjective term based on students' readiness levels to tackle new learning and how much effort they need to successfully complete a task (Sousa, 2017). For ELs/MLs, it is especially important to distinguish between difficulty and complexity because these notions are often mistaken or misunderstood. Figure 6.6 further exemplifies how to navigate and scaffold instruction that ELs/MLs receive by examining whether the learning experience has high versus low complexity and high versus low difficulty. The matrix provides four combinations of scenarios and offers scaffolding approaches that are best aligned with instruction when

1. High complexity is combined with high difficulty
2. High complexity is combined with low difficulty
3. Low complexity is combined with high difficulty
4. Low complexity is combined with low difficulty

Figure 6.6 Complexity Versus Difficulty Matrix Applied to Scaffolding

	HIGH COMPLEXITY	LOW COMPLEXITY
High Difficulty	Avoid working at the frustration level Prevent unproductive struggle Focus on foundational skills and essential background information Build on what students already know and can do	Build stamina Invite experimentation with the language or the task Support a collaborative approach to learning Develop tolerance for ambiguity
Low Difficulty	Build strategic thinking Attend to complex text with high familiarity of the subject Be able to tackle high interest reading materials (hard to do it alone) Have access to complex learning via multimodal, multilingual, and multilevel resources	Build fluency Have added practice with target skills Develop automaticity Transfer knowledge and skills to new areas Practice application of critical thinking skills and answering higher-order questions

How to Get Started With Instructional Scaffolding

One critical component of instructional scaffolding for ELs/MLs is intentional modeling. For example, modeling writing (rather than merely assigning writing tasks) is a powerful opportunity to ensure students begin to develop complex skills. Think of at least four ways you can employ instructional scaffolding via modeling in the context of writing instruction:

1. **Task modeling:** Explain the expectations and break down the writing task, writing purpose, or writing prompt to ensure clarity.
2. **Process modeling:** Show the steps of the writing process to your students and "write aloud" and "edit aloud" for your students to see the metacognitive and metalinguistic processes that take place in your mind as you write.
3. **Product modeling:** Show what the final product may look like so your ELs/MLs see the big picture and can better visualize what their classmates on similar linguistic proficiency levels have done or what they themselves will be producing.
4. **Linguistic modeling:** Make explicit connections between how the spoken words you use carry meaning (this is what we say) and then how it is transferred to a written piece (this is how we write about it) and offer language models, sentence starters, word banks, paragraph frames, and other structural support.

A SNAPSHOT FROM THE FIELD

Kristen Douglass, ESL teacher in an eighth-grade co-taught English class, of Northwood Middle School, Illinois, codeveloped the following model with Linda Kahn and Lisa Ballenger-Petitte to support their students in writing a problem–solution constructive response. In addition to the prompt that offered guided questions, Kristen provides her students with a list of articles that will help them in deciding what societal problems they could write about as well as a Google slideshow to guide them step-by-step in the process. Figure 6.7 is the color-coded constructed response-outline organizer (the abbreviation DQ stands for direct quote).

Figure 6.7 Constructed Response-Outline Organizer

- ❑ **Lead: Interesting fact**
  - ❑ Ex: "Fully 97% of teens ages 12–17 play computer, web, portable, or console games" (Pew Research Center, 2008, para. 3).

- ❑ **Reword or restate the question to form a topic sentence.**
  - ❑ Ex: A problem that needs to be solved is ________ and it should be solved by ________.
- ❑ **Answer all parts of the prompt. Include a general statement or inference.**
  - ❑ Ex: This ________ is an issue because ________.

(Continued)

(Continued)

- ❑ **Explain the problem.**
  - ❑ Give background information on how the problem began.
    - ❑ Introduce text
    - ❑ Give a DQ explaining the background of the problem
      - ❑ This is a problem because ____________.
- ❑ **Explain the solution.**
  - ❑ Introduce text.
  - ❑ Give a DQ explaining the solution.
  - ❑ This is a solution because ____________.
  - ❑ This solution will help solve the problem by ____________.

- ❑ **Conclude**
  - ❑ Restate the prompt again.
  - ❑ Give an example and explain why this is important
  - ❑ Call to action

- ❑ **Bibliography**
  - ❑ Use Easy Bib app on your Chromebook.

Figure created by Kristen Douglass, Linda Kahn, and Lisa Ballenger-Petitte. Used with permission.

Another key element of instructional scaffolding is guided practice. As suggested by its name, it is a transitional phase between teacher modeling or teacher-led instruction and independent work. During guided practice, students begin to take control of their own learning while teachers continue to offer guidance, monitor student engagement, and assess and offer feedback on student progress. Structuring guided practice includes the following:

1. Teachers directing the whole class or large groups
2. Teachers guiding small groups
3. Teachers conferring with individual students
4. Students engaging in peer learning with teacher guidance

Guidance and repeated opportunities to practice learning targets allow for committing new learning to long-term memory!

A SNAPSHOT FROM THE FIELD

James Tuck, ESOL teacher, Hanover County Public Schools, Virginia, shared the following vignette and tool with us exemplifying the importance of guided practice.

I co-teach eighth-grade math as an ESOL teacher with Courtney Long, a math content teacher. I created the Comparing Real Numbers cloze notes and corresponding anchor chart as a supplemental content and language review tool for our heterogeneous class of English learners, English speakers, and students with Individualized Education Plans and 504 plans. In our research as co-teachers, we came to understand that anchor charts are most effective when students take part in creating them. So we developed this resource to better engage our students. First, we gave copies of the cloze notes to students and displayed the anchor chart at the front of the classroom. Then, section-by-section, we completed the anchor chart by modeling how to read each sentence and having the class chorally repeat them (see Figure 6.8). This strategy supported each student in saying the math processes aloud for converting fractions, percentages, and scientific notation to decimals. After that, we had students apply their knowledge to complete the practical word problem at the bottom as guided practice with us. Finally, students were allowed to use these notes to help complete their quiz review individually. We were happy to see that so many students, ELs and non-ELs, showed growth in this unit.

(Continued)

(Continued)

Figure 6.8 Guided Practice With Anchor Chart

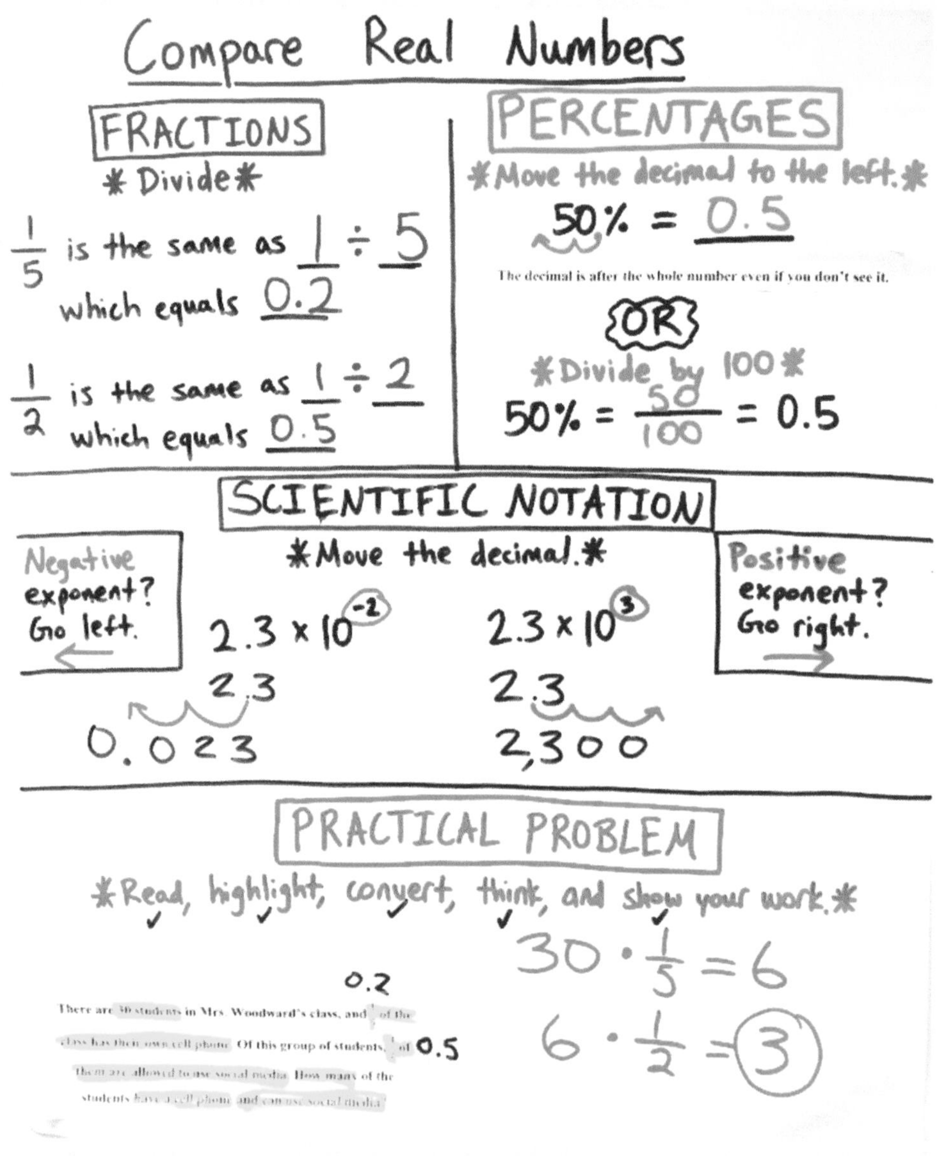

Figure created by James Tuck. Used with permission.

Instructional Scaffolding via Experiential or Project-Based Learning

Experiential learning opportunities and project-based learning may be central or supplemental to your teaching; either way, instructional scaffolding is essential for successful implementation. Ayer (2018) suggests four key steps to follow:

Step 1. Plan with the end in mind.

Step 2. Assist students in developing their own questions.

Step 3. Encourage students to think like experts.

Step 4. Make sure the projects are presented or published for an authentic audience.

When you scaffold a project or experiential activity for ELs/MLs, you recognize that it allows for academic language and literacy development alongside discovery learning tied to content goals. Key conditions for experiential or project-based learning for ELs/MLs to be successful are the following:

1. Before you begin, analyze the content demand, linguistic demand, and social-emotional learning opportunity embedded in the project you are planning for ELs/MLs. Consider the following guiding questions for instructional scaffolding:
   - What kind of background knowledge or contextual understanding is required for the project?
   - Are there any prerequisite content or linguistic skills ELs/MLs need to work on the project?
   - What are some ways ELs'/MLs' social-emotional well-being or growth may be integral to the project?
2. Create collaborative work groups that ensure active participation by all learners, including ELs/MLs. Reflect on how to achieve that with these questions:
   - How can I strategically place ELs/MLs in heterogeneous groups with English-proficient peers as well as other ELs/MLs to maximize collaboration and interaction?
   - To what extent can ELs/MLs effectively also use their full language and literacy repertoires while working on the project?
3. Scaffold ELs'/MLs' participation in one or more of the four key language uses (WIDA, 2020b) and consider how to engage them in
   - *Informing* others about the project and negotiating all aspects of the group work
   - *Explaining* the purpose and the outcomes of the work the students have engaged in
   - *Arguing* a perspective they had to take during or as a result of the project
   - *Narrating* the key steps taken or essential components of the project
4. Consider how to ensure students have the tools to communicate about their projects and what language scaffolds and other types of scaffolds are needed for them to do so. (See the rest of this chapter to explore them all.)

2. Linguistic Scaffolding

What Is It?

Through linguistic scaffolding, the full range of multilingual repertoires students and teachers possess are leveraged and multiple techniques are used to offer language-specific support.

Words of Wisdom

"Rather than framing students' uses of [their home languages] as markers of deficiency, teachers can recognize, praise, and investigate student language use to inform classroom meaning-making" (Pacheco et al., 2019, p. 77).

Why Is It Important?

Language is the means to communication and learning. When you use linguistic scaffolds, you recognize that students might be ready cognitively to work with complex concepts and develop new academic skills across the core content areas, yet the language that is necessary to communicate and to attain academic growth requires additional support.

How Does It Specifically Relate to ELs'/MLs' Needs?

While supporting academic language and literacy development are critical for all learners, ELs/MLs are especially in need of supports that respond to their unique linguistic needs and address the linguistic dimension of comprehension and participation. Linguistic scaffolding is essential to bolster ELs'/MLs' spoken and written discourse. It provides them with extended opportunities to develop appropriate use of linguistic forms and functions.

How to Get Started With Linguistic Scaffolding

When you plan to offer linguistic scaffolds, your instruction may include the following:

- Use of native language or home dialect
- Use of redundancy or rephrasing for multiple, varied linguistic modeling and input
- Contextualized definition of key terms within sentences
- Modification of sentence patterns
- Opportunities to interact with proficient English models
- Interactive word walls and word/phrase banks
- Language frames for oral interaction
- Sentence starters, paragraph frames, and essay outlines for written communication

A SNAPSHOT FROM THE FIELD

Matt Hajdun, assistant director of Learning for Language Development at The Columbus School (TCS) in Medellín, Colombia, shared with us how he and his colleagues add linguistic scaffolds to their Character Counts curriculum.

For many emergent bilinguals, vocabulary often feels like a ceiling to expression. We are working towards students being able to recognize how many words they actually know by building cognate bridges to Spanish and/or by exploring affixes. In the example (Figure 6.9), students explore words related to the six pillars of Character Counts and later explore "paired sentences" to see how adding affixes can change meaning, while focusing on the base word and amplifying student vocabulary knowledge.

Figure 6.9 Linguistic Scaffolding to Support Metalinguistic Awareness

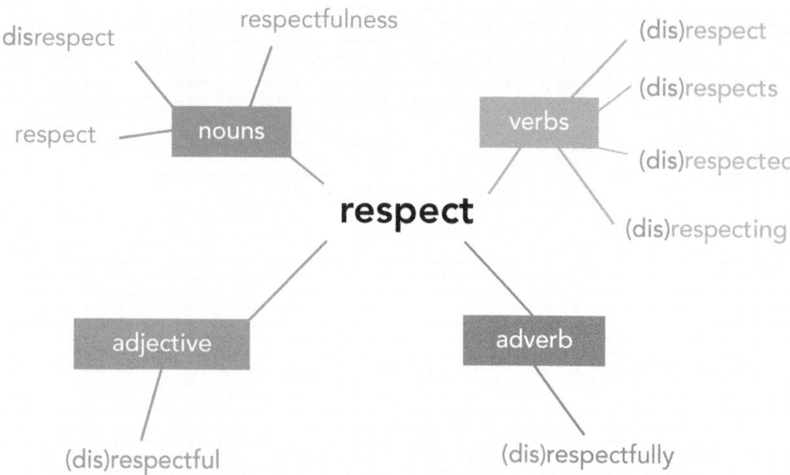

Figure created by Matthew Hajdun. Used with permission.

* * *

Jennifer Pomagier, English language (EL) teacher, Kristin Cochrane, English language arts (ELA) teacher, and Miriam Schuman, special educator, created color-coded scaffolds for their students to see the parts of a paragraph consisting of a speech tag, a direct quote, and an explanation (see Figure 6.10).

(Continued)

(Continued)

Figure 6.10 Color-Coded Paragraph Model With Annotations

In the article "The Black Hole of Technology," the author says, "Not once do we stop . . . Now I am always consumed by my tech" (para. 1*). This clearly shows that with technology we're unable to enjoy anything else around us.

Yellow = speech tag

Green = actual direct quote

Pink = page number

Blue = explanation

*Khan (2015).

Figure created by Jennifer Pomagier, Kristin Cochrane, and Miriam Schuman. Used with permission.

3. Multimodal Scaffolding

What Is It?

Multimodal scaffolding allows access to information and provides opportunities for self-expression through multiple modes of communication, such as spoken and written language. Student learning is supported by getting information and producing new content in text and non-text formats and watching short video clips on social media and responding to them using text, images (emojis and memes), video recordings, and so on.

Words of Wisdom

"Multimodality allows all students to use multiple means to engage, interpret, represent, act, and express their ideas in the classroom. For example, as students read, they also might refer to illustrations or diagrams, and as students write, they might also represent their ideas numerically or graphically" (WIDA, 2020b, p. 19).

Why Is It Important?

Through multimodal scaffolding, students have access to the same information through several channels or modalities. Multimodality is also inherent to and essential for how students make meaning, access new information, respond, or engage in disciplinary practices. All students are able to both interpret and express ideas with greater flexibility when using multimodal resources, including multiple languages. Kristina Robertson reminds us that "depending on grade level the majority of students are focused on reading and listening throughout the school day, ELs/MLs need language production practice to ensure comfort with new academic concepts and language. They need to be able to use academic language independently to become proficient" (personal communication, March 6, 2021).

Consider your own classroom or a classroom you visit frequently as a coach, colleague, or administrator:

- What types of resources are available?
- What modes of communication are privileged and supported?
- Are students afforded multiple interpretations of the target text?
- Do students have a choice to express themselves in different ways?

How Does It Specifically Relate to ELs'/MLs' Needs?

When more than one modality is available simultaneously to support language and literacy development, ELs/MLs can listen, read, write, talk, or SWIRL (speak, write, interact, read, and listen) as well as watch or view image- or video-based resources. They can also demonstrate their own understanding through textual and visual representations, having the opportunities to develop both foundational skills and meaning-making across language domains and modalities.

How to Get Started With Multimodal Scaffolding

When you plan to offer multimodal scaffolds, you may incorporate the following teaching strategies as well as create opportunities to use the same as learning strategies:

- Using multimodal texts such as picture books, graphic novels, and richly illustrated print-based readings
- Accessing multimodal digital resources such as films, video clips, and interactive webpages (see more under digital scaffolding)
- Presenting minilessons through multiple modalities including oral, written, and visual modes
- Creatively combining graphics that represent complex concepts with labels, captions, short descriptions, and spoken explanations
- Inviting student choice in selecting and analyzing resources that will support their learning as well as in demonstrating new learning (oral and written text, visual representations, graphic organizers, videos, animation, etc.)
- Engaging in project-based learning that allows for students to "comprehend and compose meaning across diverse, rich, and potentially complex forms of multimodal text, and to do so using a range of different meaning modes" (Victoria State Government, 2018, para. 6)

A SNAPSHOT FROM THE FIELD

Michelle Gill and her colleague Bharwat Vaid, both of the ELL Division of the Abbotsford School District, British Columbia, use Book Creator (Figure 6.11), which allows students to access information in both a text and video-based format, work collaboratively, and record their answers in multiple ways while also allowing teachers to provide feedback as they have access to the student-created books.

Figure 6.11 Book Creator Excerpt

Notice and Wonder

1. **Watch the short video posted.**
2. **What did you notice and wonder?**
3. **Reflect and Share**

On the next page, share what you noticed and what you wondered from the video. Include:

- 2 things you noticed: something you learned that stood out to you
- 2 questions

Thursday

Photo: iStock.com/kali9

Watch the Scholastic Video Wheelchair Racer

Figure created by Michelle Gill and Bharwat Vaid. Used with permission.

4. Multisensory Scaffolding

What Is It?

Multisensory scaffolding invites learners to simultaneously use multiple senses to process and retain information or to engage in academic and literacy practices. The four primary senses are visual, auditory, tactile, and kinesthetic corresponding to developing visual, auditory, and small or large motor memories.

Words of Wisdom

"The evidence suggests that using multisensory activities that promote student engagement during a learning episode improves student learning and retention" (Sousa, 2017, p. 63).

Why Is It Important?

Sight is used for processing text or visual input, reading information, watching teachers doing a demonstration, observing peers' actions and participation in learning, and so on. Hearing is the pathway to processing what teachers or classmates say or what may be heard while listening to podcasts or other auditory materials. When students watch their teachers attach language to actions (as they talk while modeling a task) or attach language to objects (as they describe something) or when students view videos, sight and hearing are combined. When additional senses are incorporated into the learning process—especially through the use of touch and movement—the brain has more pathways to develop tactile and kinesthetic (muscle) memories.

How Does It Specifically Relate to ELs'/MLs' Needs?

ELs/MLs are simultaneously learning a new language and content so when multiple senses are involved in creating new memories, they have multiple ways of processing and remembering information and developing new skills. When visual input is paired with verbal communication (also referred to as dual coding), students' working memory is enhanced. A well-established language pedagogical practice called TPR (Total Physical Response) invites students to participate in learning through gestures and motions. Manipulatives and tactile surfaces, such as sand or rice trays, Play-Doh, felt, and similar items have been successfully used in early childhood classes with both ELs/MLs and English-proficient students. Games and game-like activities that involve singing, clapping, and other whole-body movements help students learn basic skills (such as numbers and the alphabet) as well as hard-to-remember or more elusive complex concepts (such as states of matter, chemical balance, and more; see www.songsforteaching.com).

How to Get Started With Multisensory Scaffolding

When you plan to offer multisensory scaffolds, your instruction may include the following:

- Real objects (realia)
- Manipulatives
- 3D models or displays
- Illustrations (photographs, pictures, illustrations, diagrams, sketch notes)

- Visual representations, such as visual notetaking
- Videos, animations, interactive websites
- Songs with or without movement

See Figures 6.12 and 6.13 for additional tips on how to maximize multisensory support for ELs/MLs.

Figure 6.12 Visual Support

VISUAL SUPPORT	TIPS TO BETTER SUPPORT ELS/MLS
Show a two- to three-minute video to preview or review the material.	Use www.screen-cast-o-matic.com to create your own videos and try flipped learning.
Create or have students create illustrated one-pagers that synthesize all the key information needed for the lesson.	Have an advanced EL/ML or English-speaking peer create summary charts to synthesize a unit or chapter for extra credit or service learning credit.
Create partially completed graphic organizers with key ideas as well as visual cues already inserted.	Use the one-pager you or your students created and remove some information from it. If needed, add a word or phrase box to offer additional scaffold.
Co-generate anchor charts with visuals.	Co-create charts and graphs with your students so they can participate in the process of capturing and illustrating the same information.

Figure 6.13 Tactile/Kinesthetic Support

TACTILE/KINESTHETIC SUPPORT	TIPS TO BETTER SUPPORT ELS/MLS
Hand motions and gestures added to speech, songs, rhymes	Keep it simple and make it meaningful
TPR (Total Physical Response)	Play Simon Says
Manipulatives	Commercially produced and teacher-created manipulatives should be augmented or replaced by student-created ones
Foldables	See and adapt resources from Dinah Zike at https://dinah.com/
Dramatic representation/Acting out	Invite students' creative talent and participation

A SNAPSHOT FROM THE FIELD

When Jaymie Hogg and her co-teacher Beth Harju, Boise Public Schools, Idaho, present students with the week's vocabulary words, they use a multisensory approach. One teacher connects each word with a unique hand motion, picture, and chant while the other teacher posts the vocabulary, the definition, and a picture on the word wall. The students echo the teacher and mirror her hand motions. To consolidate their learning, students turn to one another and practice the new vocabulary words by reciting them and using the hand motions.

5. Digital Scaffolding

What Is It?

The narrowest definition of digital scaffolding may refer to the dynamic cues that many word processing programs offer through auto-correct and auto-completion algorithms or the use of digital dictionaries or translation apps. We use this term here in a much broader sense: Digital scaffolding accounts for a range of digital resources and tools that strategically support students' learning.

Words of Wisdom

"Digital media offers many possibilities when working with ELs. The use of multiple modalities through visual and video support can provide teachers with scaffolding resources that foster different types of instructional practices" (Parris et al., 2016, p. 28).

Why Is It Important?

Access to digital technology is quickly expanding both in schools and in students' homes. Digital tools have the power to provide multimodal and multisensory experiences for students as they watch and listen to videos, simulations, or animations; as they take virtual tours of national parks, monuments, and museums; as they use educational apps such as EdPuzzle, Seesaw, Nearpod, and so on to practice skills, students develop proficiency with the target content and language as they also develop 21st century technology skills. We must also recognize that most students no longer merely receive and interpret information or develop new skills or enhance them via digital supports; they can take a more active role and also create digital content.

How Does It Specifically Relate to ELs'/MLs' Needs?

Digital scaffolds may offer the much-needed opportunities to ELs/MLs to have access to new learning by (a) frontloading (preteaching or previewing) upcoming lessons, such as in flipped learning; (b) being available in the moment, such as using electronic dictionaries or using apps, such as www.rewordify.com; (c) serving as tools for reviewing or revisiting teacher-recorded or curated materials; and (d) offering enrichment and extended learning opportunities through educational games, such as Kahoot!, BrainPOP ESL, EdPuzzle, and more.

How to Get Started With Digital Scaffolding

When you plan to offer digital scaffolds, your instruction may include the following:

- Multimedia presentations created by the teacher and the students (Padlet, Nearpod)
- Digital recordings (Screencastify, Loom)
- Digital storytelling (Book Creator, Adobe Spark, VoiceThread, Lego Movie Maker, Make Beliefs Comix)
- E-books, blogs, and web-based reading materials (Epic, Newsela, NewsinLevels, Starfall)
- Digital whiteboards (Jamboard, Whiteboard)
- Instructional apps or extensions to digital platforms (Flipgrid, EdPuzzle, Peardeck)
- Web-based learning games (Kahoot, Gimkit)
- Student and parent messaging tools (TalkingPoints, Remind, WhatsApp)
- Adaptive software to practice content skills (Doodle Math, Zern, Prodigy, Mathspace)

A SNAPSHOT FROM THE FIELD

Todd Middendorf, sixth-grade science teacher, and his colleagues Danielle Kolze and Steven Wolf at Northwood Middle School offer their students digital support by presenting a well-organized digital landing page for the upcoming lesson (see Figure 6.14). This provides clear daily expectations for students, as well as having a place to easily access relevant resources.

Figure 6.14 Digital Landing Page

NORTHWOOD SCIENCE 6

Mr. Todd Middendorf - tmiddendorf@nssd112.org - 224-765-3341 - @MrMiddendorf

DAY-TO-DAY RESOURCES	LAB RESOURCES	BRING TO CLASS DAILY
FUN SCIENCE LINKS	NW LAB REPORT FORMAT	Chromebook in Original Case with Cord
RETAKES PAGE	-EQUIPMENT PACKET -SAFETY CONTRACT -(SPANISH VERSION)	Agenda Book
CLASSROOM EXPECTATIONS	GIZMO WEBSITE	Science Folder with current curricular materials
CHAMPS EXPECTATIONS	AMPLIFY MODULES (coming soon)	Writing Utensil (pencil preferred so we can learn from mistakes)

Date Directions/KUDs WARM UP Links/Resources HW/Due Dates Assessments

What are you learning today? The Earth's lithospheric plates move around due to convection currents, and interact in different ways at Boundary Points.
Why do you need to know this? So we can understand how features on our planet are formed.
How will you apply this in the real world? We can understand the thermodynamics and the forces involved in shaping planets, in the past, present, and future.

Figure created by Todd Middendorf and Danielle Kolze. Used with permission.

6. Graphic Scaffolding

What Is It?

Similar to the preceding visual support, graphic representations of complex concepts, difficult content, new skills, or language input can also contribute to (a) better understanding, (b) easier access to new learning, and (c) more support for self-expression.

Words of Wisdom

"Materials [must] incorporate carefully chosen, age-appropriate visuals and graphic supports to activate prior knowledge and scaffold conceptual development. These graphics should be used to clarify concepts and relationships within the text that are critical to comprehension. All graphics and visuals that are chosen must be culturally respectful" (Council of the Great City Schools, 2014, p. 14).

Why Is It Important?

Graphic representations of complex concepts have been a commonly used technique in teaching and learning. Both teachers and their students may initiate processing or presenting ideas using a graphic tool. Frequently used graphic supports include graphic organizers, summary charts, tables, diagrams, outlines, maps, timelines, and many other formats. Some tools such as Thinking Maps™ (www.thinkingmaps.com) help students organize their thoughts as they activate their prior knowledge, build background knowledge, process information presented in a lesson, or plan to speak or write about a topic.

How Does It Specifically Relate to ELs'/MLs' Needs?

Graphic tools support students in at least two major ways. They help with their interpretive processes, and they help with their expressive processes during content learning and language, literacy, and social-emotional development. Some graphic representations, such as one-pagers (also referred to as one-sheeters) may offer quick, visual access to complex concepts while also helping synthesize key information. As the name suggests, all key information about a topic is summarized on a single sheet in a graphic format. Graphic scaffolding is versatile, and it can support students to organize, summarize, categorize, and connect pieces of information. It can also be created simply and duplicated effortlessly.

How to Get Started With Graphic Scaffolding

When you plan to offer graphic scaffolds, your instruction may include the following:

- Outlines (to help organize a paper, to arrange topics and subtopics, to differentiate between the main idea and supporting details)
- Charts (to display complex data in a visually accessible way)
- Tables (to summarize key features of a phenomenon or group information or data together)
- Timelines (to follow historic events)
- Number lines (to aid in mathematical computations)
- Graphs (to illustrate relationships among data)
- Maps (to visualize geographical regions)
- Thinking Maps™
- Graphic organizers (to identify relationships between ideas or concepts)
- Partially completed graphic organizers (to aid in writing or presenting)

A SNAPSHOT FROM THE FIELD

Shannon Machacek, fifth-grade ELA teacher, and her colleague Rabab Magid, fourth- and fifth-grade EL teacher from North Palos District 117 in Hickory Hills, Illinois, shared with us a specific strategy on how they scaffold up using graphic scaffolds infused with linguistic and digital scaffolds:

Rabab Magid and I co-teach a class of twenty-eight students, and eleven of them are English learners. We created a "game" to review the vocabulary words that our students would have a quiz on the following day. I created the questions, and then Rabab put them into Google Slides, added Arabic words, and also added pictures to each slide. I teach another ELA class before Rabab's and my class, so I am able to present the material to those students first. As that class plays the game, I "refine" the slides. Then, when Rabab and I co-teach our class, everything is perfect for our EL students! The pictures and the Arabic words help our EL students work on grade-level material (see Figure 6.15).

Figure 6.15 Examples of Graphic Scaffolding for Vocabulary Development

Relationship علاقات رسمية

1. Would you rather have a **positive relationship** with your dentist or your mailman? Why?

2. What would happen if you had a **negative relationship** with your dentist? Mailman?

Express التعبير

Example/non-example (Thumbs-up if this is an example of the word **"express"** or thumbs-down if it is not an example.)

a. **Writing a letter to someone you love**
b. **Playing on a playground**
c. **Talking to a friend about how you feel**
d. **Writing a poem**
e. **Watching a television show**
f. **Painting a picture**
g. **Writing rap lyrics**
h. **Singing a song**

Image sources: (Relationships) istock.com/MaksimYremenko; (Mailman) istock.com/sababaJJ; (Dentist) istock.com/Teerapol24; (Thumbs Down emoji) istock.com/yayayoyo; (Thumbs Up emoji) istock.com/yayayoyo

(Continued)

(Continued)

Affecting تأثير

1. Name some things that are **affecting** your mood right now.
2. How is the weather this week **affecting** the road and sidewalk conditions?

Minority الأقلية

1. Who is the **minority** in this class–boys or girls?
2. What is the opposite of **minority?**

Image sources: (Grumpy Girl) istock.com/KanKhem; (Icy Road) istock.com/philipp_g; (US Map) istock.com/RLT_Images; (Minority) istock.com/Pict Rider

Figure created by Shannon Machacek and Rabab Magid. Used with permission.

7. Collaborative Scaffolding

What Is It?

Also referred to as interactive support, collaborative scaffolding refers to a process where meaning-making and language and literacy development and engagement happen in the company of others.

Words of Wisdom

"In engaging with others, we recognize that learning unfolds in the company of others and is a social endeavor. We learn in, from, and with groups. The group supports our learning as well as challenges it, allowing us to reach higher levels of performance" (Ritchhart & Church, 2020, p. 8).

Why Is It Important?

Since learning takes place in a social context, students need to experience a variety of interactive structures, such as whole-class or large-group lessons and activities in small groups as well as pairwork, triads, or other configurations. When students collaborate with their peers about the topic, time is allotted for them to formulate their own ideas and practice using academic language. Learning stations, learning centers, and other cooperative-group structures allow students to co-construct meaning, collaboratively tackle a new problem, or complete an academic task. While doing so, they take ownership of new learning and the academic language and literacy skills that are connected to them.

How Does It Specifically Relate to ELs'/MLs' Needs?

Language is socially constructed and only develops when used authentically, frequently, and meaningfully. Collaborative scaffolds shape ELs'/MLs' participation in language and literacy activities and disciplinary practices because "knowledge and understanding are co-constructed through interaction, and through the practice of scaffolding, whereby the learner's understandings and attempts to express these in words are supported and assisted through dialogue" (Cullen et al., 2013, p. 426). Based on the instructional context or focus, collaborative support may be offered by the teacher or one or more peers.

How to Get Started With Collaborative Scaffolding

When you plan to offer collaborative scaffolds, your instruction may intentionally shift between and among various interactive configurations:

- Whole class
- Large-group versus small-group instruction
- Learning centers
- Learning stations
- Pairwork
- Buddy system

A SNAPSHOT FROM THE FIELD

Jamie Albon, sixth-grade ELA collaborating teacher at Conrady Junior High in North Palos District 117, Hickory Hills, Illinois, shared with us how she uses Kagan structures to help ELs/MLs to read, write, speak, and listen for a variety of purposes and in different situations.

As part of the sixth-grade unit, Teaching through Tragedies, the students learn about several different tragedies and how society changed as a result of them. After reading about the topic in class, students completed a written response as well as a team-building activity. Next, students were asked to turn to talk to their shoulder partners. Students were already seated using the Kagan method, allowing them to sit near someone who was within their ability. Each partnership took turns sharing what they wrote. Initially, students, especially EL students, were more comfortable reading off their screens. As the weeks progressed, all students were encouraged to close their Chromebook screens and

(Continued)

(Continued)

simply discuss what they wrote. Students were timed giving a total of 5 minutes to practice speaking to one another. Students had to be clear and concise with their speaking, as the next component required students to demonstrate their listening skills.

Upon sharing their own personal writing, students were then asked to meet with their face partners to share what their partners wrote about. At first, this was challenging since many students wanted to talk about what they wrote. However, as weekly practice continued, students became very astute at sharing what their shoulder partners wrote with their face partners.

The final component of this activity brought the whole class together. During this time, the teacher would spot-check students by calling on students to share what they heard. The scenario would look like this (also see Figure 6.16):

- *A/B and C/D are shoulder partners—sharing their personal writing*
- *A/D and B/C are face partners—sharing their shoulder partner's response*
- *Whole group: Student C would report Student A's writing via the conversation with Student B*

Figure 6.16 Face Partners and Shoulder Partners Work Together

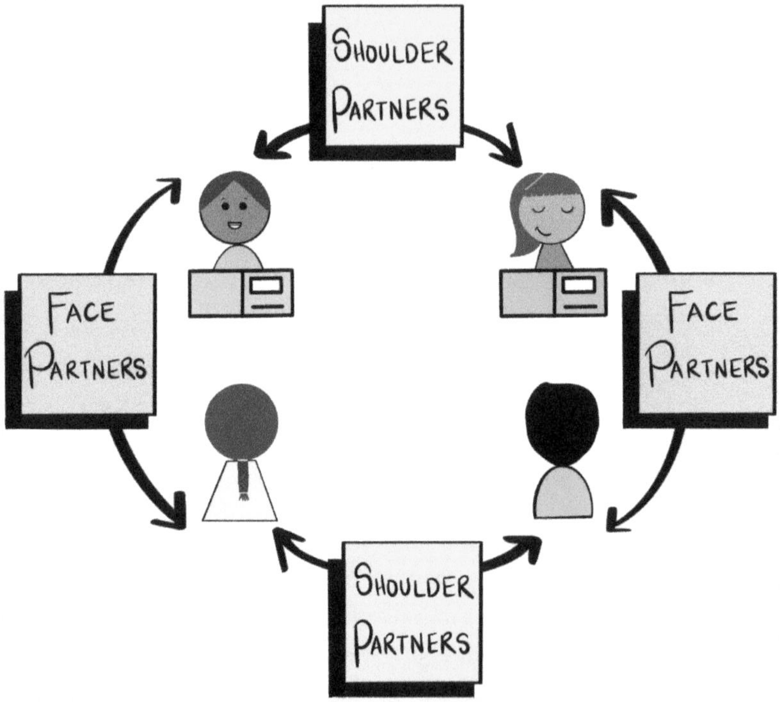

As each week passed, the students became more confident in all areas. Giving the students time to prepare their ideas prior to sharing with a classmate allowed them to gather their thoughts, which ultimately led to strong oral interactions with their peers. The entire process led to increased proficiency in three target areas (writing, listening, and speaking) for all students.

8. Social-Emotional Scaffolding

What Is It?

Social-emotional scaffolding is a purposeful, pedagogical use of linguistic and non-linguistic communication tools that help students build relationships and support their social development as well as emotional response to learning.

Words of Wisdom

"Society needs individuals who can effectively communicate with and learn from one another. Students deserve the opportunity to learn how to articulate their thoughts and ideas, listen effectively to decipher meaning, knowledge, values, attitudes and intentions, and communicate effectively within diverse communities" (Spies & Xu, 2018, p. 29).

Why Is It Important?

Students' emotional well-being and ability to develop the necessary social knowledge, skills, and disposition to be a confident part of a learning community are of utmost importance. Meyer and Turner (2007) emphasize the need to focus on "sustaining students' understanding of challenging concepts, students' demonstration of their competencies and autonomy, students' involvement and persistence, and students' emotional or personal experiences" (p. 245). We must recognize and appropriately respond to all the pedagogically important emotions (such as motivation, excitement, and agency) that students exhibit as well as the ones that may hinder learning (anxiety, fear of failure, boredom, negative self-talk, and so on). It is also our role as educators to create a positive affective space where our students' social development is supported, emotional well-being is addressed, and authentic student participation, agency, and autonomy are nurtured. One way to achieve this is through social-emotional scaffolding.

How Does It Specifically Relate to ELs'/MLs' Needs?

ELs/MLs—as well as many of their peers—arrive with complex social-emotional backgrounds and experiences to school each day. Whether they are immigrant children or children of immigrants, many of them have faced numerous challenges to adjust to a new life, new expectations, or a new language. To enjoy a sense of belonging, students must develop the social-emotional knowledge and skills of how to recognize, regulate, and communicate their emotions, how to make friends, how to interact with peers and adults in an academic context, and how to be a productive part of a class community. By focusing on students' social-emotional needs in an academic context, teachers provide a much-needed sense of security for students. Morcom (2015) reports on collaboratively establishing class agreements that represent various ways to support social-emotional development for all students (see the target skills listed in parentheses):

1. Mutual respect (interpersonal)
2. Appreciating others (interpersonal)

3. Attentive listening (communication)
4. Participation/right to pass (inclusion)
5. Personal best (positive learning mindset) (p. 21)

How to Get Started With Social-Emotional Scaffolding

When you plan to offer social-emotional scaffolds, your instruction may include the following:

- Setting a positive, affirming emotional tone for the classroom through community building
- Co-constructing classroom norms and expectations with your students
- Showing respect and patience to all students
- Teaching language associated with core emotions and more complex feelings alike
- Daily emotional check-ins
- Modeling ways students can manage and express their emotions, such as through positive self-talk, affirmations, I-statements, and journaling
- Using multiple group configurations to encourage interaction and relationship building among all students
- Micro-teaching (supporting individual students as needed)
- Offering frequent and targeted feedback
- Co-developing anchor charts that include appropriate talk moves
- Accepting only lift-ups and no put-downs

A SNAPSHOT FROM THE FIELD

Matt Hajdun, assistant director of Learning for Language Development at The Columbus School (TCS) in Medellín, Colombia—previously featured in this chapter—shared with us how he and his colleagues focus on student social-emotional and language development at the same time.

In our school, which builds on responsive classroom techniques, we encourage all our teachers to do two things: build language norms as part of their classroom routines and expectations as well as ensure that the classroom community is built at the beginning of the year. In order to do this, we provided teachers with a bank of team builder activities that had linguistic scaffolds as well as social-emotional scaffolds to support all learners (see Figure 6.17 for an example). Teachers who were not yet comfortable designing these resources could use them as developed. Other teachers, after seeing the examples, expanded upon some of the modeled scaffolds and modified the supports to match their favorite social-emotional and community-building activities.

Figure 6.17 Social-Emotional Scaffolds

I am not like a waterfall because . . .

I differ from a waterfall because . . .

One reason I'm different than a waterfall is . . .

I am like a waterfall because . . .

I am the same as a waterfall because . . .

One reason I'm similar to a waterfall is . . .

Figure created by Matt Hajdun. Used with permission.

* * *

Mary Pettit, NBCT fifth-grade teacher in South Country Community School District, New York, introduced journaling about social-emotional learning with fifth graders. She has taught her students about the difference between being *mind-full* and *mindful*, and she asked her students to visually represent and write about what these concepts mean to them. See Figure 6.18 for a fifth grader's response, who reflected on moments in her own life when she felt the stress due to things outside of her control ("mind-full") as well as the times when she was able to refocus her thoughts about things in life she has control over ("mindful").

Figure 6.18 Student Journaling With Social-Emotional Scaffolds

Figure created by Danielle Rivas. Used with permission.

9. Environmental Scaffolding

What Is It?

Environmental scaffolding helps ensure that the physical or virtual setting is one in which learning takes place successfully; it creates a supportive environment designed to build a socio-cultural context for students' academic, linguistic, and social-emotional growth and development.

Words of Wisdom

"Non-threatening, nurturing environments fulfilling students' cognitive, linguistic, and socioemotional needs contribute to higher academic achievement and motivation to learn science among bilingual students" (Morrison et al., 2020, p. 257).

Why Is It Important?

Although the quote above specifically mentions science and bilingual students, there is ample evidence to make the same claim for all students. Both the physical (or tangible) and socio-cultural (intangible) contexts for learning must ensure what Ryan and Deci (2020) refer to as three psychological needs of autonomy, competence, and relatedness. Autonomy is the need to work independently and to feel empowered and in control while learning; competence is the ability to accomplish work and experience success with tasks; and relatedness is the need to belong and feel accepted. They are all connected to students' self-determination and participation in learning as productive and engaged members of the classroom community. When the physical environment is inviting and conducive to learning, it is characterized by bright but not overpowering colors, natural light, comfortable and age-appropriate furniture, and easy accessibility to the tools needed for learning. Our hope is that the English language development (ELD) classrooms in your school are not repurposed closets, a partitioned piece of the hallway, old dressing rooms behind the stage, the classroom situated next to instrumental music, basement rooms that are far removed from other spaces used for learning, or classrooms no one else wants!

How Does It Specifically Relate to ELs'/MLs' Needs?

Schools and classrooms are learning spaces where ELs/MLs not only master the core curriculum or develop language and literacy skills but also spend a considerable part of every day of their lives, build relationships with peers and adults, and spend a considerable amount of time. As suggested by CASEL (2019), it is essential to create an equitable learning environment characterized by the following:

- Equity of voice: All participants are encouraged to speak and are respectfully heard.
- Inclusion: All degrees of participation are welcomed and acknowledged.
- Collectivism: All engage in and contribute to a "for the good of the group" experience. (p. 7)

How to Get Started With Environmental Scaffolding

When you plan to offer environmental scaffolds, be creative, even if you do not have the most ideal space assigned to you in your building, and ensure that your classroom includes

- A welcoming, stress-free or stress-reduced physical classroom set-up
- High expectations maintained for all students
- A multilingual, print-rich environment
- Decorations respectful of cultural and linguistic diversity honoring students' background knowledge and experiences
- Co-constructed anchor charts or agendas that clearly indicate shared classroom norms and expectations
- Multimodal and multisensory, multilingual, multilevel instructional resources
- Areas with formal seating (tables, desks, and chairs) and informal seating (area rugs, bean bag chairs, floor cushions)
- Spaces that are brightly lit, and spaces that offer low lights
- Easy access to tissues, hand sanitizer, and other items to keep safe and healthy
- Designated space where personal belongings can be kept safe

A SNAPSHOT FROM THE FIELD

Valentina Gonzalez, educational consultant and author at Seidlitz Education, shared with us her collaborative experience designing language and literacy rich environments:

Mrs. Gardner is a master third-grade teacher in Texas with vast experience teaching language arts, social studies, math, and science. One year, I had the privilege of coming into her classroom for in-class ESL support. Because her class consisted of newcomer students and many ELs at various English proficiency levels as well as English-proficient students, we worked together to create an environment that leveraged and honored students' assets. Mrs. Gardner and I were intentional about the environment we created.

(Continued)

(Continued)

For us, a language-rich environment was not just about what was on the wall; it was also how students felt and what students did. For example, the math word wall was filled with math words and real objects. Students were also encouraged to bring in objects to place on the wall. When we taught units for science, we used graphic organizers, visuals, and comparison charts that students later referenced as they discussed and wrote about the topics. We exhibited poems, input charts, and graphic organizers, which remained on the wall throughout the units (see Figure 6.19 for an example). During each unit of study, we chanted poems as a class using gestures to practice language structures and fortify vocabulary. We frontloaded vocabulary and built background using colored input charts through whole-group direct teaching. And we helped students organize their learning with graphic organizers like content frames and Venn diagrams. All of these were springboards for peer-to-peer conversations and writing.

Figure 6.19 Creating a Language-Rich Environment

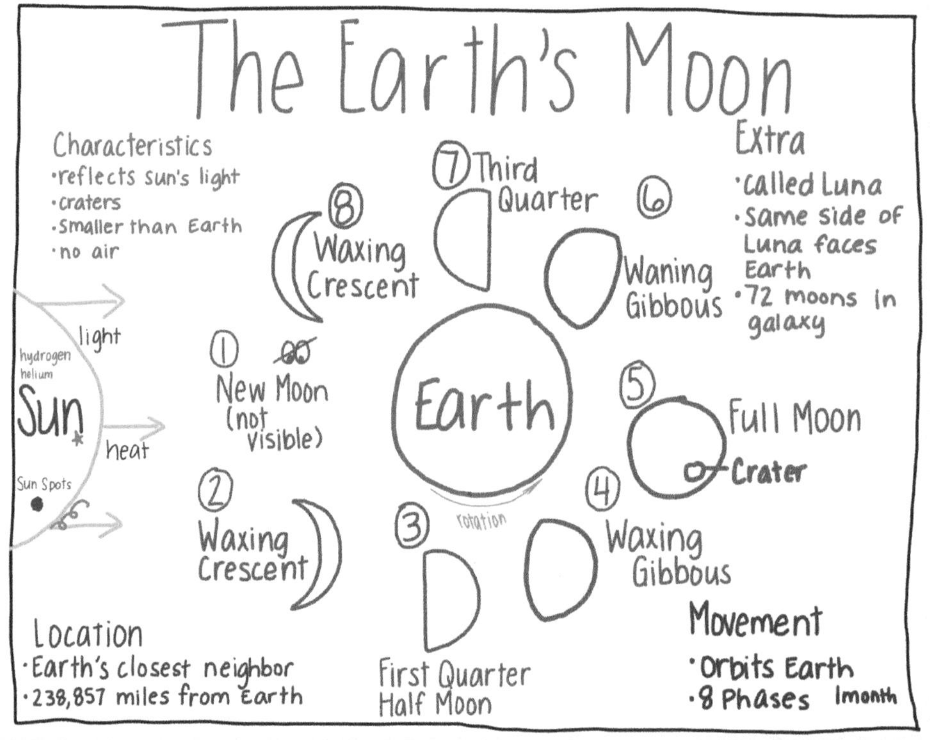

Figure created by Valentina Gonzalez. Used with permission.

Justin Garcia, Grade 1 teacher and ELA team leader, Chiang Mai International School, Thailand, shared with us how they scaffold the fishbowl activity by creating a classroom setup and instructional tools in support of his ELs/MLs (see Figure 6.20).

I decided to implement the fishbowl activity as an exercise to boost the confidence in my students' speaking abilities. I've been intentionally utilizing more strategies that facilitate student output (writing and speaking) as I noticed that their writing and speaking confidence wasn't as strong as their reading and listening. I weaved this

activity through our unit on animals, and at the end of the unit, students were explaining what they discovered about animals' unique features. I was also inspired by my colleague who was focusing on building up students' understanding of peer observations. He showed me the types of checklists he used for peer critiquing, and I decided to adapt one of my own to this speaking activity. I started with simple criteria, so the students would have more of an opportunity to get used to this new skill. In this case, students were listening for complete sentences and responses to their peers' ideas.

I started out this activity with having the students write out their explanations, first on a note card. This way, I could ensure that students were using complete sentences. Plus, it gave them time to think about what they wanted to say. More confident speakers wrote out multiple sentences while students who took more time to piece together their thoughts focused on one. We rehearsed our sentences with partners and then shared them with the larger group.

When it came time for the fishbowl, the class sat in a circle while four to five students sat in chairs in the center. Students in the outer circle marked their checklist as they listened for complete sentences and responses. I didn't expect students to blossom into having full-length conversations, but I wanted to expose them to this type of activity, so we could continue to practice having academic conversations in the future. Some of the discussions surprised me, though! One student shared how "Humboldt squids can shred skin with their tentacles" (look at that awesome Tier 2 word!), and another student responded, "I agree with you because their tentacles have lots of sharp teeth." Success!

Figure 6.20 Setting Up for the Fishbowl Activity

Figure created by Justin Garcia. Used with permission.

Collaborative Planning Using the Nine Dimensions of Scaffolding

The selection and development of appropriate scaffolded approaches for learning for ELs/MLs are a part of general and specific conversations when teams collaboratively plan instruction. In this chapter, we have focused on two aspects of scaffolding—the 4 Rs and the nine dimensions of scaffolding. The 4 Rs of scaffolding concentrate on what we might consider the "big ideas" of supportive instruction for ELs/MLs. They identify how to maintain rigor and relevance in ELD lesson delivery, build relationships with students to bolster their learning, and implement research-informed practices to promote student success. On the other hand, the nine dimensions are organized to further explore the practice of scaffolding by pinpointing and applying various instructional supports for specific purposes. Due to the multiple approaches that scaffolding strategies provide and considering the complex tasks that collaborative planners often must address, we have created another handy checklist incorporating the nine dimensions for scaffolded instruction for ELs/MLs as an additional tool for your toolbox (see Figure 6.21).

Figure 6.21 Checklist for Collaboratively Planning: Nine Dimensions of Scaffolding

SCAFFOLDING DIMENSIONS	WAYS TO MEET THE DIMENSIONS
Instructional	— Questioning techniques: Surface to deep (Bloom's taxonomy) — Modeling — Demonstrating — Guided practice — Chunking information — Mentor texts — Teacher clarity

Linguistic	— Translanguaging
	— Contextualizing key terms
	— Sentence frames and starters
	— Building fluency through collaborative participation—for example,
	    — Fishbowl
	    — Literature circles
	    — Reader's Theatre

Multimodal	— Richly illustrated print-based text — Digital resources—films, video clips, interactive webpages — Incorporating speaking, writing, interacting, reading, and listening (SWIRL) — Graphic representations of concepts — Student choice

SCAFFOLDING DIMENSIONS	WAYS TO MEET THE DIMENSIONS
Multisensory	— Realia (real objects) — Manipulatives — Illustrations — Audio representations — Video representations — Songs, dance, and movement
Graphic	— Outlines — Charts — Maps — Tables — Timelines — Thinking Maps™ — Graphic organizers
Digital	— Multimedia presentations — Digital recordings — Digital storytelling — E-books, blogs, web-based books — Digital whiteboards — Instructional apps
Interactive/ Collaborative	— Whole-group learning — Small-group learning — Paired learning — Reciprocal teaching — Peer tutoring — Jigsaw reading — Project-based learning
Social-emotional	— Community building — Micro-teaching (supporting individual students as needed) — Offering frequent and targeted feedback — Using multiple group configurations to encourage interaction — Daily emotional check-ins — Individual goal setting — Collaboratively establishing norms and expectations
Environmental	— Maintaining high expectations for all students — Multilingual, print-rich classroom — Class displays reflect students' cultural and linguistic diversity — Instructional resources meet students' learning preferences — Areas for learning meet with students' preferences for feeling safe and comfortable

online resources Available for download at **resources.corwin.com/CoPlanningforELs**

Tools of the Trade

GO TO Strategies

Dr. Linda New Levine, Ms. Laura Lukens, and Dr. Betty Ansin Smallwood collaborated on a grant-supported project, the outcome of which is an open-access toolkit consisting of strategies and scaffolding tools arranged by language proficiency level.

https://www.cal.org/what-we-do/projects/project-excell/the-go-to-strategies

Project-Based Learning

https://www.pblworks.org/

Thinking Maps™

Thinking Maps™ (www.thinkingmaps.com) offers a consistent and systematic way of supporting ELs'/MLs' thinking. Each of the eight maps is specific to certain thinking processes, thus the cognitive and metacognitive processes are concisely connected to eight visuals, each with its own protocol. (Thinking Maps ™ is a registered trademark of Thinking Maps, Inc.)

Celebrations

Mary Sue Ragsdale, K–6 EL teacher, and Regan Landers, fifth-grade teacher at Mary E. Castle Elementary School, Indianapolis, Indiana, shared a protocol born out of the conga line interaction from SIOP (Echevarria et al., 2016). Please see Figures 6.22 and 6.23 for an illustration and an explanation of the process for comprehending difficult text.

As co-teachers, we were trying to develop reliable processes for facilitating the skills a student may need as they are tackling and digesting a tough text, while also giving student practice using all four domains (listening, speaking, reading, and writing) to promote language development. Once the students became familiar with the process, transitions became fairly seamless, and we were able to add variations to assist in the rigor of the grade-level text. Students gained comfort and skill because this protocol gave them anticipatable steps. We were able to fashion questions that were anywhere from text-dependent to evaluative, all standards-driven from the onset. All of this work was done during collaborative planning, and it was wonderful to see this process evolve as student thinking grew and developed within each of our mentor/anchor texts that we used.

Figure 6.22 Process Protocol for Tackling Tough Text

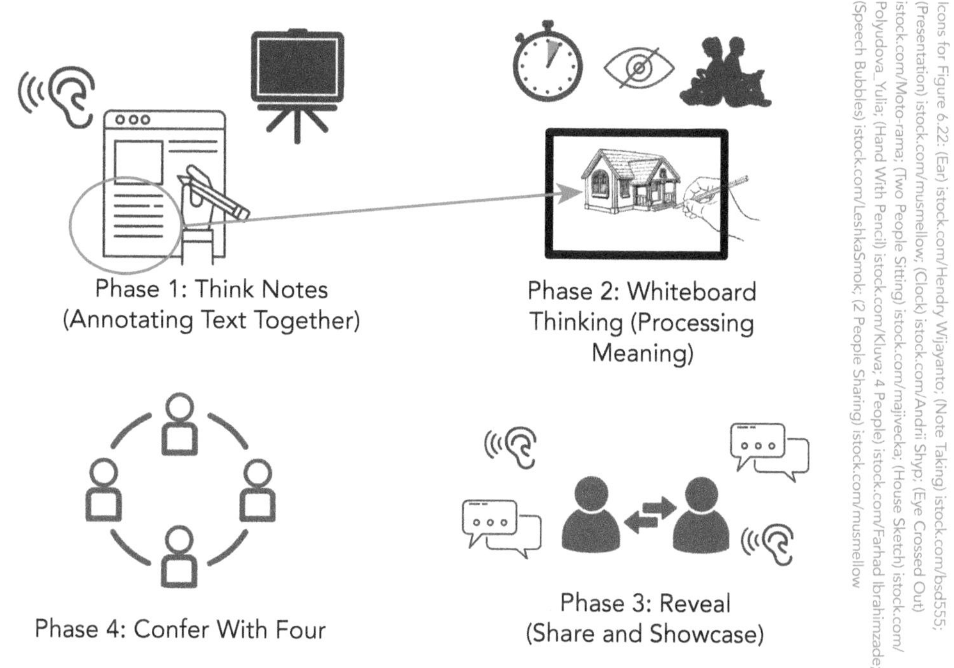

Figure created by Mary Sue Ragsdale and Regan Landers. Used with permission.

Figure 6.23 Process Explanation: Tackling Tough Text

PHASE	DESCRIPTION	PURPOSE
Think Notes *Whole-group instruction: Place students next to others (back-to-back on the carpet) for purposeful talk to negotiate meaning. Students bring text, whiteboard, & writing utensils*	For challenging grade-level texts, chunk the text into paragraphs or sections. Consider the levels of ELs or language demand of the text in order to preteach/preread with students prior to the following: 1. Read through section of text aloud; students listen for gist with writing utensils down. 2. Display text and reread the same section, this time stopping to rephrase ideas or explain new language. Annotate text with synonyms, short definitions, pictures, or icons to aide comprehension. Students annotate their text along with the teacher.	The purpose of doing "think notes" or annotating the text is to track thinking and build comprehension of grade-level ideas and language within texts.

(Continued)

(Continued)

PHASE	DESCRIPTION	PURPOSE
	*Stretch & Climb As the year progresses, students read each section with a partner and anticipate what ideas need to be talked about based on the standards and learning targets and the language they need to understand or clarify; they can ask for comprehension help with partners, other teams, or the teacher.	
Whiteboard Illustrations *Students remain back-to-back with each other, illustrating the section read for 3–5 minutes.*	Students need a whiteboard and marker. Read text aloud one more time. Students choose to illustrate something from that section of the text, for example, new vocabulary, text organization—problem/solution, cause/effect, and so on. Students use stick figures, icons, and speech bubbles to illustrate characters' thoughts/or feelings. *Stretch & Climb Specify which vocabulary terms/phrases or ideas students should illustrate; think notes are not as powerful unless the text is previewed and the important ideas students needed selected to solidify understanding. Drawing the concepts and ideas or illustrating new vocabulary often brings students freedom and comfort.	We wanted to give students the chance to create comprehensible output first without pressure. Their pictures become a source and tool for more refined language production later.
Sharing & Showcasing *(Balance of partnering—peer language models, L1 partners, friends, random, girl/boy, etc.)* **OR** *Flipgrid & Feedback on each other's videos*	This is the "reveal" part of the protocol. Model first how to "share" an idea for the section read, specifically model the language needed and proactive/purposeful listening. This works best with two teachers (co-teaching). Students face the person they are sitting back-to-back with, and one shares what was illustrated, showcasing their work while the other listens. Then they reverse roles. Scaffold sharing with sentence frames: "My illustration is a _______, which I drew to represent _______ from the text. (They would cite the source.) This detail from the text helps me to understand _______. This detail helps to support the idea that _______." Take anecdotal notes of the language students used while sharing.	After all students developed a "visual tool" on their whiteboards, they get a chance to share their illustrations. Stop and model academic language that students should emulate. Track their progress as they rehearse and share with each other. Give them feedback about their spoken language. This activity helps students to build critical listening skills. At times, pause the process before letting the other partner share; have the listening partner share what the speaking partner just offered. 

PHASE	DESCRIPTION	PURPOSE
	*A great variation** to this was to have students create a **Flipgrid** instead of face-to-face sharing. In this way, students can practice, record, re-record, decorate, or glam up their video before production and get feedback from their peers. ***Stretch & Climb** As the year progresses, increase the rigor of what to model and what to expect students to share verbally with each other.	
Repeat the Process & Write • *Think Notes* • *Whiteboard Illustrations* • *Sharing and Showcasing* • *Write, Write, Write*	Repeat the process of chunking and digesting the text piece by piece, sometimes over a span of a few days. Encourage students to retrieve information and contribute to growing conceptual ideas throughout the unit of study. Have them practice writing about what they read, whether it is responding to a specific question, a personal application, or analysis and evaluation of the text.	Repeat the process for each section of the text. Sometimes, select only part of the text for this process, depending on its length.
Confer With Four	Depending on the difficulty of the skills, standard concepts, or language and the amount of practice ELs need, tag on this final step after the entire text has been read. Center this task on rigorous essential questions about the text. Pose an essential question, have students review and scour the text for whatever evidence or ideas they need, and then illustrate those concepts on their whiteboards. Have two partners (back-to-back) confer with another set of partners (preferably another pair next to them), to reveal whiteboard thinking to three partners instead of just one. Numbering or identifying students by letter (A, B, C, or D) is another way of grouping students for sharing. For example, all of the As in each group share their thoughts, then the Bs, and so on. An additional question might be devised for Cs and Ds to answer so there are fewer repetitive responses.	Avoid giving EL students too much teacher support when the rigor increases. Instead, increase their support for each other. Increase the group size from two to four so that more perspectives are shared, clarified, and rehearsed before a whole-group conversation is held. Purposefully group students based on what strengths each student has.

Figure created by Mary Sue Ragsdale and Regan Landers. Used with permission.

Icons for Figure 6.23: (Ear) istock.com/Hendry Wijayanto; (Note Taking) istock.com/bsd555; (Presentation) istock.com/musmellow; (Clock) istock.com/Andrii Shyp; (Eye Crossed Out) istock.com/Moto-rama; (Two People Sitting) istock.com/majivecka; (House Sketch) istock.com/Polyudova_Yulia; (Hand With Pencil) istock.com/Kluva; (4 People) istock.com/Farhad Ibrahimzade; (Speech Bubbles) istock.com/LeshkaSmok; (2 People Sharing) istock.com/musmellow

COLLABORATIVE REFLECTION QUESTIONS

1. The 4 Rs offer four critical rationales for scaffolding instruction for ELs/MLs. Which of them seem most aligned to your current practice, and which might you want to focus on studying or go about implementing?
2. Macro-, meso-, and micro-scaffolding were introduced and illustrated at the beginning of the chapter. How do you make sure that scaffolding on all three levels helps ELs/MLs engage in and demonstrate learning similar to their English-proficient peers?
3. On the (many) pages of this chapter, we have redefined scaffolding around the 4 Rs of rigor, relevance, relationships, and research-informed best practices. Next, we unpacked nine scaffolding approaches. What does scaffolding mean to you now that we have examined it in depth? How will it impact your instructional practice?
4. Which of the nine scaffolding approaches would you consider low-prep and which one(s) hi-prep?
5. Scaffolding instruction supports students to become independent learners. What are some qualities independent learners exhibit? Why might it also be important to foster interdependent learners who are able to work collaboratively?

Watch Andrea and Maria discussing some highlights of Chapter 6. What would you add to their argument in favor of scaffolding? In what ways did they affirm or challenge your thinking about this topic?

COLLABORATIVE ACTION STEPS

Consider pathways to enhance your instruction for ELs/MLs by collaboratively planning for scaffolding.

1. Assess you and your collaborating teachers' familiarity with the 4 Rs of scaffolding.
2. Determine which of the 4 Rs you are going prioritize as a next step regarding enhancing your collaborative planning.
3. Consider the remaining Rs and develop a short-term and long-term plan for systemic, purposeful implementation of each.
4. Review the nine scaffolding dimensions. Choose one that you think is most important to incorporate when planning for your students. Identify three specific instructional strategies you can incorporate into your instructional routines that address your chosen dimension.
5. Draft an implementation plan that will prioritize the scaffolding techniques and align them with your curriculum and instruction. Use one of the chapter's checklists (Figure 6.3 or 6.21) as a guide for planning.

References

Aguilar, E. (2013). *The art of coaching: Effective strategies for school transformation*. Wiley.

Alber, R. (2017). *3 ways student data can inform your teaching.* https://www.edutopia.org/blog/using-student-data-inform-teaching-rebecca-alber

Akhavan, N. (2009). *Teaching writing in a Title I school, K–3.* Heinemann.

Almarode, J. T., & Vandas, K. (2018). *Clarity for learning: Five essential practices that empower students and teachers.* Corwin Press.

Anderson, J., & La Rocca, W. (2017). *Patterns of power: Inviting young writers into the conventions of language, grades 1–5.* Stenhouse.

Applebee, A. N., Langer, J. A., Nystrand. M., & Gamoran, A. (2003). Student performance in middle and high school English discussion-based approaches to developing understanding: Classroom instruction and student performance in middle and high school English. *American Educational Research Journal, 40,* 685–730.

August, D. (2018). Educating English language learners: A review of the latest research. *American Educator, 42*(3). https://www.aft.org/ae/fall2018/august

August, D., & Shanahan, T. (Eds.). (2006). *Developing literacy in second-language learners: Report of the National Literacy Panel on Language-Minority Children and Youth.* Erlbaum.

Avila, K. (2015). The call to collaborate: Key considerations as ELDs and classroom teachers begin to align new standards. *ORTESOL Journal, 32,* 33–43.

Ayer, L. (2018). *4 things all project-based learning teachers should do.* https://www.teachthought.com/education/4-things-project-based-learning-teachers/

Bacon, C. K. (2017). Multilanguage, multipurpose: A literature review, synthesis, and framework for critical literacies in English language teaching. *Journal of Literacy Research, 49*(3), 424–453. https://doi.org/10.1177/1086296X17718324

Baker, S., Lesaux, N., Jayanthi, M., Dimino, J., Proctor, C. P., Morris, J., Gersten, R., Haymond, K., Kieffer, M. J., Linan-Thompson, S., & Newman-Gonchar, R. (2014). *Teaching academic content and literacy to English learners in elementary and middle school* (NCEE 2014-4012). http://ies.ed.gov/ncee/wwc/publications_reviews.aspx.

Bambrick-Santoyo, P. (2019). *Driven by data 2.0: A practical guide to improve instruction.* Jossey-Bass.

Banse, H. W., Palicios, N. A., & Martin, A. (2019). How do effective upper elementary teachers of English language learners show support? *Teachers College Record, 121*(7), 1–42. https://www.tcrecord.org/content.asp?contentid=22688

Beck, I. L., McKeown, M. G., & Kucan, L. (2002). *Bringing words to life: Robust vocabulary instruction.* Guilford.

Beck I. L., McKeown, M. G., & Kucan, L. (2008). *Creating robust vocabulary: Frequently asked questions and extended examples.* Guilford.

Beninghof, A. M. (2020). *Co-teaching that works: Structures and strategies for maximizing student learning* (2nd ed.). Jossey-Bass.

Bialystok, E., & Ryan, E. B. (1985). A metacognitive framework for the development of first and second language skills. In D. L. Forrest-Pressley, G. E. MacKinnon, & T. G. Waller (Eds.), *Metacognition, cognition and human performance* (Vol. 1, pp. 207–252). Academic.

Blachowicz, C., Fisher, P., Ogle, D., & Watts-Taffe, S. (2006). Vocabulary: Questions from the classroom. *Reading Research Quarterly, 41,* 524–539.

Boushey, G., & Moser, J. (2014). *The daily five: Fostering literacy in the elementary grades* (2nd ed.). Stenhouse.

Boutle, I., Joshi, M., Mayne, N., et al. (2020). How can dust make planets more suitable for life? *Physical Science Journal for Teens.* https://sciencejournalforkids.org/wp-content/uploads/2020/07/dust_article.pdf

Brisk, M. E. (2015). *Engaging students and academic literacies: Genre-based pedagogy in K–5 classrooms.* Routledge.

Bruner, J. (1983). *Child's talk.* Norton.

Bruner, J. S. (1960/2009). *The process of education.* Harvard University Press.

Bunch, G. C. (2013). Pedagogical language knowledge: Preparing mainstream teachers for English learners in the new standards era. *Review of Research in Education, 37*(1), 298–341. https://doi.org/10.3102/0091732X12461772

Bunch, G. C., & Walqui, A. (2019). Educating English learners in the 21st century. In A. Walqui & G. C. Bunch (Eds.), *Amplifying the curriculum: Designing quality learning opportunities for English learners* (pp. 21–41). Teachers College Press.

Bunch, G. C., Walqui, A., & Kibler, A. (2015). Attending to language, engaging in practice: Scaffolding English language learners' apprenticeship into the Common Core English Language Arts Standards. In L. C. de Oliveira, M. Klassen, & M. Maune (Eds.), *The Common Core State Standards in English Language Arts for English language learners, Grades 6–12* (pp. 5–23). TESOL.

Calderón, M. (2016). A whole-school approach to English learners. *Educational Leadership, 73*(5). http://www1.ascd.org/publications/educational_leadership/feb16/vol73/num05/A_Whole-School_Approach_to_English_Learners.aspx

Calderón, M. E., Dove, M. G., Staehr Fenner, D., Gottlieb, M., Honigsfeld, A., Ward Singer, T., Slakk, S., Soto, I., & Zacarian, D. (2019). *Breaking down the wall: Essential shifts for English learners' success.* Corwin Press.

Carr, J., Sexton, U., & Lagunoff, R. (2006). *Making science accessible to English learners.* WestEd.

CASEL. (2019). *SEL 3 signature practices playbook: A tool that supports systemic social and emotional learning.* https://schoolguide.casel.org/uploads/2018/12/CASEL_SEL-3-Signature-Practices-Playbook-V3.pdf

CASEL. (2020). *The CASEL guide to schoolwide SEL essentials.* https://schoolguide.casel.org/uploads/sites/2/2019/09/2020.10.22_School-Guide-Essentials.pdf

CAST. (2018). *Universal design for learning guidelines version 2.2.* http://udlguidelines.cast.org

Chappuis, J. (2015). *Seven strategies of assessment for learning* (2nd ed.). Pearson Education.

Chval, K. B., Smith, E., Trigos-Carrillo, E., & Pinnow, R. J. (2021). *Teaching math to multilingual students: Positioning English Learners for success.* NCTM.

Coe, R., Rauch, C. J., Kime, S., & Singleton, D. (2020). *Great teaching toolkit: Evidence review.* https://www.cambridgeinternational.org/Images/584543-great-teaching-toolkit-evidence-review.pdf

Cohan, A., Honigsfeld, A., & Dove, M. G. (2020). *Team up, speak up, fire up! Teamwork to empower English learners.* ASCD.

Compton, T. N. (2018). *Access to culturally responsive teaching for English language learners: Mainstream teacher perceptions and practice on inclusion.* Electronic Theses and Dissertations. Paper 2949. https://doi.org/10.18297/etd/2949

Council of the Great City Schools. (2014). *A framework for raising expectations and instructional rigor for ELLs.* https://www.cgcs.org/cms/lib/DC00001581/Centricity/Domain/4/Framework%20for%20Raising%20Expectations.pdf

Council of the Great City Schools. (2017). *Re-envisioning English Language Arts and English language development for English language learners.* https://www.cgcs.org/cms/lib/DC00001581/Centricity/domain/4/darrell/CGCS_ReinvisEngLang_pub_Rev_final.pdf

Cox, T. L., Malone, M. E., & Winke, P. (2018). Future directions in assessment: Influences of standards and implications for language learning. *Foreign Language Annals, 51*(1), 104–115.

Cullen, R., Kullman, J., & Wild, C. (2013). Online collaborative learning on an ESL teacher education programme. *ELT Journal, 67*(4), 425–434.

Danielson, C. (2007). *Enhancing professional practice: A framework for teaching* (2nd ed.). ASCD.

Davison, C. (2006). Collaboration between ESL and content area teachers: How do we know when we are doing it right? *The International Journal of Bilingual Education and Bilingualism, 9*(4), 454–475.

de Oliveira, L. C. (2016). A language-based approach to content instruction (LACI) for English language learners: Examples from two elementary teachers. *International Multilingual Research Journal, 10*(3), 217–231. doi.org/10.1080/19313152.2016.1185911

de Oliveira, L. C. (2019). Key concepts and issue in TESOL in K–12. In L. C. de Oliveira (Ed.), *The handbook of TESOL in K–12* (pp. 1–7). Wiley.

de Oliveira, L. C., & Smith, S. L. (2019). Interactions with and around texts: Writing in elementary schools. In N. Caplan & A. Johns (Eds.), *Changing practices for the L2 writing classroom: Moving beyond the five-paragraph essay* (pp. 65–88). University of Michigan Press.

DESE. (2019). *Collaboration tool.* http://www.doe.mass.edu/ell/curriculum.html

Dodge, J., & Honigsfeld, A. (2014). *Core instructional routines: Go-to structures for effective literacy teaching, K–5.* Heinemann.

Donohoo, J. (2017). *Collective efficacy: How educators' beliefs impact student learning.* Corwin Press.

Donohoo, J., Hattie, J., & Eells, R. (2018). The power of collective efficacy. *Educational Leadership, 75*(6), 40–44.

Dove, M. G., & Honigsfeld, A. (2014). Analysis of the implementation of an ESL co-teaching model in a suburban elementary school. *NYS TESOL Journal, 1*(1), 62–67. http://journal.nystesol.org/jan2014/60dove.pdf

Dove, M. G., & Honigsfeld, A. (2018). *Co-teaching for English learners: A guide to collaborative planning, instruction, assessment, and reflection.* Corwin Press.

Dove, M. G., & Honigsfeld, A. (2020a). Is there magic in co-teaching? In M. G. Dove & A. Honigsfeld (Eds.), *Co-teaching for English learners: Evidence-based practices and research-informed outcomes.* Information Age Publishing.

Dove, M. G., & Honigsfeld, A. (Eds.). (2020b). *Co-teaching for English learners: Evidence-based practices and research-informed outcomes.* Information Age Publishing.

Dove, M. G., Honigsfeld, A., & Cohan, A. (2014). *Beyond core expectations: A schoolwide framework for serving the not-so-common learner.* Corwin Press.

Drake, S. M., & Burns, R. C. (2004). *Meeting standards through integrated curriculum.* ASCD.

DuFour, R., & Eaker, R. (1998). *Professional learning communities at work: Best practices for enhancing student achievement.* Solution Tree.

Duke, N., Caughlan, S., Juzwik, M., & Martin, N. (2011). *Reading and writing genre with purpose in K–8.* Heinemann.

Dutro, S., & Kinsella, K. (2010). English language development: Issues and implementation at grades six through twelve. In *Improving education for English learners: Research-based approaches* (pp. 151–207). California Department of Education.

Echevarria, J., Vogt, M., & Short, D. J. (2003). *Making content comprehensible for English learners: The SIOP model* (2nd ed.). Pearson.

Echevarria, J., Vogt, M., & Short, D. (2010). *Making content comprehensible for elementary English Learners: The SIOP model.* Pearson.

Echevarria, J., Vogt, M., & Short, D. J. (2012). *Making content comprehensible for English learners: The SIOP model* (4th ed.). Pearson.

Echevarria, J., Vogt, M. E., & Short, D. (2016). *Making content comprehensible for English learners: The SIOP model* (5th ed.). Pearson.

Eisner, E. W. (2017a). Educational objectives—Help or hindrance? In D. J. Flinders and S. J. Thorton (Eds.), *The curriculum studies reader* (5th ed., pp. 129–136). Routledge.

Eisner, E. W. (2017b). What does it mean to say a school is doing well? In D. J. Flinders and S. J. Thorton (Eds.), *The curriculum studies reader* (5th ed., pp. 313–322). Routledge.

EL Education. (n.d.). *Language dives.* https://curriculum.eleducation.org/sites/default/files/curriculumtools_languagedives_072017.pdf

Ergas, O. (2017). *Reconstructing 'education' through mindful attention: Positioning the mind at the center of curriculum and pedagogy.* Palgrave/MacMillan.

Ernst-Slavit, G., & Egbert, J. (2006). *Planning meaningful instruction for ELLs: Integrating academic language and content in K-12 classrooms.* https://opentext.wsu.edu/planning-meaningful-instruction-for-ells/

Fang, Z. (2012). Language correlates of disciplinary literacy. *Topics in Language Disorders, 32*(1), 19–34. doi:10.1097/TLD.0b013e3182 4501de

Fang, Z., & Robertson, D. A. (2020). Unpacking and operationalizing disciplinary literacy: A review of *Disciplinary Literacy Inquiry and Instruction. Journal of Adolescent and Adult Literacy, 64*(2), 240–242. https://doi.org/10.1002/jaal.1070

Fearn, L., & Farrnan, N. (2001). *Interactions: Teaching writing and the language arts.* Houghton Mifflin.

Fendick, F. (1990). *The correlation between teacher clarity of communication and student achievement gain: A meta-analysis.* Unpublished doctoral dissertation. https://ufdc.ufl.edu/AA00032787/00001

Fillmore, L. W. (2009). *English language development: Acquiring the language needed for literacy and learning.* http://assets.pearsonschool.com/asset_mgr/current/201010/English%20Language%20Development.pdf

Fisher, D., & Frey, N. (2014). *Better learning through structured teaching: A framework for the gradual release of responsibility* (2nd ed.). ASCD.

Fisher, D., Frey, N., & Akhavan, N. (2020). *This is balanced literacy, Grades K–6.* Corwin Press.

Fisher, D., Frey, N., Amador, O., & Assof, J. (2019). *The teacher clarity playbook: A hands-on guide to creating learning intentions and success criteria for organized, effective instruction.* Corwin Press.

Fisher, D., Frey, N., Hattie, J., & Thayre, M. (2017). *Teaching literacy in the visible learning classroom: 6–12 classroom companion.* Corwin Press.

Fisher, D., Frey, N., & Lapp, D. (2016). *Text complexity: Stretching readers with texts and tasks* (2nd ed.). Corwin Press.

Fisher, D., Frey, N., & Uline, C. (2013). *Common Core English Language Arts in a PLC at work.* Solution Tree.

Flores, E., & Cordeiro, K. (2020). *Using a co-planning template to design instruction.* [Video] YouTube. https://www.youtube.com/watch?v=Ir6z8OQbETk

Foltos, L. (2018). *Teachers learn better together.* http://www.edutopia.org/article/teachers-learn-better-together

Friend, M., & Cook, L. (2012). *Interactions: Collaboration skills for school professionals* (7th ed.). Allyn & Bacon.

Froehle, J. (2017). *What the standards-based movement got wrong: We can modernize academic standards with three simple questions.* https://www.edweek.org/ew/articles/2017/11/29/what-the-standards-based-movement-got-wrong.html

Fullan, M. (2016). *The new meaning of education change* (5th ed.). Teachers College Press.

Fullan, M., & Hargreaves, A. (2016). *Bringing the profession back in: Call to action.* Learning Forward.

Fullan, M., & Quinn, J. (2016). *Coherence: The right drivers in action for schools, districts, and systems.* Corwin Press.

Gallagher, K. (2011). *Write like this: Teaching real world writing through modeling & mentor texts.* Stenhouse.

García, O., & Kleifgen, J. A. (2018). *Educating emergent bilinguals: Policies, programs, and practices for English language learners.* Teachers College Press.

García, O., & Wei, L. (2014). *Translanguaging: Language, bilingualism, and education.* Palgrave Macmillan.

Genesee, F., & Lindholm-Leary, K. (2013). Two case studies of content-based language education. *Journal of Immersion and Content-Based Language Education, 1,* 3–33. doi:10.1075/jicb.1.1.02gen

Genesee, F., Lindholm-Leary, K., Saunders, W., &. Christian, D. (2006). *Educating English language learners.* Cambridge University Press.

Gibbons, P. (2015). *Scaffolding language scaffolding learning: Teaching English language learners in the mainstream classroom.* Heinemann.

Glatthorn, A. A., Boschee, F., Whitehead, B. M., & Boschee, B. F. (2019). *Curriculum leadership: Strategies for development and implementation.* Sage.

Goleman, D., & Senge, P. (2014). *The triple focus: A new approach to education.* More Than Sound.

Goodwin, B. (2018). *Student learning that works: How brain science informs a student learning model.* McREL International.

Gorski, P. C. (2020). *Understanding multicultural transformation.* http://www.edchange.org/multicultural/curriculum/concept.html

Goss, M., Castek, J., & Manderino, M. (2016). Disciplinary and digital literacies: Three synergies. *Journal of Adolescent & Adult Literacy, 60*(3), 335–340. https://doi.org/10.1002/jaal.598

Gottlieb, M. (2021). *Classroom assessment in multiple languages: A handbook for teachers.* Corwin Press.

Gottlieb, M., & Ernst-Slavit, G. (2014). *Academic language in diverse classrooms: Definitions and contexts.* Corwin Press.

Gottlieb, M., & Honigsfeld, A. (2020). From assessment of learning to assessment for and as learning. In *Breaking down the wall: Nine essential shifts for EL achievement.* Corwin Press.

Grapin, S. (2019). Multimodality in the new content standards era: Implications for English learners. *TESOL Quarterly, 53*(1), 30-55.

Greenberg Motamedi, J., Vazquez, M., Gandhi, E., & Holmgren, M. (2019). *English language development minutes, models, and outcomes: Beaverton School District.* https://educationnorthwest.org/resources/english-language-development-minutes-models-and-outcomes-beaverton-school-district

Greene, M. (2017). Curriculum and consciousness. In D. J. Flinders, & S. J. Thorton (Eds.), *The curriculum studies reader* (5th ed., pp. 147–160). Routledge.

Hammond, J., Cranitch, M., & Black, S. (2018). *Classrooms of possibility: Working with students from refugee backgrounds in mainstream classes.* NSW Government. https://app.education.nsw.gov.au/serap/ResearchRecord/Summary?id=46

Hargreaves, A., & Fullan, M. (2012). *Professional capital: Transforming teaching in every school.* Teachers College Press.

Harris, P., Harris, J., & Smith, B. M. (2012). Standardized tests do not effectively measure student achievement. In D. Bryfonski (Ed.), *Standardized testing* (2nd ed., pp. 33–45). Greenhaven Press.

Harvard GSE. (2020). *Wise about data.* https://www.gse.harvard.edu/hgse100/story/wise-about-data

Hattie, J. (2009). *Visible learning: A synthesis of over 800 meta-analyses relating to achievement.* Routledge.

Hattie, J. (2012). *Visible learning for teachers: Maximizing impact on learning.* Routledge.

Hattie, J. (2015). *What works best in education: The politics of collaborative expertise.* https://www.pearson.com/content/dam/corporate/global/pearson-dot-com/files/hattie/150526_ExpertiseWEB_V1.pdf

Hattie, J. (2018). *Collective teacher efficacy (CTE).* https://visible-learning.org/2018/03/collective-teacher-efficacy-hattie

Heineke, A. J., & McTighe, J. (2018). *Using Understanding by Design in the culturally and linguistically diverse classroom.* ASCD.

Heritage, M., & Wylie, C. E. (2020). *Formative assessment in the disciplines: Framing a continuum of professional learning.* Harvard Education Press.

Holder, C., Bell, J., & Toppel, K. (2019). *Using The SIOP® Model to support successful co-planning.* https://blog.savvas.com/using-the-siop-model-to-support-successful-co-planning/

Honigsfeld, A., & Dodge, J. (2015). *Core instructional routines: Go-to structures for 6–12 classrooms.* Heinemann.

Honigsfeld, A., & Dove, M. (2017). The coteaching flow inside the classroom. In M. Dantas-Whitney, & S. Rilling (Eds.), *TESOL voices: Secondary education* (pp. 107–114). TESOL.

Honigsfeld, A., & Dove, M. G. (2010). *Collaboration and co-teaching: Strategies for English learners.* Corwin Press.

Honigsfeld, A., & Dove, M. G. (Eds.). (2012). *Coteaching and other collaborative practices in the EFL/ESL classroom: Rationale, research, reflections, and recommendations.* Information Age Publishing.

Honigsfeld, A., & Dove, M. G. (2013). *Common core for the not-so-common learner, Grades 6–12: English language arts strategies.* Corwin Press.

Honigsfeld, A., & Dove, M. G. (2015). *Collaboration and co-teaching for English learners: A leader's guide.* Corwin Press.

Honigsfeld, A., & Dove, M. G. (2019). *Collaborating for English learners: A foundational guide to integrated practices.* Corwin Press.

Honigsfeld, A., McDermott, C., & Cordeiro, K. (2018). Preparing social studies and ESOL teachers for integrated language and content instruction in support of ELLs. In L. de Oliveira & K. Obenchain (Eds.), *Teaching history and social studies to English language learners: Preparing pre-service and in-service teachers* (pp. 127–158). Palgrave Macmillan.

Hopkins, M., Gluckman, M., & Vahdani, T. (2019). Emergent change: A network analysis of elementary teachers' learning about English learner instruction. *American Educational Research Journal, 56*(6), 2295–2332. https://doi.org/10.3102/0002831219840352

Illinois Priority Learning Standards. (2020). https://www.isbe.net/Documents/Illinois-Priority-Learning-Standards-2020-21.pdf#page=6

Jung, L. A., Frey, N., Fisher, D., & Kroener, J. (2019). *Your students my students our students: Rethinking equitable and inclusive classrooms.* ASCD.

Kagan, S., Kagan, M., & Kagan, L. (2016). *59 Kagan structures: Proven engagement strategies.* Kagan Publishing.

Kaufman, J. H., Steiner, E. D., & Baird, M. D. (2019). *Raising the bar for K–12 academics: Early signals on how Louisiana's education policy strategies are working for schools, teachers, and students.* https://www.rand.org/pubs/research_reports/RR2303z2.html

Kersaint, G., Thompson, D. R., & Petkova, M. (2009). *Teaching mathematics to English language learners.* Routledge.

Khan, L. (2015). *The black hole of technology.* https://www.huffpost.com/entry/the-black-hole_1_b_6253550

Kibler, A., Valdés, G., & Walqui, A. (2014). What does standards-based educational reform mean for English language learner populations in primary and secondary schools? *TESOL Quarterly, 48*(3), 433–453.

Knight, J. (2012). *High impact instruction.* Corwin Press.

Knips, A. (2019). *6 steps to equitable data analysis.* https://www.edutopia.org/article/6-steps-equitable-data-analysis

Kolko, J. (2020). *Design is a mess.* https://modernststudio.com/corporate-education/design-is-a-mess

Kuusisaari, H. (2014). Teachers at the zone of proximal development – Collaboration promoting or hindering the development process. *Teaching and Teacher Education, 43*, 46–57.

Leana, C. (2011, Fall). The missing link in school reform. *Stanford Social Innovation Review.*

https://ssir.org/articles/entry/the_missing_link_in_school_reform

Learned, J. E. (2018). Doing history: A study of disciplinary literacy and readers labeled as struggling. *Journal of Literacy Research, 50*(2), 190–216. https://doi.org/10.1177/1086296X17746446

Lee, C. D., & Spratley, A. (2010). *Reading in the disciplines: The challenges of adolescent literacy.* Carnegie Foundation.

Lee, O. (2019). Aligning English language proficiency standards with content standards: Shared opportunity and responsibility across English learner education and content areas. *Educational Researcher, 48*(8), 534–542.

Lesaux, N. K. & Harris, J. (2015). *Cultivating knowledge, building language: Literacy instruction for English learners in elementary schools.* Heinemann Publishing.

Lesaux, N. K., Kieffer, M. J., Kelley, J. G., & Harris, J. R. (2014). Effects of academic vocabulary instruction for linguistically diverse adolescents: Evidence from a randomized field trial. *American Educational Research Journal, 51*(6), 1159–1194.

Levine, L. N., Lukens, L., & Smallwood, B. A. (2013). *The GO TO strategies: Scaffolding options for teachers of English language learners, K-12.* https://www.cal.org/what-we-do/projects/project-excell/the-go-to-strategies

Linton, C. (2011). *Equity 101: The equity framework.* Corwin Press.

Martin-Beltrán, M., & Madigan Peercy, M. (2012). How can ESOL and mainstream teachers make the best of standards-based curriculum in order to collaborate? *TESOL Journal, 3*(3), 425–444. https://doi.org/10.1002/tesj.23

Martin-Beltrán, M., & Madigan Peercy, M. (2014). Collaboration to teach English language learners: Opportunities for shared teacher learning. *Teachers and Teaching, 20*(6), 721–737. https://doi.org/10.1080/13540602.2014.885704

Menken, K. (2008). *English learners left behind: Standardized testing as language policy.* Multilingual Matters.

Meyer, D. K., & Turner, J. C. (2007). Scaffolding emotions in classrooms. In P. A. Schutz & R. Pekrun (Eds.), *Emotion in education* (pp. 243–258). Elsevier.

Miranda, L. (2015). *Hamilton: An American musical* [MP3]. New York: Atlantic Records.

Moje, E. B. (2015). Doing and teaching disciplinary literacy with adolescent learners: A social and cultural enterprise. *Harvard Educational Review, 85*(2), 254–278. https://doi.org/10.17763/0017-8055.85.2.254

Morcom, V. (2015). Scaffolding social and emotional learning within 'shared affective spaces' to reduce bullying: A sociocultural perspective. *Learning, Culture and Social Interaction, 6,* 77–86. https://doi.org/10.1016/j.lcsi.2015.04.002

Morrison, J. H., Ardasheva, Y., Newcomer, S., Lightner, L., Ernst-Slavit, G., & Carbonneau, K. (2020). Supporting science learning for English language learners. *Journal of Educational Research & Practice, 10*(1), 254–274.

Motley, N. (2016). *Talk, read, talk, write.* Seidlitz.

Murawski, W. W. (2009). *Collaborative teaching in secondary schools: Making the co-teaching marriage work!* Corwin Press.

Murawski, W. W. (2010). *Collaborative teaching in elementary schools: Making the co-teaching marriage work!* Corwin Press.

Murawski, W. W., & Lochner, W. W. (2017). *Beyond co-teaching basics: A data-driven, no-fail model for continuous improvement.* ASCD.

Murphy, A. F., & Torff, B. (2019). Teachers' beliefs about rigor of curriculum for English language learners. *The Educational Forum, 83*(1), 90–101.

National Academies of Sciences, Engineering, and Medicine. (2017). *Promoting the educational success of children and youth learning English: Promising futures.* The National Academies Press. https://doi.org/10.17226/24677

The New York State Education Department. (2019). *Culturally sustaining-responsive framework.* http://www.nysed.gov/bilingual-ed/culturally-responsive-sustaining-education-framework

Noddings, N., & Brooks, L. (2017). *Teaching controversial issues: The case for critical thinking and moral commitment in the classroom.* Teachers College Press.

Norton, J. (2016). Successful coteaching: ESL teachers in the mainstream classroom. *TESOL Connections.* http://newsmanager.commpartners.com/tesolc/issues/2016-10-01/3.html

Novak, K. (2014). *UDL now! A teacher's Monday-morning guide to implementing Common Core Standards using Universal Design for Learning.* CAST Professional Publishing.

NYSED. (2018). *Program options for English language learners/multilingual learners.* http://www.nysed.gov/bilingual-ed/program-options-english-language-learnersmultilingual-learners

NYU Steinhardt. (2018). *An asset-based approach to education: What it is and why it matters.* https://teachereducation.steinhardt.nyu.edu/an-asset-based-approach-to-education-what-it-is-and-why-it-matters/

Oczkus, L. D. (2007). *Guided writing: Practical lessons, powerful results.* Heinemann.

O'Hara, S., Pritchard, R. (2016). Framing teaching for Common Core literacy standards: SOAR teaching frames for literacy. *Psychology Research, 6*(2), 92–101.

Oliveira, A. W., Weinburgh, M., McBride, E., Bobowski, T., & Shea, R. (2019). Teaching science to English language learners: Current research and practices in the field of science education. In L. C. de Oliveira (Ed). (2019). *The handbook of TESOL in K–12* (pp. 277–290). Wiley.

Ottow, S. B. (2019). *The language lens for content classrooms: A guide for K–12 teachers of English and academic language learners.* LSI.

Pacheco, M. B., Daniel, S. M., Pray, L. C., & Jiménez, R. T. (2019). Translingual practice, strategic participation, and meaning-making. *Journal of Literacy Research, 51*(1), 75–99. https://doi.org/10.1177/1086296X18820642

Parker, W. C. (2015). Social studies education eC21. In W. C. Parker (Ed.), *Social studies today: Research and practice* (pp. 1–13). Routledge.

Parris, H., Estrada, L., & Honigsfeld, A. (2016). *ESL frontiers: Using technology to enhance instruction for English learners.* Corwin.

Pawan, F. & Ortloff, J. (2011). Sustaining collaboration: ESL and content area teachers. *Teaching and Teacher Education, 27*, 463–471.

Pawan, F., & Sietmann, G. B. (Eds.). (2007). *For all our students: Collaborative partnerships among ESL and classroom teachers.* TELD/ESL.

Pearson, P. D., & Gallagher, G. (1983). The gradual release of responsibility model of instruction. *Contemporary Educational Psychology, 8*, 112–123.

Pearson, P. D., Cervetti, G. N., Palincsar, A. S., Afflerbach, P., Kendeou, P., Biancarosa, G., Higgs, J., Fitzgerald, M. S., Berman, A. I., & Hurt, M. (2020). Expanding reading for understanding: Understanding our vision of the science of reading. *Literacy Today, 38*(2), 26–28.

Peercy, M. M., Ditter, M., & Destefano, M. (2017). "We need more consistency:" Negotiating the division of labor in ESOL–Mainstream teacher collaboration. *TESOL Journal, 8*(1), 215–239. https://doi.org/10.1002/tesj.269

Peery, A. (2019). *The co-teacher's playbook: What it takes to make co-teaching work for everyone.* Corwin Press.

Pew Research Center. (2008). *Teens, video games and civics.* https://www.pewresearch.org/internet/2008/09/16/teens-video-games-and-civics/

Pratt, S. M., Imbody, S. M., Wolf, L. D., & Patterson, A. L. (2016). Co-planning in co-teaching: A practical solution. *Intervention in School and Clinic, 52*(4), 1–7.

Pritchard, R., & O'Hara, S. (2016). Framing the teaching of academic language to English learners: A Delphi study of expert consensus. *TESOL Quarterly, 51*(2), 418–428.

Ritchhart, R. (2015). *Creating cultures of thinking: The 8 forces we must master to truly transform our schools.* John Wiley and Sons.

Ritchhart, R., & Church, M. (2020). *The power of making thinking visible: Practices to engage and empower all learners.* Jossey-Bass.

Ritchhart, R., & Church, M. (2020). *The power of making thinking visible: Practices to engage and empower all learners.* Jossey-Bass.

Rivera, F. (2020). *Ask Fatima: What are WIDA Can Do student portraits?* https://wida.wisc.edu/memberships/isc/newsletter/ask-fatima-what-are-wida-can-do-student-portraits

Rizga, K. (2019). *How to keep teachers from leaving the profession.* https://www.theatlantic.com/education/archive/2019/09/teachers-need-other-teachers-succeed/598330/

Robb, L. (2016). *Read, talk, write.* Corwin Press.

Roberts, M. (2020). *Shifting from me to we: How to jump-start collaboration in a PLC at work.* Solution Tree.

Rubin, H., Estrada, L., & Honigsfeld, A. (in press). *Digital age teaching for ELs* (2nd ed.). Corwin Press.

Ryan, R. M., & Deci, E. L. (2020). Intrinsic and extrinsic motivation from a self-determination theory perspective: Definitions, theory, practices, and future directions. *Contemporary Educational Psychology, 61.* https://doi.org/10.1016/j.cedpsych.2020.101860

Santiago, S. (2019). *Telling ELs' story with data visualizations.* https://www.youtube.com/watch?v=EyyeD-F0Yv2I&list=PLFywV8JrSRQX1Evn6t3136QYJG-drfuX0E&index=5

Santos, M., Darling-Hammond, L., & Cheuk, T. (2012). *Teacher development to support English language learners in the context of Common Core State Standards.* http://ell.stanford.edu/publication/teacher-development-appropriate-support-ells

Saunders, W. G., & O'Brien, G. (2006). Oral language. In F. Genesee, K. Lindholm-Leary, B. Saunders, & D. Christian (Eds.), *Educating English language learners: A synthesis of research evidence* (pp. 14–48). Cambridge University Press.

Scanlan, M., Frattura, E., Schneider, K. A., & Capper, C. A. (2012). Bilingual students with integrated comprehensive service: Collaborative strategies. In A. Honigsfeld & M. G. Dove (Eds.), *Coteaching and other collaborative practices in the EFL/ESL classroom: Rationale, research, reflections, and recommendations* (pp. 3–13). Information Age Publishing.

Schiro, M. S. (2013). *Curriculum theory: Conflicting visions and enduring concerns* (2nd ed.). Corwin Press.

Schmoker, M. (2019). Focusing on the essentials. *Educational Leadership, 77*(1), 30–35.

Shanahan, T., & Shanahan, C. (2008). Teaching disciplinary literacy to adolescents: Rethinking content-area literacy. *Harvard Educational Review, 78*(1), 40–59.

Shanahan, T., & Shanahan, C. (2014). Teaching history and literacy. In K. A. Hinchman & H. K. Sheridan-Thomas (Eds.), *Best practices in adolescent literacy instruction* (2nd ed., pp. 232–248). Guildford Press.

Shanahan, C., & Shanahan, T. (2020). Disciplinary literacy. In J. Patterson (Ed.), *The SAT® suite and classroom practice: English language arts/literacy* (pp. 91–125). College Board.

Singer, T. W. (2014). *Opening doors to equity: A practical guide to observation-based professional learning.* Corwin Press.

Singer, T. W. (2018). *EL excellence every day: The flip-to guide for differentiating academic literacy.* Corwin Press.

Sleeter, C. E., & Carmona, J. F. (2017). *Un-standardizing curriculum: Multicultural teaching in the standards-based classroom.* Teachers College Press.

Snow, M. A., Met, M., & Genesee, F. (1989). A conceptual framework for the integration of language and content in second/foreign language instruction. *TESOL Quarterly, 23*(2), 201–217.

Solórzano, D. G., & Yosso, T. J. (2002). Critical race methodology: Counter-storytelling as an analytical framework for education research. *Qualitative Inquiry, 8*(1), 23–44.

Soto-Hinman, I., & Hetzel, J. (2009). *The literacy gap: Bridge-building strategies for English language learners and standard English learners.* Corwin Press.

Sousa, D. (2017). *How the brain learns* (5th ed.). Corwin Press.

Spencer, J. (2016, August 17). Cooperation vs. collaboration: When to use each approach. [Video]. YouTube. https://www.youtube.com/watch?v=Gr5mAboH1Kk&vl=en

Spies, T. G., & Xu, Y. (2018). Scaffolded academic conversations: Access to 21st-century collaboration and communication skills. *Intervention in School and Clinic, 54*(1), 22–30. https://doi.org/10.1177/1053451218762478.

Stanford University. (n.d.). *Understanding language: Overview.* https://ell.stanford.edu/about

Stein, E. (2016). *Elevating co-teaching through UDL.* CAST Professional Publishing.

Taboada Barber, A. M. (2016). *Reading to learn for ELs: Motivation, practices and comprehension strategies for informational texts.* Heinemann.

Taylor, J. (2015). *9 effective communication skills.* https://www.habitsforwellbeing.com/9-effective-communication-skills/

Theoharis, G., & O'Toole, J. (2011). Leading inclusive ELL social justice leadership for English language learners. *Educational Administration Quarterly, 47*(4), 646–688.

Thinking Maps. (2018). *What are Thinking Maps?* https://www.thinkingmaps.com/why-thinking-maps-2/

Thompson, T. (2021). Are you scaffolding or rescuing? https://choiceliteracy.com/article/are-you-scaffolding-or-rescuing/

Torres, C. (2019). *Assessment as an act of love.* http://www.ascd.org/publications/newsletters/education-update/feb19/vol61/num02/Assessment-as-an-Act-of-Love.aspx

U.S. Department of Education and the National Center for English Language Acquisition. (2016). *The English learner tool kit for state and local agencies (SEAs and LEAs).* http://www2.ed.gov/about/offices/list/oela/english-learner-toolkit/index.html

U.S. Department of Education, Office for Civil Rights, & U.S. Department of Justice. (2015). *Dear colleague letter: English learner students and limited English proficient parents.* http://www2.ed.gov/about/offices/list/ocr/letters/colleague-el-201501.pdf

Vangrieken, K., Dochy, F., Raes, E., & Kyndt, E. (2015). Teacher collaboration: A systematic review. *Educational Research Review, 15*, 17–40.

Victoria State Government. (2018). *Literacy teaching toolkit: Multimodal literacy.* https://www.education.vic.gov.au/school/teachers/teachingresources/discipline/english/literacy/readingviewing/Pages/litfocusmultimodal.aspx

Villa, R. A., & Thousand, J. S. (2005). *Creating an inclusive school* (2nd ed.). Alexandria, VA: Association for Supervision and Curriculum Development.

Villa, R. A., Thousand, J. S., & Nevin, A. I. (2013). *A guide to co-teaching: New lessons and strategies to facilitate student learning* (3rd ed.). Corwin Press.

Villegas, L., & Pompa, D. (2020). *The patchy landscape of state English learner policies under ESSA.* https://www.migrationpolicy.org/research/state-english-learner-policies-essa

Vygotsky, L. S. (1978). *Mind in society: The development of higher psychological processes.* Harvard University Press.

Walqui, A. (2019a). Designing the amplified lesson. In A. Walqui & G. C. Bunch (Eds.), *Amplifying the curriculum: Designing quality learning opportunities for English learners* (pp. 43–69). Teachers College Press.

Walqui, A. (2019b). Shifting from the teaching of oral skills to the development oracy. In L. C. de Oliveira (Ed.), *The handbook of TESOL in K–12* (pp. 181–197). John Wiley and Sons.

Walqui, A., & Heritage, M. (2012). *Instruction for diverse groups of ELLs.* Stanford Graduate School of Education. http://ell.stanford.edu/publication/instruction-diverse-groups-ells

Walqui, A., & van Lier, L. (2010). *Scaffolding the academic success of adolescent English language learners: A pedagogy of promise.* WestEd.

WIDA (2020a). *WIDA guiding principles of language development.* WIDA. https://wida.wisc.edu/sites/default/files/Website/Misc%20Pages/2020StandardsVision/2020-vision-guiding-principles-flyer.pdf

WIDA. (2020b). *WIDA English Language Development Standards Framework, 2020 edition: Kindergarten—Grade 12.* https://wida.wisc.edu/sites/default/files/resource/WIDA-ELD-Standards-Framework-2020.pdf

WIDA. (2020c). *WIDA resources: Sample Can Do students portrait.* https://wida.wisc.edu/resources/sample-can-do-student-portrait

Wiggins, G., & McTighe, J. (2005). *Understanding by design* (2nd ed.). ASCD.

Yoon, B. (2008). Uninvited guests: The influence of teachers' roles and pedagogies on the positioning of English language learners in the regular classroom. *American Educational Research Journal, 45*, 495–522.

Zwiers, J. (2008). *Building academic language: Essential practices for content classrooms, grades 5–12.* Jossey-Bass (with IRA).

Zwiers, J. (2014). *Building academic language: Meeting Common Core Standards across disciplines, Grades 5–12.* Jossey-Bass.

Zwiers, J. (2019). *Next steps with academic conversations: New ideas for improving learning through classroom talk.* Stenhouse.

Author Index

Subject Index

Helping educators make the greatest impact

CORWIN HAS ONE MISSION: to enhance education through intentional professional learning.

We build long-term relationships with our authors, educators, clients, and associations who partner with us to develop and continuously improve the best evidence-based practices that establish and support lifelong learning.